THE
OBSOLETE
EMPLOYEE

How Businesses Succeed Without Employees –

And Love It!

Michael J. Russer

Virtual Source **Press**

The OBSOLETE EMPLOYEE
How Businesses Succeed Without Employees —And Love It!

Virtual Source **Press**

315 Meigs Rd., Suite A356
Santa Barbara, CA 93109 U.S.A.
orders@virtualsourcepress.com; http://www.virtualsourcepress.com

Unattributed quotations are by Michael Russer

Russer, Michael J.
    The obsolete employee : how businesses succeed
    without employees —and love it! / Michael J. Russer.
    p. cm.
    Includes bibliographical references and index.
    LCCN 2007920727
    ISBN-13: 978-0-9662484-6-3
    ISBN-10: 0-9662484-6-5

    1. Contracting out. 2. Organizational effectiveness.
    3. Personnel management. I. Title.

    HD2365.R87 2007   658.4'058
                            QBI07-600025

Table of Contents

Acknowledgements

When I first contemplated writing this book, the thought of using "virtually" outsourced talent to help me produce it seemed like a clever idea. Boy, was I wrong! There is a big difference between "clever" and absolutely essential. To say I "walked my talk" by using all the tools and secrets shared in this book to help me finish it is one thing. To realize that this book could not have happened without these resources is quite another.

It turns out that the successful completion of this book required the focused efforts of a small army of talented individuals. Most of the people listed below were found, evaluated and hired using the resources and methods found in this book. And, with only two exceptions, I have never met any of these wonderfully talented individuals face-to-face, yet each and every one made an important contribution:

Research:
Lisa Morgan – Senior Researcher (Springfield, OH)

Case Story Research & Interviews:
Lorraine Lucciola – Case Story Interviewer/Editor (Fall River, MA)
Dawn Smith, Team Double-Click^sm – Case Story Researcher (Atlanta, GA)

Editing & Proofreading:
Lisa Birckhead, Team Double-Click^sm - Proofreader (Gordonsville, VA)
Rita Cook, Team Double-Click^sm – Proofreader (North Hollywood, CA)
Lesley Bates, Team Double-Click^sm - Proofreader (Brooksville, FL)

Typesetting & Book Design:
JustYourType.biz (San Antonio, TX)

Cover Design:
Brad Carroll, Dakno Marketing (Raleigh, NC)

Graphic Design:
Creativeskulls (New Delhi, India)

Marketing & PR:
Robin Parker, Team Double-Click^sm – Marketing Director (Berlin Center, OH)
Jennifer Wright, Team Double-Click^sm – Marketing Assistant (Avon, IN)

This list is not quite complete. That is because, as this is being written, there remain other types of virtual support required for the successful launch of this book that I have yet to hire. The ability to have affordable, "just in time" talent on demand is one of the many advantages of Virtual Outsourcing you will discover in this book.

There were also many friends, colleagues and professional associates who helped me to refine this work. In particular, Robert Tucker, a fellow NSA speaker and author who helped me stay focused so business readers see benefits on every page. Dr. Terry Paulson, who gave unending encouragement and suggestions. Dan Poynter, who is the best mentor an author and publisher could hope for. And to the rest of my Gold Coast Speakers Institute colleagues who so generously gave their support and suggestions to make this book the best it can be.

Over the past few years, my ideas about Virtual Outsourcing crystallized to what they are today due in large part to the many hours of discussion and debate with my friend and reality checker, Tom Courts. A special thanks to Ken and Scott Goodfellow for their input on the business side of Virtual Outsourcing. To Chris Durst and Michael Haaren, my collaborators on another book, for their insights on the origins of Virtual Assistants and the military spouse Virtual Assistant program. To Lisa Morgan for her insights on the use of executive level Virtual Assistants. I owe my insights into the Virtual Service Provider Marketplace business model to Fabio Rosati, CEO of Elance.com and Inder Guglani, CEO of Guru.com. Likewise, a deeper experiential understanding of how scalable Virtual Assistant business models may just be possible, thanks to the pioneering work of Gayle Buske and her company Team Double-Click[sm]. I am also greatly appreciative of the talented individuals outsourced through Gayle's company who were instrumental in the production of this book. And, of course to Michael E. Gerber, who has been my inspiration to business being as it should be —a faithful servant, and for writing the foreword to this book.

On a more personal note, I want to thank my brother-in-law Richard Cowan for providing initial, critical feedback that only someone who has actually owned and run a small business could provide. To my dear friend Linda Doss who was unwaveringly supportive with her review comments. And to my wife Sean who so selflessly put up with my "virtual obsession" of writing this book and spreading the word about Virtual Outsourcing through speaking engagements while running our not-so-virtual household.

And finally, to Vickie Smith, my #1 Virtual Assistant whose efforts to keep my other enterprises running smoothly allowed me the time to complete this book.

In an earlier phase of my life, I was young, dumb and arrogant enough to think that the assistance of other people was not necessary to accomplish things of value. Perhaps it is the benefit of hard-won (and often painful) experience that I now see value in the very process of accomplishing worthy objectives with the collaborative help of other people. Thanks to Virtual Outsourcing, my scope of possible collaboration now spans the entire world.

To Jacqueline and Max
—you are the bright lights of my life!

Warranties and Disclaimers

OK, here's the requisite lawyer talk. (Too bad more attorneys couldn't be virtual!)

If you do not wish to be bound by the following, you may return this book to the publisher for a full refund.

This book is designed to provide information on Virtual Outsourcing and the impact it may have on your business. It is sold with the understanding that the publisher and author are not engaged in rendering legal, accounting or other professional services. If legal or other professional assistance is required, the advice of the respective competent professional should be sought.

EXCEPT AS EXPRESSLY PROVIDED HEREIN, ALL INFORMATION IN THIS BOOK IS PROVIDED "AS IS" WITHOUT WARRANTY OF ANY KIND, EITHER EXPRESS OR IMPLIED, INCLUDING, BUT NOT LIMITED TO, THE IMPLIED WARRANTIES OF MERCHANTABILITY, FITNESS FOR A PARTICULAR PURPOSE, OR NON-INFRINGEMENT. THE AUTHOR ASSUMES NO RESPONSIBILITY FOR ERRORS OR OMISSIONS IN THE INFORMATION OR OTHER DOCUMENTS WHICH ARE REFERENCED IN THIS WORK. IN NO EVENT SHALL THE AUTHOR AND/OR HIS RESPECTIVE SUPPLIERS BE LIABLE FOR ANY SPECIAL, INDIRECT OR CONSEQUENTIAL DAMAGES OR ANY DAMAGES WHATSOEVER RESULTING FROM LOSS OF USE, DATA OR PROFITS, WHETHER IN AN ACTION OF CONTRACT, NEGLIGENCE OR OTHER TORTIOUS ACTION, ARISING OUT OF OR IN CONNECTION WITH THE USE OR PERFORMANCE OF INFORMATION AVAILABLE IN THIS BOOK.

THIS BOOK COULD INCLUDE TECHNICAL OR OTHER INACCURACIES OR TYPOGRAPHICAL ERRORS. CHANGES MAY BE PERIODICALLY ADDED TO THE INFORMATION HEREIN; THESE CHANGES MAY BE INCORPORATED IN NEW EDITIONS OF THIS BOOK. THE AUTHOR MAY MAKE IMPROVEMENTS AND/OR CHANGES IN THE PRODUCT(S) DESCRIBED IN THIS BOOK AT ANY TIME.

Any third party resources or services mentioned in this book are done so for informational purposes only. Their mention is not to be construed as an endorsement or statement of suitability of said services or resources either by the publisher or author. Always do a thorough due-diligence prior to using any of the services or resources mentioned in this book.

Any businesses mentioned in this book that have achieved certain levels of financial and/or operational success through the use of virtual outsourcing or the methods described herein are unique to those businesses. Your results may vary. The publisher and author make no promises or warranties about the level of results you will experience by applying the resources and methods described herein.

Foreword

Some books are timeless. Others are exactly the opposite; they come at exactly the right time, for exactly the right reason, and perform exactly the right job in exactly the right way.

This book, Michael Russer's THE OBSOLETE EMPLOYEE, is of the second sort.

It's not timeless, it's just brilliant.

Brilliantly written, brilliantly appropriate, brilliantly to the point, and brilliantly essential to anyone who wants to start a small business, owns a small business, or wants to grow a small business into a very big business.

This book is a Brilliant Resource for any or all of the above.

Read it. I did. And it changed the way I think about hiring forever.

I will follow Michael Russer's instruction for the rest of my days as I grow my many small to large businesses with a new lease on life. Thank you, Michael. You are my hero. And, just think, I would have never met you had you not sent me this manuscript to read. Thank God you did!

—Michael E. Gerber
Founder and Chairman
E-Myth Worldwide and
In The Dreaming Room LLC
And author of The E-Myth books

"Any time you do something outside your core competency, you pay top dollar for amateur results."

Preface

It didn't take too long in my career as a founder and owner of several small businesses to discover I was a lousy manager of people. I just wanted the work to get done so I could focus on growing my business. Unfortunately, it was never quite that simple. It seemed like we were always looking for talented help we could depend on and not have to baby-sit. Not being a highly trained Human Resources person and lacking the intuition of a psychic meant that we went through a lot of new hires before we found ones who actually showed promise. As you are probably well aware, finding good help is an expensive, frustrating and time-consuming process. And that is just the beginning.

Like most businesses, occasionally we would be lucky enough to find someone with a sparkle in their eye and fire in their belly. When we hired these special human beings, we knew that what stood before us was the raw clay that someday, with the help of our careful, loving, molding hands, would turn into the "Perfect Employee!" (Excuse me a second, I have to wipe a tear from my eye.)

OK, so it takes a lot of time, effort and patience to do all that molding —but it's worth it, isn't it? Look at what you have when you're done. Another high-performance member of your "team," another cheerleader for your company's success, another champion that gets one for the Gipper!

A funny thing happens on the way to the ball game of business though. Unlike you, who are always charged up and ready to take on the best every day, your team players need to be given the locker room pep talk fairly regularly. That means more time, more energy and more focus away from doing what you do best in your business —which, for most small business owners, clearly isn't managing people. Not only was I not good at it, I hated doing it; as a result, it sucked the joy out of being in business. I simply couldn't understand why my employees, even the best of them, couldn't bring it upon themselves to be as excited about my business as I was.

Then I realized one day with stunning clarity (you know, the kind when you hear choirs of angels sing and have that dumb, distant look on your face) what the problem was. No matter how good, talented or well intentioned —they were still "employees." It was the inherent exploitive/parasitic relationship between employer (me) and employees (them) that was the cause of all the problems. It was at that instant that I resolved to never again hire another employee —ever! (Cue the angelic trumpets...) And I further resolved that I would find a way to get all the things done within my business that needed to be done —dependably, affordably and without requiring the inspired wisdom of the One Minute Manager or a Peter Drucker —all while freeing me up to focus on what I do best and enjoy most.

I did find a way to accomplish all this and much more —through what I call "Virtual Outsourcing" (not to be confused with the typical enterprise outsourcing used by big businesses). I've discovered an incredibly powerful way to have awesome talent accomplish brilliant work for me for far less than the cost and hassle of having employees. For the last 10 years, I've used Virtual Outsourcing to transform the way my businesses work for me. I have no employees, yet I have teams of people (most of whom I've never met) that do what needs to be done, often brilliantly, without management or training. This book is for you if you are a business owner, manager, entrepreneur, independent professional, salesperson or even a nonprofit organization and any of the following rings true for you:

- You feel you have to do everything yourself in order to stay "in control," only to find that you stay exhausted instead;

- You have projects and strategies that would make you rich and your business thrive if only you could find and afford the talent to pull them off;

- You can't quite put "brilliant talent," "easy to manage" and "affordable" all in the same sentence with a straight face;

- You hire and train great employees only to find they are soon shopping their newly acquired talents to others for more money;

- You want to aggressively grow your business, but are afraid you cannot afford the required additional infrastructure or staffing;

- You assume only the "big boys" can afford to hire exceptional talent;

- You believe the pool of available talent for your business is just too small to ever have a hope of consistently hiring people who have the "right stuff";

- You've gone through four personal assistants and hope against hope that the next one you bring on will somehow be different and actually work out;

- You just want the work to get done —with no excuses, no whining, no complaining, no threats and no standing over people's shoulders to make sure it's done right and on time;

- You absolutely hate the hiring process;

- You dread bringing onsite support staff into your home-based business;

- You dislike training people and don't feel you're good at it;

- Your idea of enlightened management is "My way or the highway!";

- You could give a rat's a** about becoming a "more enlightened" manager;

- You can't stand it when employees always seem to "want more," especially just when things are starting to look up for your business;

- You often feel as though you are working for your employees rather than they for you;

- You've been sued for wrongful termination (or you're terrified that if you even think of firing someone, you might as well file for bankruptcy and get it over with);

- You're weary of countless interviews with talented people whose primary focus is what you can do for them rather than demonstrating how they can help you;

- You're tired (no, worn out!) from slaving 18 hours a day and wondering if your business will ever turn around.

This book is for you if you have ever dreamed about having a business or career where you could focus nearly all your time on what you do best and love to do, make a great living doing it and have all the free time you want to enjoy your success. This book is for you if you are truly committed to having a business that serves you and not the other way around.

As business people, we cannot succeed by our own efforts alone; we need help. This means access to dedicated, talented people who are committed to helping us achieve our vision. Now, through Virtual Outsourcing, you have access to every kind of talent you could ever need, often in just minutes, for far less than you thought possible. This is a dream-come-true for thousands of businesses around the world that have discovered the secrets of using Virtual Outsourcing. If this is the kind of business (and life) you always wanted, then this book is for you.

—Michael J. Russer
January 4, 2007

How To Get The Most Out Of This Book

As a communicator to the adult masses, I have found a proven formula for getting across any important message. First, have people get in touch with their "pain," and then offer a practical solution to relieve it and give best practices for its effective application. As a result, "pain" transforms into "opportunity."

For the most part, the layout of this book follows this principle of **PAIN** → **SOLUTION** → **APPLICATION**. However, experience has also taught me that everyone has different learning styles. Some people need to know the nook and crannies of every detail, nuance and corroborative evidence. Others just want to get to the essence of an idea and find out as quickly as possible how to apply it. For this reason, I've laid out the major sections of this book below so you can determine which is most important to you in terms of reading order preference:

Chapter 1: **Why (some) Employees Don't Work** Chapter 2: **Familiarity Breeds Contempt**	**PAIN:** If you ever had any lingering doubts that the employer/employee relationship is fundamentally flawed and expensive, these two chapters will help you get in touch with your inner scream of managerial frustration. *NOTE: For the "Get to the meat!" folks, these two chapters are not necessary for the understanding or application of Virtual Outsourcing. Feel free to skip right to Chapter 3.*
Chapter 3: **Virtual Outsourcing**	**SOLUTION:** This is a critical chapter that covers the emergence and foundational principles of Virtual Outsourcing and its two major categories of Virtual Consultants and Virtual Assistants. *NOTE: This is the chapter to start with if you want to dive right into what Virtual Outsourcing is all about.*
Chapter 4: **Virtual Consultants** Chapter 5: **Virtual Assistants** Chapter 6: **Virtual Outsourcing and Your Business**	**APPLICATION / BEST PRACTICES:** These chapters go into the step-by-step details of how to find, evaluate, hire and work powerfully with Virtual Consultants and Virtual Assistants, and how to incorporate these resources seamlessly with your current onsite staff. *NOTE: It is strongly suggested that you read Chapter 3 prior to these last three chapters.*

At the end of chapters 1 thru 6, there is a summary of the key points to help you "lock in" what was covered. The last chapter (7), The Future of Virtual Outsourcing, covers how the Virtual Outsourcing paradigm is likely to grow and impact you, your business and society at large over the next five to 10 years.

Also included throughout the book are many "case stories" which are actual first-person accounts from individuals either using Virtual Outsourcing in their business, or providing those services to others. These case stories are designed to help you see how Virtual Outsourcing may be incorporated within your business by vicariously experiencing it through the eyes of others. And for those who love to wallow in detail, an extensive End Note and Index are included at the back of the book.

Only a fool tries to please everyone. However, it is my sincere hope that this book's content structure will appeal to the widest range of adult learning styles, with yours being among them.

Why (some) Employees Don't Work

Now don't get me wrong, I'm not anti-employee. I fully recognize that without great supporting talent, an organization hasn't got a chance to succeed in the long run. However, "great supporting talent" and "employees" are not necessarily synonymous, especially for small and entrepreneurial businesses. In fact, that's one of the central premises of this book. In this chapter, we'll explore why the traditional employer/employee relationship is systemically flawed. As you will see, it simply doesn't work in many cases no matter how it's configured or how "enlightened" the respective parties are. To conclude, I'll introduce Virtual Outsourcing as a whole new way to get things done that sidesteps all of these issues.

Devil's Bargain

It wasn't until we made the shift from an agrarian society to an industrial society that the modern concept of "employee" really came about. People left farms in droves to go to the cities for a "better" life. What many of them found instead was a devil's bargain; they sold their time, blood, sweat and tears, often doing soul-robbing, dangerous, mindless tasks for just enough money to survive. On the farm, they sometimes had good years and often had bad years. But at least they were connected with Mother Earth, the work was on their terms and, depending how hard (and smart) they worked, they had some influence on the outcome. By choosing to work in the cities, they traded nature for brick and their misery of uncertainty for the certainty of their misery —but at least they would make enough money to live, if only barely.

Back then (the good old days), employers held all the cards. They dictated everything, including pay, working conditions and time off. They were the kings of the new era of prosperity, (which only they seemed to singularly enjoy) while everyone else (their employees) were mere pawns to do their bidding. The reason for this inequity was really quite simple: Living in the city without a job was an oxymoron. There was no "living" in the city without a job —you either had one or you starved. Survival was a strong motivator back then. Needless to say, there wasn't a big market for motivational speakers to pep up the troops. The phrase "You're fired!" did the trick quite nicely since it nearly equated to "You're going to starve and die!"

This period of dictatorial employers didn't last too long for several reasons. First, it was important that employees receive enough pay to cover basic needs and have money leftover to buy the things being manufactured. Employers also realized that if they kept their employees working 16 hours a day, no matter how much they paid them, the employees would be too exhausted to enjoy the fruits of their labor (and thus probably not purchase the employer's products).

As employees started receiving more and actually enjoying life a bit, they of course wanted more. It didn't take them very long to figure out that if they organized, they would finally be in the same card game with the employers. Thus, the unions were born. And like any kind of birth, it was a bit messy, even bloody at times. But with the emergence of unions, the entire employer/employee dynamic changed dramatically.

Once unions realized just how much power they had, they wielded it fiercely and without mercy. Who could blame them? Individual employees had been under the thumbs of greedy employers for years, and now (by popular support) it was time those robber baron bastards got some of what they gave. The unions wouldn't hesitate to shut down a major manufacturing plant until the board of directors "cried uncle" and they had their demands met. Now the tables were turned and the employers were wondering about their own survival (or at least the potential loss of a cushy lifestyle).

For several decades after World War II, unions were able to maintain a position of strength and power equal to those that employed their members. There was always tension between the companies and unions. They hated each other, yet needed one another. Certainly the unions needed the companies to survive, otherwise everyone would lose. And companies saw certain advantages in collective bargaining with relatively few representatives rather than with the many thousands of individuals who worked for them. Though there was tension, there was stability as well. People knew their place, be it a union wage earner on the line, or white-collar middle management in the office. Keep your nose clean and to the grindstone and you'll do OK. During this period, people looked at employment as a lifetime contract. Do your job and we (the company) will make sure you have one until you retire, and maybe even throw in a pension for good measure. Your life may not be at the pinnacle of Maslow's hierarchy of needs, but hey, it's a living and you get Saturdays and Sundays off with the family, plus maybe a few weeks a year for vacation.

Nothing stays the same for very long though (other than underlying principles, that is). Eventually, our industrial society commenced its transition to a service-based society and then to one based upon the intangible 1's and 0's of the Information Age. This happened around the same time as the Japanese "invasion" where a significant number of manufacturing jobs were lost forever to the other side of the Pacific. Now both companies and unions were feeling equally threatened (there's that survival thing again). And after a while, they both realized that they better work collaboratively rather than inimically, otherwise there would be little left to fight over. Suddenly it seemed everyone was embracing the Rodney King school of better management: "Why can't we all just get along?"

Largely due to this dynamic, the "enlightened workplace" emerged. You know, the one where corporate managers and leaders take special courses (usually involving ropes and team cheers of various kinds) to learn how to motivate the troops to do their best and even feel great about it. Some management actually became quite skilled at this and, particularly in highly exciting, innovation-driven environments, employees fought to have the chance to work there. Not because they needed to for survival, but because they would be part of something "big" and their efforts would be rewarded and sincerely acknowledged. In other words, employees flocked to work in places like these because they would be doing interesting work, get paid well and be treated like human beings instead of some cog in the great churning wheels of commerce.

Filling the Hole of Fulfillment

Now keep in mind, even at the height of this era, relatively few companies were that great to work for. Most fit somewhere along the continuum of "I wouldn't work there if it were the last place on earth!" to "I'd give my left reproductive gland for a chance to work there!" Certainly most employees found their work to be more diverse and interesting, though not necessarily fulfilling. And you know, it's funny how as human beings we feel the need to constantly "fill" the hole of missing personal fulfillment. As employees, no matter how enlightened the management or interesting the work, people still must do what their management tells them to do. They (typically) have to show up at a certain time, put in a certain number of hours, do certain types of work (whether they enjoy it or not) and work with other people they may or may not even like. The very definition of employment implies that employees must conduct their work under terms largely dictated by the employer. Personal fulfillment will always be limited under those conditions.

> The very definition of employment implies that employees must conduct their work under terms largely dictated by the employer. Personal fulfillment will always be limited under those conditions.

This is an important point. I contend that business owners will always have issues with their support staff as long as they don't feel truly fulfilled by their work, no matter what perks the employer gives them. By definition, high levels of personal fulfillment are impossible under the typical employer/employee model because employees must do their work on the employer's terms, not their own.

Granted, many people find comfort in being an employee. This is because they don't have to take responsibility for much else other than doing their job, while "Mother Company" takes care of all the rest. However, a growing contingent of employees are demanding more autonomy and freedom in the ways they produce their work product.[1] These demands are really a cry for wanting to feel more fulfilled in doing their job —a fact that most employees may not realize consciously, but feel nonetheless.

Entitlement Mentality

Recognizing the importance of the fulfillment factor and realizing that good help was getting harder to find (especially during boom times), many companies actively sought to create workplace environments that most people would find highly attractive. Efforts to improve employee satisfaction waxes and wanes depending on the relative supply of and demand for skilled workers. Before enterprise outsourcing was a big deal, high-tech companies would fall all over themselves to attract and retain top employees. Then corporate America discovered that there were highly skilled people many time zones away who could do the same work for a fraction of the hourly wage/benefits paid to a typical domestic worker. Now, all of a sudden, the tables switched yet again in favor of the employers. Few companies were popping champagne corks with this turn of affairs though. That is because by now local, state and federal government employment regulation had become so entrenched in "protecting" employee rights, (at great expense to employers big and small) that there was really very little to celebrate. And besides, "outsourcing" was just for the big guys; small business, which makes up the largest segment of the U.S. economy, was still getting legislated to death and without the benefit of having access to affordable labor.

Whether driven by market conditions or threat of regulatory sanction, employees in general have been elevated to a form of "protected species." On the job, this equates to the "enlightened employee" who so articulately asks the question: "What are you [Mr./Ms. Employer] going to do for me today?" This is what I call the "Employee Entitlement Mentality" and, unfortunately, it is quite prevalent in today's society. As a business owner, I have a real problem with this (some might even say an "attitude") and maybe you can relate. By definition, you (as the business owner) are working for the person who asks the question: "What can you do for me today?" Now, our customers ask this question every day and we bust our rumps answering it to the best of our ability and hopefully get paid well for our efforts.

However, when our "enlightened" employees ask that question, it almost certainly means our costs will go up, typically without any commensurate increase in revenue. When this happens, you are effectively working for your employees —period. And don't expect it to get better any time soon. In fact, it will get worse, a lot worse —especially for the small to midsized companies who don't have the legal or HR resources to effectively deal with these growing burdens.

To give you an idea of just how bad it can get, take a look at Germany and France. In these "civilized" havens of employee nirvana, among other things, employers are required to provide:[2]

Five weeks of paid vacation for French employees over the age of 21, even if newly hired. Also, most European Union employers give a full month's Christmas bonus and extra pay just before vacation;

Up to 16 weeks of maternity leave at 100 percent pay for women and 11 paid days of paternity leave for new fathers. After that, women are entitled up to three years and fathers up to 18 months of unpaid leave with the right to return to their original jobs;

Two months notice before termination for cause for employees with two or more years of service. Termination for reasons other than just cause is often a lengthy and expensive process for the employer.

And this is just the tip of the iceberg that clearly explains why EU workers are nowhere near as productive as their U.S. counterparts —so far any way.

Some *Really* Hard Costs

In addition to there being a general trend toward a profound "Employee Entitlement Mentality," today's employees are just darned expensive. Here's a breakdown of costs from hiring to firing and everything in between for a typical small to midsized business:

Wages:	$18.82/hr[3]
Cost to hire:	$1,370[4]
Interviewing	
Testing	
Evaluation	
Cost to train:	$955[5]
Logistics (office space & equip.):	$10,000/yr[6]
Benefits:	$5.22/hr[7]
Vacation	
Sick pay	
Holiday pay	
Health insurance	
Paid family leave	
Company functions	

Retirement and savings
Awards
Regulatory compliance: $2.16/hr[8]
Taxes
Insurance
Payroll and accounting: $459/yr[9]
Termination: $2,288[10]
Exit interview
Regulatory compliance
Payroll/accounting adjustments
Legal costs ($25,000+ if sued[11])

And those are just the hard costs. This doesn't even take into account the tremendous loss of productivity due to factors such as commute stress and discord among employees and/or management. Or, that it takes an average of eight weeks for new clerical workers to reach full productivity.[12] These costs are there whether you have work for them or not. This fact causes many small business people to drive their staff relentlessly to maximize their per-person productivity —which, of course doesn't help with boosting the employee's morale or job satisfaction. To paraphrase Dr. Steven Covey, author of *The Seven Habits of Highly Effective People*, running people or machines full out to squeeze every last drop of productivity will eventually cause something to break. And in so doing, you lose the very thing you sought after.

Hell's Revenge

And God help the employer who actually has to let someone go. With the threat of wrongful termination suits always hovering over their head, employers practically have to call their attorney every time they consider letting someone go. In states that have taken employee entitlement to such ridiculous levels (like my state of California), you might as well just file for bankruptcy and get it over with. Don't believe me? Here is an example from a former business owner who shared his rather interesting run in with the employee from Hell...

Peace, Love and Lunacy

HELLLP! I have been held hostage by the weirdest, oddest, most disturbed employees on the planet…and I owned the business! Does this sound familiar? If you are an employer in California, this may have happened to you, too. It's not the case in New York (where I come from) or other parts of the country.

For years, California has maintained its reputation as a liberal, "wiggy" state. In business and in everyday life, a certain mindset still seems to prevail, decades after the Mamas and the Papas crooned "California Dreamin" and the nation's rebellious young were making daisy chains and sewing peace signs on their grungiest jeans.

Difficult or downright strange employees in California are a new breed of workers, intent on dictating to management how they will perform the duties of a given job. State labor laws have limited the power and legal right of an employer to simply fire someone who is disrupting business or clearly not doing their job.

The message to employees is one of "entitlement," which often compromises the policies of a business and causes workers to expect the demands of the job to conform to them.

When I owned my software business, I got stuck for a year and a half with the employee from hell. When we hired this man, we didn't know he was gay. We didn't need to know this kind of information; it's not important or relevant to one's ability to do the job.

After just two hours on the job, he walks into the Human Resources office and says he's "highly disturbed" at some gay jokes he heard being told by some of his fellow workers. He files a report, goes home and doesn't come to work for the next two days, claiming illness. On the third day, he comes into my office with a letter from his psychiatrist, which stated that the joke had such a disturbing effect on him that he was now in therapy.

He claimed job-related "mental injury," as one would claim physical injury in the workplace and was seeking compensation. My hands were tied. I had a letter from his psychiatrist as proof of an "illness" and I could not legally fire him.

When he finally came back to work, about two months later, we had to hire specialists to conduct sensitivity training workshops; we had to re-train him, as well.

He was eventually fired and leveled a law suit against the company. In the course of preparing our case, our lawyers found out that this person had a history of exploiting other employers in the same or similar fashions.

I went to Verizon the other day. I said to the 25-year-old kid behind the counter, "My stylus keeps popping off my PDA. I turned my PDA upside down and the stylus just fell out. This appears to be a problem. I've purchased three packages of styluses this week. I think we need to do something about the phone." He gives me a dull stare and says, "Well…it doesn't happen to my phone. Maybe you don't know how to put a stylus in." Now, the guy is in my face and I'm thinking that I just want to get my phone repaired. I'm not looking for an attitude.

The problem is that he can't be fired, either. He may have a record of being abusive to people, but here, in this state, you can't call him into your office and say, "Hey! You're fired!"

If an employer wants to discharge an employee, they have to go about creating a file, compiling complaint letters and negative reports from customers …and if you do fire him, you'd better have your attorney waiting in the wings to combat charges of discrimination or unfair practices.

Hiring and firing initiatives in the state of California would be better served by preparing job seekers for the realities of the working world, rather than enabling them to skirt the issues of healthy employment.

I sold my business two years ago. If I were ever to start a new business, the first thing I'd want are people with the kinds of behaviors and learned life skills most of us get at home long before we join the workforce.

Marc Davison, Former Owner
Software Company

As a result, the proven success formula of "hire slow, fire fast" has turned into the profit-sucking quagmire of "hire fast, fire slow." For most companies, especially small ones (those without the big budgets), the function of hiring and firing has become so miserable, time-consuming and soul-robbing that "HR" often stands for "Hells Revenge."

It Takes Two To Be Loyal

At first glance, one might think that a progressive way out of this mess is to treat employees so well that they would always strive to give their best and never even think of leaving —ha! Just because you offer afternoon yoga/ meditation breaks, days off for discordant biorhythms and conjugal visits every other Friday doesn't mean that your employees will show any semblance of loyalty or work more effectively (they may smile more though…).

In today's world of revolving-door employees, "loyalty" is a laughable cliché, and frankly it is one that turns both ways. Why should employees be loyal to an employer that can downsize, outsource or offshore them in a moment's notice, make them train their barely English-speaking replacements, and have their pensions disappear in a puff of smoke when things get tough financially. There is no way around this particular problem. That is because you can only have employer/employee loyalty when it is mutual and the business environment for both parties is perceived as stable and equally beneficial. Without perceived stability, you can never have loyalty. Survival instincts kick in too strongly for anything like loyalty to last very long. And, as we all know, the days of stable business environments are long gone. Innovation and the change it causes is happening at a double-exponential rate[13] which hardly fosters warm cozy feelings of "everything is going to be just fine."

Key Ideas and Chapter Review

All right, this is a good time to take a quick review of key points covered so far in this chapter. I started out by declaring that the employer/employee relationship is systemically flawed and will almost always produce conflict, no matter how it is configured or how enlightened each party happens to be. The underlying reasons for this are:

- Employers (especially small businesses) just want the work done without having to spend a great deal of time, money and energy on the people they hire to get the work done. And employers typically don't have the management skills and/or the desire to use them in order to maintain high levels of productivity and employee satisfaction (more on this in the next chapter);

- In the traditional setting, employees are forced to provide their work product under the terms and conditions (location, people, dress code, etc.) dictated by employers. As a result, many employees are left "wanting" for more because of their largely unconscious need for personal fulfillment which the traditional workplace cannot provide;

- Costs of hiring, training, paying, managing, supporting and terminating employees continues to rise meteorically, thanks largely to an increasingly business-unfriendly regulatory environment;

- Increasing employee turnover rates (due to a perceived increasingly insecure business environment) magnify the costs of maintaining employees.

So what's the answer? Well, you can do what I did 13 years ago and swear off from ever hiring an employee again (which I've held true to for all that time). No, I haven't gone into seclusion or become one of those business burn-outs that have little X's where their eyeballs used to be. In fact, my businesses are more dynamic, fun and profitable than ever before.

This Virtual Outsourcing approach to staffing my business has transformed the way my businesses work for me. I am no longer working for my employees because I don't have any. And, because my "staff" consists entirely of independent contractor specialists (who, like me, are business people in their own right), I have none of the employer/employee issues discussed earlier or in the next chapter.

Let me reassure you that you don't have to go "cold turkey" by eliminating all your employees when you incorporate the benefits of Virtual Outsourcing within your business. Later on I will give you the battle-tested proven protocols, operating procedures and methods to seamlessly integrate Virtual Outsourcing with those valuable employees you consider crucial to your business.

In the next chapter, we will explore why most independent business people are quite frankly terrible (OK, fine..."unskilled") at managing people. And, why any time you have two or more employees working under the same roof, you're just asking for problems. Then we'll look at how Virtual Outsourcing mitigates these concerns as well.

NOTE: At this point you may feel you really "get" the issues inherent in the traditional employer/employee relationship and don't need to explore it further. If so, skip the next chapter for now and *go directly to Chapter 3:* **Virtual Outsourcing –** *The New Way To Get Things* **Done**

Familiarity Breeds Contempt 2

Why "Do this" Doesn't Work

OK, I admit it —I'm one of the world's worst managers of people. Back in the (definitely not) "good old" days when I actually had employees, I never quite understood why they didn't get the concept of "Do - this!" Is it the "Do" they didn't get or the "this?" I didn't have the time, desire or skills to become an "enlightened" manager of people. I just wanted the freak'n work done! Don't tell me about the bad date you had last night with your boyfriend, or how the car wouldn't start or why germs seem to be particularly virulent on Fridays and Mondays. If you don't get along with your office mates —too bad, work it out and don't waste my time with the details. If you have a great idea to improve our business, awesome —put it in the suggestion box. Please don't interrupt whatever I happen to be doing when you have a stroke of brilliance just so I can pat you on the head and say, "Good job —thanks a million!"

Let me make this very, very clear. When I have a business to run, I expect my support staff to act and behave like adults. I don't want to manage, coddle, entice, motivate or threaten them —or even be their friend (oh, I do have friends; they're just not on my payroll). I expect them to do the work they were hired to do, dependably and without complaint. I just want to spend my time doing what I do best for my business and what I most enjoy, while my support staff takes care of the rest, without me having to watch their every move to make sure things get done right and on time.

Is this too much to ask? You can bet your bottom dollar it is —if your support staff consists of typical onsite employees. In fact, if you're reading this and have had any experience managing people at all, you're probably laughing one end of your anatomy or the other off this very moment. That's because everyone knows that it's impossible to have a group of adult human beings in the same room, office or building and expect them to act like adults all the time. It can't happen —we are genetically pre-programmed to revert to six-years-olds when working in the same space for any length of time (the same reason why Dilbert® is such a massively popular comic strip —humor is often a caricaturized mirror of truth). The only way around this is to have a skilled manager constantly working the team to maximize their performance while minimizing employee-induced disruption. And, if you're the typical small to midsized business owner or independent professional, that skilled manager of people is most likely not you. Even if you are a skilled manager, is this really the best use of your time?

> *we are genetically pre-programmed to revert to six-years-olds when working in the same space for any length of time.*

The E-Myth Revisited —Again

In his seminal book *The E-myth* (and now *The E-myth Revisited*), author Michael Gerber powerfully lays out why most small businesses fail. By the way, if you haven't read that book, run, don't walk to your nearest bookstore and pick up a copy. Consider it a prerequisite for getting the most out of *this* book. One of the many things I like about the E-myth is that it reveals several fundamental operating principles that hold true no matter what business you're in.

For example, every business needs three types of skills to enjoy long-term success. These skills embodied in people are the Entrepreneur, Manager and Technician. Most small businesses come into being because their owners/founders are good at "doing" something. That is, they are the Technician. Because they are good at doing what they do, their business starts to grow. In order to grow effectively, you need to know where and how you plan on growing. This takes vision to see what others don't and courage to act where others won't —which defines the job of the Entrepreneur. And the bigger and faster you want your business to grow, the more vision and courage it will require. While not every business owner/Technician has strong entrepreneurial skills, many do, otherwise they would still be working for someone else.

Where things really start getting sticky for small businesses is when their growth demands that they must add staff to handle it. And with this comes the whole package of skills embodied in a Manager. It has been my experience, both personally and anecdotally, that most small business owners and independent professionals are woefully lacking in those skills. In fact, according to American Management Association (AMA), 75 percent of managers lack appropriate "soft" people-management skills necessary to keep their employees happy and productive. Furthermore, a Dunn & Bradstreet study estimates that 90 percent of small businesses that fail do so because of poor management ability[14]. And, these skills are not particularly easy to learn. While a few business owners also happen to be gifted managers of people, most clearly are not.

If having good management is so crucial, yet typically lacking at the ownership level, you might be wondering why most business owners just don't go out and hire a good manager. Sure, no problem, we'll just go out and get one and all our problems will be solved! Oh, wait a minute, isn't good hiring an important skill of being a good manager? Well, I guess we could always hire a good headhunting firm to find one for us —it might be a bit expensive though (especially for a limited budget). OK, screw the budget, let's say we hire a great placement firm to find an awesome manager. Now, who is going to manage the manager? After all, they are a real live person, too. And, if I turn over the reigns to them, I might feel just a bit vulnerable relinquishing that much control to a non-partner.

Michael Gerber goes on to mitigate some of these management concerns by delineating another fundamental principle of successful business — McDonaldization. What Ray Kroc saw as he delivered his order of milkshake machines to the McDonald brothers in 1954 was not the best hamburger being offered at the time. Instead, his entrepreneurial eyes captured a glimpse of how strict, standard business processes could be set up so that the customer experience and the procedures and costs of delivering that experience were the same no matter which McDonald's restaurant provided the meal. By creating explicit written processes and procedures for every aspect of the restaurant's operation and training, management at the restaurant level would not have to be extraordinarily "gifted." This approach to the service industry (akin to Ford's introduction of the assembly line) created a business environment where results were consistent and measurable no matter how large it became.

It also made it easier to hire less skilled employees and keep them on track without having to stand over their shoulders.

The Other E-Myth —The *Employee* Myth

I'm an enthusiastic proponent of creating written processes for each function within your business. In fact, as you will see, this is also a fundamental principle behind the success of Virtual Outsourcing. This way, the people executing the process become interchangeable and should always provide the same result no matter who is doing the job. That's the theory at least. However, in the traditional world of onsite employees, even with written processes to guide them, there are still issues to contend with. The "E" in Michael Gerber's "E-myth" stands for "Entrepreneurial." I suggest that it could also stand for "Employee" as in the "Employee Myth."

Just because you have written a set of business processes and procedures that are so beautifully documented that any idiot should be able to execute them, doesn't mean they will. People are people and always will be, especially when you put two or more of them in the same room.

All For One & One For All —*Until…*

Sometimes employee problems can sneak up on you like a thief in the night. For example, when businesses are just getting started, employer and employees tend to rally to the common cause of a successful launch. They will enthusiastically work together as a cohesive team dedicated to innovation, great customer service and efficiency. Why wouldn't they? Both parties are smart enough (most of the time) to know that a business just starting out needs every edge it can get. And, frankly, it can be darned exciting to be part of a team that launches a new enterprise.

So, for the first few years of the startup "struggle" phase, everyone is working together like one big happy family. Your employees know that, as a new business, you cannot afford the pay, benefits or perks of a more established enterprise. Everyone comes into work (often early) bright-eyed and bushy-tailed, and many times they stay late. You beam with pride at the dedication your crew is showing, especially under the less-than-ideal circumstances typical of most businesses starting up (funky furniture and equipment, crowded quarters, location not in the best part of town, little or no parking, etc.) As the business owner and visionary, you can see where this is all headed. With a team like this, you can conquer the world. Nothing, given a little more time and a lot of coordinated blood, sweat and tears, will stand in your way. You can actually see your picture on the cover of *Forbes* magazine!

OK, even if you don't see yourself on the cover of *Forbes*, you are still darn proud of your team. Enjoy these times while you can, however; even start a scrapbook to help remember them (I did) because the moment your business turns the corner, all the Kum Ba Yah feelings with your "team" will go out the door. A funny thing about people is that we have a strong, innate desire to help others in need. It seems to be part of our makeup, our very DNA. We're ready and willing to rebuild the neighbor's barn after it burned down and give shelter to natural disaster victims. The reason I say this is a "funny" thing is that the very moment the person or organization we are helping appears to have their need fulfilled, or worse, attained something more than we (the giver) have, those altruistic tendencies vanish in a puff of smoke.

You Owe Me!

After years of struggle, your business is now starting to show consistent growth and maybe even some serious cash flow. Congratulations —you made it! Right… your troubles are just getting started. Actually, they started way back when you first opened your doors and everyone was working together like a well-oiled, finely-tuned machine. You see, whether you knew it or not, you made a bargain with those first employees. They were willing to give up the finer accouterments of working with a more established company and toil like a dog for you —assuming they would see some rewards after your company started to make it. You may have even made this an explicit understanding upon hiring your first people. It doesn't really matter because it's almost certain that your employee's idea of "just rewards" and yours will never coincide.

And what's worse is that the more money your company makes (or more accurately, is perceived to make), the more your employees will hit you with demands. Everything was hunky-dory during the struggle phase, but the moment they perceive you getting "more" as the business owner, they'll start feeling resentment. And a team that is full of people resenting the team leader is no team at all. This behavior shouldn't surprise you since it is a fundamental principle of human nature. We love to help others in need, yet we can't stand it the moment someone else has more.

What exacerbates this is the fact that employees are physically present at your place of business. As a result, they see firsthand the kind of money you make off their hunched over backs. From their perspective, you're getting fat from their efforts, and it's just not fair. This type of issue is often seen by highly successful independent salespeople (real estate, insurance, securities, etc.) who hire assistants to help them take care of the details, which frees them up to drum up more business. These high-performance salespeople are the rainmakers for their business; without their finely honed skills, there would be no business. Unfortunately, great salespeople are rarely great managers. One of the first mistakes they make is to find a great assistant who will take care of everything for them. Now let's say they get "lucky" and find that someone, a genuine Girl/Guy Friday who's just amazing!

Pay Me More — Or Else!

For the first couple of weeks (the honeymoon period), our high-performance salesperson comes into the office every day whistling. In her mind, everything is now right in the world because she has someone taking care of all the details. All she has to do now is sell. However, because her assistant is taking care of all the details, they also see every one of those fat commission checks that our hapless high-performance sales gal brings in. It doesn't take long for this "awesome" assistant to figure out that the high-performance salesperson cannot live without their support. And if they are really, really good, they'll make damn sure of it.

Our high-performance salesperson is now faced with a conundrum (or more accurately, an extortion threat): "Give me a piece of the action, or I walk." And now, because this amazing assistant is the only one who knows the intricacies of running the business, making good on this threat would cause a serious disruption to our heroine's income stream, not to mention her peace of mind. More often than not, the sales person/employer will cave. In fact, the more successful and busy the salesperson, the more likely they are to give in to the demands of a key assistant. I know of one very successful mortgage loan officer who confided in me that he was paying some of his assistants over $200,000/year —for essentially administrative work!

That's just crazy —and as you will soon discover, so unnecessary. The key factors here that inevitably lead to this problem are: *a)* the assistant ends up knowing more about the details of running the business than the business owner does, thus becoming "indispensable," and *b)* their very presence makes them aware of just how much money is being made (on their backs, of course).

As we will see in the next chapter, Virtual Outsourcing eliminates these factors and hence the problem because: *a)* no one person is indispensable when each job function is handled by an outsourced specialist using a well-defined, written process, and *b)* since they are supporting you off premises, they are never reminded or made aware of just how much money your company generates (out of sight, out of mind). Nor, do they particularly care because they have their own business to run.

Avoiding compensation creeps (or leaps) is just one of the many advantages of incorporating Virtual Outsourcing. Another is greatly reducing, in fact nearly eliminating, one of the most onerous, unproductive, enervating and politically charged practices in modern business...

Death by Meeting

From 1986 until 1993 when we retired from it, my wife and I owned a highly profitable high-tech mortgage consulting firm that eventually grew to about 25 or so employees. Having painstakingly trained nearly every one of them myself, I fairly glowed in the notion that they were the highest performance team in our market area —if not in the entire state of California. In an effort to maintain that high-pitched competitive edge, it seemed necessary at the time to meet in some form nearly every day. We'd have a company-wide meeting once a week, meticulously planned and enthusiastically lead by yours truly, and smaller sub-group meetings throughout the day —day in, day out. The bigger, more complex our organization became, the more meetings we needed. It just seemed to be the logical way to maintain control, provide managerial guidance and empower the troops to give their best. We tried everything in the book(s) to help make our meetings more inspired, creative, interactive and time worthy. We even tried stand up meetings —exactly one time (my revved up troops didn't care much for the "meet with your feet" technique).

Boy, was I a dope! In my very sincere and eventually desperate effort to shepherd the growth of the company through meetings, I was actually taking valuable time away from my people, and quite frankly, me. The more we met, the more distracted and less productive we all became. And by the way, have you ever noticed how meetings are like rabbits? Once they get started, they can generate multiple generations of offspring in a single day! Being the hard-charging, creative bunch that we were, we'd have ad hoc meetings in the hallway, near the water cooler, the copy room, the foyer, or just about any place where you could fit at least two bodies together. If any of us had a great idea, we'd charge into an office and share it with someone. Every day was exciting, the energy was palpable —and, it was *totally* unproductive; no, make that counterproductive. These meetings were so interruptive that less and less real work was getting done. It got so bad that we started putting signs up on our office doors that said: "Don't even THINK of interrupting me unless the building is burning!"

However, try as you might, whenever you have two or more people present in the same workspace, it's impossible to escape meetings. We are highly social beings, we can't help ourselves, and we will rationalize meeting with our workmates in any number of creative ways. The more people you have in the same location, the worse it is. In fact, in larger organizations, it is not uncommon to have "meta-meetings" or even "meta-meta-meetings" (i.e., meetings to determine the time, structure and content of future meetings). Meetings are ostensibly a tool to sharpen the focus of an organization's work force, but they often quite effectively do the opposite.

Here is my take as to why this is inherently the case. By their very nature, meetings:

- Break the focus of the participants. If your people are not fully engaged in the execution of their business objectives, then by definition, they have lost focus. Maintaining laser-like focus is the foundation for personal and organizational productivity;

- Are a rich nutrient in the petri dish of organizational politics, which can eat away at a company like a cancer. The nonverbal and often unconscious communications flying around a meeting room are unbelievably rich and complex. This sets up personal dynamics between a company's staff that's rooted in one's own "CYA"; the focus is on moving up the ladder of success or on preventing others from obtaining the same. These are all major distractions from the business objectives at hand;

- Are expensive! You can figure you will lose a minute and a half of productive time for each attendee for every minute you have your staff in a meeting. This is because most meetings are considered ineffective[15] and it takes time to ramp down to prepare for the meeting and ramp back up to full focus afterwards.

As you can probably tell by now, I'm not very fond of meetings —"loathe" probably better describes my feelings toward them. And that's whether it involves meetings within my own businesses, which are very far and few between, or participating in those of others. As a consultant to several major organizations, I get to attend other company's high-level management meetings. In addition to participating, a part of me also tends to step back and watch as a passive observer; what I witness is usually not very pretty. The politics, BS, jockeying for position, the herd mentality, CYA and drama —it's all there, all except the productivity and focus that the meeting was meant to produce.

Were you ever part of a business meeting where the attendees acted like they were bit-players in some B-movie? Unfortunately, it seems that far too many people have. This former corporate business analyst experienced it first-hand…

The Staff Meeting from Hell

When I think of my last "corporate meeting to end all meetings," I compare it to a room with multiple layers of wall paper, one plastered over the other, to the point where a wall no longer looks like a wall, but an upholstered surface; better yet, a padded cell!

Business meetings should have a purpose; they should accomplish something. Not this meeting. Not the one that convinced me to leave the corporate world forever. I felt as if I was in the middle of a bad soap opera —complete with egotistical leads, jealous supporting players and cheap extras from central casting.

For 12 years, I worked for one of the world's largest mega-banking corporations. My bruises are healing, and the lingering, foul odor is almost gone! When I decided to leave, my division had already gone through its fourth restructure in six months.

I'm a big movie buff and, as I sat in those fateful meetings, I actually heard the very same words I had heard in the film, *The Godfather*, when Michael says to Fredo, "You don't say anything outside the family!" You don't have to be Italian to know that this was not a gentle warning. It was an order.

The straw that broke my back was the result of a huge faux pas on the part of upper-level management, run by the twins of the Evil Empire division. Together, they succeeded at thrashing every principle of decency I ever held dear. Let's just call them Ava and Alex for the purposes of my story.

They were ready to swear on a stack of bibles that they had assigned a particular project to me much earlier than they actually did. The day of reckoning had approached to discuss the progress of the project, which would be the topic at a standard executive meeting.

When Ava realized that I was insistent on the date I received the project and willing to say so in a meeting, she said, "No. You didn't get it then." Hmm. I knew right then and there that this stain was going to bleed across the entire afternoon.

So, she and I had a pre-meeting, so she could instruct me as to what I could or could not say. We had just walked into the meeting, when she immediately approached Alex and said to him, "I already gave her the Fredo speech!" I couldn't believe what I was hearing! I was caught between indignation and a desire to laugh as I never had before!

Misinformation and egomania dominated the meeting that followed, after which Ava called for pre-meeting number two, for just the three of us. I was warned not to say anything. "What if I'm asked a question?" I inquired. "Alex will answer it," said Ava.

"I see what's going on here," said Alex. "I think we're armed for battle." This was beginning to feel very surreal. Suddenly, I began to understand Dali and Picasso.

We carted off into the super-big, top-of-the-charts meeting, now. I was told exactly where to sit —right between Ava and Alex, close enough for either or both of them to kick me under the table to stifle or reprimand me, whichever seemed appropriate.

As meeting number three progressed, I wondered if there was a first aid kit anywhere in the room. My legs were feeling awfully bruised! I wasn't going to shut up about the timeline of this project and they weren't prepared to take the blame.

Ava proposed another meeting with me and Alex. I practically limped into her office, only to be detained once more for a tête-à-tête between just Ava and me.

My entire day was spent going from office to office and conference room to conference room. In the next business quarter, yet another restructuring took place. This time, I was actually offered a promotion. Have you guessed the ending to my story?

For the past three years I have been running two successful businesses from home, while enjoying the advantage of being there for my 10-year-old son. I am a strategic planner and marketing specialist. I tell clients that when they are out selling properties, I am efficiently running their offices from my location.

I make my own rules for the way my business runs. I don't think I could ever work for someone else, again. No more idiotic meetings, meta-meetings or meta-meta-meetings filled with thinly veiled movie dialog threats. I've never been happier in my life.

Lisa Morgan
Executive Level Virtual Assistant

Studies have shown that the more meetings you have, the greater negative impact on staff morale and job satisfaction.[16] "Hmmm, that seems like a serious problem —let's have a meeting to discuss setting up a task force to study it further..."

Why have I bothered to make such a big deal about meetings? Because, as we have just seen above, they are by their very nature counterproductive. And (here's the kicker), meetings *will happen* any time you have two or more people within the same physical workplace. And finally, the more people you have in the same location, the more numerous and disruptive the meetings become.

There are two ways to avoid this "Slow Death by Meeting." The first is to minimize the number of people within the same physical workspace. The second is to make sure every one of your staff has a clearly written set of business objectives with well-defined processes, procedures, goals, timelines and reporting. Having these in place will eliminate the need for most meetings. And, when you do meet, have a darned good reason for it and avoid meeting in person. This will tend to keep the meetings shorter and more focused and eliminate most of the nonverbal cues that can be so counterproductive.

At this point, you might be thinking: "This guy has lost his mind!" I can assure you that I am quite sane (my wife's opinion notwithstanding) and live what I preach. You see, with Virtual Outsourcing, your "staff" are geographically dispersed and hence never located in the same place. And, because virtually outsourced staff are business people in their own right, they are very comfortable working independently and executing according to written business processes. You will find that once you have incorporated Virtual Outsourcing into your business, your "need" and tolerance for meetings will be greatly diminished. And that means you and your virtual staff are freed up to do what you and they do best and what brings highest value to your business.

Management by Process

As mentioned earlier, one of the ways to avoid unnecessary meetings is to have all your business processes well documented. This also happens to be one of the primary keys to incorporating virtually outsourced staff within your organization. No matter what kind of staff you have, it's important for many reasons to create and maintain your company's own set of standard business practices and procedures. When working with someone you never meet (a Virtual Assistant or Consultant), it's absolutely critical that their job function is unambiguously defined. In fact, a written process for what they do literally defines their relationship with your company.

Having formal written business processes for every significant job function is the foundation of "management by objective." This approach allows you, as the business owner/manager, to focus on what needs to get done rather than how it's done because that's already been unambiguously defined. Management by objective is a highly effective and proven way to greatly reduce or eliminate your organization's internal "friction" that mucks up the smooth running and growth of companies. However, most small to midsized business owners/managers are not schooled in the art and science of writing formal business processes. And even if they were, they simply wouldn't have the time (or likely the desire) to do it. In larger enterprises, they either have their own dedicated staff for this purpose or they outsource it to the business services unit of companies like IBM or Accenture —neither of which are likely to be very affordable or practical for small organizations.

So what is a small business to do? Well, you can do what I have done and outsource it to a Virtual Consultant who happens to specialize in creating and maintaining written business processes. In fact, as of this writing, I am currently having all of my business processes formalized in a highly structured way, designed to be easy to follow and easy to update when necessary. This person happens to live in Australia and it is highly unlikely I will ever meet her. Using the methods I'll be sharing later in this book, you will see just how easy it was to find her and understand why she is so affordable. By the way, one of the processes I intend to have her write is the process of writing and maintaining business processes for my companies! That means this important job function will be completely documented so I can easily replace her if I choose.

OK, let's do a quick review of what we covered so far in this chapter.

Key Ideas and Chapter Review

- Successfully running and growing a business with onsite staffing requires strong management skills;

- Most small business owners don't have strong management skills;

- Virtually outsourced support typically doesn't require training or management —they simply get the job done;

- When your business turns the corner, employees will typically resent you making "tons of money" off their backs, ask for a "piece of the action" and develop an entitlement attitude;

- Talented employees will sometimes strive to make themselves indispensable, thereby holding you hostage;

- An offsite virtual staff typically doesn't see how much money you make, nor do they care. As independent business people, they rarely develop an employee mentality;

- Business meetings with employees are typically counterproductive;

- The more employees you have, the more frequently unnecessary meetings will occur;

- "Management by meeting" doesn't work;

- Because they simply get the job done, far fewer meetings are required when using virtually outsourced support;

- "Management by objective" does work (when objectives and processes are well documented);

- Maintaining a well-documented and up-to-date set of business processes allows your support staff to become interchangeable;

- You can easily and affordably virtually outsource the writing and maintaining of your business processes.

Business is already tough, so is it any wonder so many small companies struggle with the whole notion of running and growing their businesses using employees? Even if the above points were not major issues, the fact of the matter is that bigger companies have a huge advantage over small businesses when hiring talent. That's because small companies typically don't have the financial or HR resources to attract, hire, train and manage people who may be pulled from a broad geographical region.

In other words, under the typical employer/employee model of support staffing, small businesses will almost always get hammered with higher costs, greater hassles, and far fewer options than larger firms. For the most part, using employees exclusively for support simply does not work (or at best, not well) for the small business owner or independent professional.

It is often said that in business, people are your greatest asset. I couldn't agree more, as long as there are as few as possible to get the job done and you don't have to train, manage, coddle, stroke, motivate, counsel or even look at them. Not only are your people your greatest asset, they can also be the biggest pain in your asset —especially when they all work under the same roof. These issues are just a function of human nature and I learned long ago never to fight it because to do so means you'll lose —every time.

Virtual Outsourcing is the revolutionary answer to this staffing conundrum. This innovative strategy eliminates most of the staffing problems and gives you access to talent that you otherwise never dreamed of being able to reach or afford. This means your business is able to be far more productive for less money and hassle than you ever thought possible.

Your business will never be the same once you've learned the secrets of tapping into this geographically independent, limitless pool of very affordable, highly skilled talent. With Virtual Outsourcing you don't have to train, manage or even provide support facilities in order for your staff to do their job. We're talking about leveling the playing field here. Not only with big business, but just as importantly, with your small to midsized competitors who may have an edge with their superior management talent —talent that becomes less relevant in this whole new world of support you are about to discover.

Now, let's explore this incredible alternative to the standard employer/employee model with respect to getting things done for you, the business owner.

Virtual Outsourcing is defined as business-related help or support from anyone who has the time, talent and desire to assist you with any aspect of your business *that can be done from a distance*. Virtual Outsourcing falls into two basic categories: *Virtual Consultants* (VCs) for project-based work and *Virtual Assistants* (VAs) for ongoing support. The chart below provides an overview of their differences. Additionally, in this chapter we will explore how very real businesses have benefited from Virtual Outsourcing, its genesis and how it is quite different from enterprise outsourcing and telecommuting. We will also explore the various sources that feed the enormous pool of virtual talent that's available right now to help your business.

Virtual Consultants vs. Virtual Assistants

The reason I make a distinction between VCs and VAs is that the processes by which you find, evaluate, hire, manage and compensate people within these two respective groups are quite different:

	Virtual Consultants (VCs)	**Virtual Assistants (VAs)**
Finding	Sophisticated online "Virtual Service Provider Marketplaces" that give you access to hundreds of thousands of VCs from around the world, skilled in just about any area of expertise you can imagine.	Virtual Assistant associations, industry-specific VA communities, source-specific VA communities, virtual staffing companies and search engines.

Evaluating	VCs bid against each other for the privilege of doing your project. You choose a VC based upon their bid response, bid amount, experience, examples of their work and objective feedback from previous users.	You choose a VA based upon their experience in the area of expertise you require, communication style, cost/terms, examples of their work and a due-diligence process similar to that used when hiring an employee.
Hiring	A simple click of the mouse indicating your acceptance of your chosen VC's bid terms. NOTE: You can hire a VC while maintaining your complete anonymity, even through the point of paying them for the completed project.	Execution of a formal independent contractor's agreement that defines all aspects of the job function to be performed, standards of work, compensation, nondisclosure, etc.
Managing	Since VCs only work on well-defined "projects," management is by objective. Also, most online Virtual Service Provider Marketplaces provide an online "workspace" or intranet that can be used to manage your project process and communicate with the VC.	Ideally by objective. That is, the ongoing job function that the VA agrees to do for you should be based upon a well-defined, written business process with straightforward and easily measured results, timelines and quality standards.
Compensating	Upon satisfactory completion of your project, you pay the online Virtual Service Provider Marketplace (where you found the VC) the agreed upon bid amount. This protects your financial information from the individual VC who could be located anywhere in the world.	Upon submission of a periodic invoice, you typically pay the agreed-upon hourly fee, retainer or results-based fee (which is preferred for reasons that will be covered in a later chapter). Most VAs will accept credit cards, checks or other types of online payment systems like PayPal.

The main differences between a VC and VA are: *a)* how you find and hire them, and *b)* that you often may use a VC only once (for a specific project) even if they did an absolutely brilliant job, while a VA is someone you use on an ongoing basis similar to an employee.

The boundary between VCs and VAs can be blurry at times. For example, you may find an awesome VC for a project and determine that they would be great for some ongoing support within your business, at which point they become a VA. Likewise, many VAs do project work as well, turning them into VCs within those particular contexts.

It simply does not make fiscal or managerial sense to hire skilled employees if you can successfully outsource their functions (either to a VC or VA) only when you truly need them. This gives you the ability to have the benefit of "talent on demand," rather than having to pay for employees all the time, whether you need them or not.

The Virtual Payoff Is Real

So what kind of financial benefits can *you* expect to see by incorporating Virtual Outsourcing into your business? If you follow the procedures that are laid out in this book, you can expect plenty! For example, here is a story of how one of my students enthusiastically incorporated the use of Virtual Assistants within his business and the results he realized because of it.

Steve (not his real name) is a very affable gentleman whose young looks belie his 40 plus years of age. He also happens to be the General Manager of a real estate brokerage in a resort location near the East Coast of the U.S. He attended one of my workshops several years ago at a real estate industry convention. As a professional speaker, I'm usually fairly aware of my audience and can tell which individuals really "get" what I'm trying to share. Clearly, Steve was one of those and you could see on his face the quiet determination to put the concepts, processes and procedures of Virtual Outsourcing to work in his business.

Not too surprisingly, his location is a fairly expensive place to do business. Wages tend to be high and office space goes for a premium. So Steve was highly motivated to reduce his operational costs any way he could, and Virtual Outsourcing appeared to be a viable option. Keep in mind that when he first started on his journey to implement Virtual Outsourcing, he felt just as uncertain about applying something so radically new to his business as you may be feeling right now. However, he started out incrementally. That is, he identified the first support function that could be handled remotely and then found the skilled VA to do the job. After it was clear that function was running smoothly and efficiently, he then virtually outsourced the next function to another VA, made sure it worked, and so on. He now has five VAs helping him run his business and he has never met a single one of them.

The payoff for Steve and his company has been substantial. In 2004, his company was named the top small to midsized brokerage in the world for his franchise. In February of 2006, I once again was speaking at a major industry conference and happened to run into him, and as always he had a big smile on his face. I asked him how things were going with his cadre of Virtual

Assistants and he enthusiastically remarked it couldn't be better. Well, that's always good to hear, but I was interested in specifics. So I asked him how much money he was saving annually in staffing costs by using his VAs. He replied that conservatively he was saving over $200,000 a year, taking into account savings on wages, benefits, payroll taxes, insurance, reduced training and management, office space and equipment.

Remember, Steve's company is not particularly large, so $200,000 a year in savings is quite substantial. As good as this is however, what he said next made it even better. With almost a look of misty-eyed disbelief, he went on to say, "Michael, the best part is that when my VAs complete a job, they THANK ME!"

While most of the case stories you will see in this book fully disclose who they are about, "Steve" insisted on remaining anonymous. The reason is that none of his local competitors have any idea how he's producing these kinds of results, and frankly, he wants to keep it that way.

Now envision the benefits that your business can realize with access to nearly any kind of talented individual you can imagine. Individuals that you don't have to manage, train, provide office space for or constantly coddle to perform at their peak. And, you only pay for what you use. In other words, imagine getting to focus exclusively on what you do best while talented others take care of the rest from a distance —for far less than what traditional onsite staffing costs you now. That is the paradigm-busting benefit of incorporating Virtual Outsourcing into *your* business.

The Virtual Pants Presser

If you own a traditional small business such as a retail shop or dry cleaner, you may be wondering how Virtual Outsourcing could benefit you. After all, there are no such things as virtual sales clerks or virtual pants pressers. You need the help of real people onsite in order to make your business run properly. For these purposes, you are restricted to hiring from a pool of potential employees who live reasonably close to your establishment.

However, there are many other important functions within your business that can easily and affordably be virtually outsourced. For example: book-keeping (my bookkeeper lives in Kansas), marketing (my marketing director is in Ohio), advertising design, Human Resources, Web site development (my developer is in North Carolina), strategic planning, telemarketing, point of sale computer systems, etc. These can all be performed by affordable specialists residing anywhere in the world, who use the Internet as the primary vehicle to deliver their work product.

The point is, no matter what your business happens to be, or how traditional it is, you will be able to benefit from Virtual Outsourcing. And as you read on, you'll see exactly how it can be integrated into your unique business for maximum benefits.

Virtual Specialists

Whether a Virtual Assistant or Virtual Consultant, they typically specialize in one or more particular business support functions. This is a very important factor. When you hire a Virtual Consultant (for project-based work) or Virtual Assistant (for ongoing support), you are hiring an independent contractor who is an expert, a "master" at what they do rather than a "jack of all trades." This means you typically don't have to train them and can expect extremely high levels of work quality and efficiency. When you think about this, it makes perfect sense. In the parlance of Michael Gerber's "E-Myth," individuals offering Virtual Outsourcing services are highly specialized "Technicians" who most likely love what they do. And, in doing it over and over for a wide range of business clients, they become quite good at it, in terms of both quality and speed. In fact, one of the keys to successfully using Virtual Outsourcing is making sure you hire specialists and avoid those that purport to offer many different types of services.

Also, as you will see in Chapter 5, communities of independent Virtual Assistants have started to form for the purpose of supporting particular industries (real estate, insurance, securities etc.) This is a very significant development for several reasons. First, having a specific industry focus means that the Virtual Assistants within those communities are more likely to have an intimate knowledge of the people within that industry and their unique needs. Second, by having an entire community of VAs support a particular industry, it allows for individual VAs to specialize in one or more sub-categories of support within that industry. These are usually very industry-specific skills and job functions that would otherwise require a great deal of training to bring an employee up to speed.

These industry-specific communities effectively enable a much broader and deeper level of support for that industry's business people than what would otherwise be available. At this point, you might be thinking: "Gee, it sounds like I have to hire a different Virtual Assistant or Virtual Consultant for each type of job function within my business." The short answer to that is "yes."

However, it's much more manageable than it may at first seem (certainly more so than a stable of onsite staff). And in Chapter 6 you'll discover how to maintain a scope of control over your virtual staffing, no matter how many you end up having.

First, though, let's delve into how the Virtual Outsourcing movement emerged and how it's different than traditional enterprise outsourcing or telecommuting.

The "V" Word

Most people (especially grounded and practical business people) are not comfortable with the term "virtual," and frankly I don't blame them. To many, the term "virtual" refers to something that is not real (i.e., Virtual Reality). As a result, when first introduced to the concept of Virtual Outsourcing as a staffing alternative, many business people are confused and a bit, well …uneasy with the term. For example, I gave a speech titled "Transform Your Business Using Virtual Assistants" to a large trade group a few years back. On a whim, prior to commencing my speech, I asked the audience how many thought my topic centered on computer hardware or software. Over one-third raised their hands. It isn't too much of a stretch to see how some people could imagine a "Virtual Assistant" as some sort of Internet-based sex doll endowed with, among other things, a healthy dose of artificial intelligence "to serve your every need —from a distance!"

"Virtual" would not have been my first choice to describe this rapidly growing industry of very real people who provide their business support services from a distance. If given the opportunity, I think the term "remote outsourcing" and its respective sub-categories of "remote consultants" and "remote assistants" better describes the interaction between business and these geographically diverse people providing their support services as independent contractors.

It's not too hard to see how someone may have thought it apropos to name the industry with the "V" word. Clearly, the entire Virtual Outsourcing industry could not exist without the Internet (and is therefore a relatively recent phenomenon). And, in the early pioneering days of the Net, it seemed that everything was being referenced as "virtual this, virtual that" and so on.

So don't let the "V" word bother you. It simply means that they (Virtual Assistants and Virtual Consultants) are "not there," but are very real nevertheless. Now that we have covered the "virtual" half of Virtual Outsourcing, we need to spend a bit of time on the "outsourcing" part. That's because Virtual

Outsourcing is very different from what we normally think of typical business outsourcing today.

Outsourcing, Offshoring and Downsizing

There has been a lot of talk and press in the last few years about "outsourcing." Typically, it's referring to large businesses shunting their non-core business functions to other organizations that specialize in assisting companies with those specific functions. This is often referred to as "enterprise outsourcing" since it was most visible at the large organization level, often affecting thousands of employees. When an enterprise outsources to a company located in another country, it is referred to (and often pejoratively, at least from an employee's perspective) as "offshoring" or "nearshoring" in the case of jobs being outsourced to Mexico and South America.

Actually, enterprise outsourcing has been going on for many years with nary a line of negative press. For example, IBM and EDS are two of the largest information systems integration outsourcing companies in the world.[17] They are very good at handling the planning, implementation and running of complex computer and information systems. Most other companies, even Fortune 500 size firms, simply cannot afford to match the skills and experience that IBM and EDS and other similar enterprise-level outsourcing firms can offer with their own in-house staffing. Many midsized to large companies also outsource the manufacturing of their products so they can focus on design, engineering and sales.

Even if you own a small business with a few employees, chances are you're using outsourcing right now to handle your payroll. This is a particularly complex and error-prone business process that most small to midsized businesses would rather not have to deal with themselves. Paychex (http://www.paychex.com), one of the largest such companies, has been handling the payroll function (and now employee benefit plans as well) for businesses of all sizes since 1971.

The reason we are seeing more companies outsource non-core business functions is that it simply works —for the following reasons:

- *Specialists Do It Better* – Companies that specialize in supporting critical, yet non-core business functions, for other organizations are more likely to be better at it. This means that "best practices" will likely be applied to a company's outsourced non-core functions without having to spend the time, money and infrastructure necessary to constantly keep up-to-date;

- *It Can Cost Less* – Since outsource firms tend to specialize in supporting a certain set of business functions, they can often take advantage of economies of scale and pass on the savings to their corporate clients. Also, outsourcing certain functions like manufacturing, warehousing and distribution means a tremendous savings of operating capital otherwise needed for plant, infrastructure and personnel. It saves money that can be better spent on a company's core business;

- *Companies Can Focus On What They Do Best* – When a company can focus on its core competency (i.e., what they uniquely do well to create value), it's much more likely to do it better than competitors who try to do everything themselves.

With all these positive benefits of outsourcing, why all the negative press? When U.S. companies outsource to other U.S. based companies, it's no big deal. Everyone is happy (except perhaps the employees who were downsized as a result) because the jobs stayed in the U.S. However, when organizations start outsourcing major business functions (sometimes involving thousands of workers) to offshore companies, the nasty stuff starts hitting the fan. In the last few years, the press has built a feverish pitch rallying against the evils of offshoring. Stories about highly paid technical workers training their considerably less paid replacement in India or Mexico or Argentina abound. No longer are jobs staying in this country; they're being exported by the "greedy" megacorporations seeking cheap labor. And the jobs being outsourced are increasingly going up the corporate ladder in terms of skills and experience. Computer programming is, of course, one example of a highly technical skill being offshored with alacrity by large companies. And beyond that, more and more upper-level corporate functions such as legal and accounting work are being offshored as well.[18]

So where does Virtual Outsourcing fit in to all this? Virtual Outsourcing is small to midsized businesses' answer to obtaining all the benefits of enterprise outsourcing, but without the cost or hassles. There are some stark differences between enterprise outsourcing and Virtual Outsourcing. First of all, as the name suggests, enterprise outsourcing is geared to big business, often really big business. Understandably, IBM and EDS would much rather work on

> *Virtual Outsourcing is small to midsized businesses' answer to obtaining all the benefits of enterprise outsourcing, but without the cost or hassles.*

multimillion-dollar system integration projects than help a Mom & Pop Print Shop set up their PCs and local area network. And, if you're looking for custom programming to be done, don't expect the large coding houses in India, Pakistan, Russia or any other place to take on your project. They're simply not set up for the small onesy-twosey jobs. As a result, enterprise-level outsourcing is just not a practical option for most small businesses. Bummer! Those darn big business guys always seem to get the breaks —*until now.*

Virtual Outsourcing, on the other hand, is available and affordable to every small to midsized business, even if you're a business consisting of one person —you. Instead of hiring a big, impersonal company to perform your outsourced non-core business functions, Virtual Outsourcing is much more intimate. When you hire a Virtual Assistant or Virtual Consultant to do a job, chances are very good you're hiring a business of one person. These individuals (whether located domestically or overseas) are set up to specifically help the small business person with a narrow range of support functions that fall within their specialty. And, in addition to helping you with your day-to-day operations, these virtual resources can also help you launch your dreams…

From $0 to $60 Million In Two Years Flat

On August 14, 2006, Kevin Rose got to experience a thrill that few 29 year olds ever will —seeing his own face on the cover of *Business Week.* Kevin is the founder of Digg.com, one of the more famous Web 2.0 sites on the Internet. Through Digg.com, Kevin figured out an easy, yet elegant way for anyone on the planet with access to the Internet to leave their two-cents worth on any kind of news story that happens to be circulating at the time.

The way Digg works is deceptively simple. Any member of Digg (which costs nothing to join) can post a link and their comments to any story they feel is relevant (if only to them). Other members who see the post either "digg it," "bury it" or simply ignore it. The more a posting is "dugg," the more it bubbles to the top of Digg.com's popularity list. This very simple model virally increased its community of members to well over one million in a very short time. And, according to the *Business Week* article, Digg.com was the 24th most popular Web site in the U.S. —right on the heels of the *New York Times* (19th) and easily eclipsing Fox News (no. 62). These kinds of numbers make Digg. com very attractive to advertisers who are willing to pay good money for access to the relatively affluent Digg membership. The essence of the inherent popularity of Digg (and other similar Web 2.0 sites) is that it gives the opportunity to otherwise obscure masses of people to achieve their 15 clicks of fame and benefit from the "social proof" of knowing what's hot and what's not.

Kevin started Digg.com from essentially just an idea (and little else) just two years prior to his celebratory *Business Week* issue (and estimated worth of $60 million). His rags to riches story would be yet another classic Silicon Valley hero's journey —with all the drama of pouring one's heart, soul and bank account into it and losing a girlfriend in the process. Typical, except for one very important detail. You see, Kevin couldn't afford to hire a programmer at going rates to transform his dream into reality. So he found a Virtual Consultant programmer who started writing his digital baby's code for all of $12/hr. The resource he used to find, evaluate and hire this talent is one of several that are covered in the next chapter.

For most small businesses, dreams remain just that, fond wishes that frustratingly never come true because of lack of know-how, cash and talent. Virtual Outsourcing can easily mitigate all of these barriers, essentially making it the 21st century dream maker.

Virtual Outsourcing isn't just for people who are in business to make money. It can often be the difference between "making a difference" or not for nonprofits with limited budgets as well…

Getting S.M.A.R.T.

My specialty is shaking skeletons out of closets. I have a very special degree —a Ph.D. of the streets. It's not about voodoo. It's about giving back.

It took me 10 years to put my program together. That program is S.M.A.R.T. Students, Inc. (Students Making Academic Rewarding Trips). After I retired from pro football, I came to San Francisco and became a juvenile probation officer and did some coaching at the local high school.

What I saw took me back to my own experiences as a kid growing up in Detroit. That life was far behind me, but the stories I heard and the stuff I saw tugged at me.

What really convinced me to establish my program were the stories of two students in particular. One was a girl, whose mother offered her up to teenage prostitution, and the other, a boy who was the child of rape.

The more research I did, the more I wanted to provide a network of counseling and educational services for "at risk" kids. Coming from a neighborhood wracked with drugs, violence and crime is, in itself, a powerful deterrent to achieving a fulfilling life. Yet, the area in which most of these kids were floundering was education —the academic kind. National statistics show that 71 percent of high school kids drop out.

However, the first and most important step in preparing these kids for studies and tutoring was "cleaning house" or getting rid of those old, dusty skeletons which prevent many of us from moving on in life.

You've got to clean out those closets before you stuff them with more junk! Often, programs for at risk kids treat the disturbing or antisocial behaviors without really delving into the personal issues and/or family dynamics that created them.

So, as a first step, we offer counseling and therapy. With the right tools, we are hopeful that minds can be healed.

When I first thought of establishing a Web site for S.M.A.R.T. Students, Inc., I knew I had good ideas, but no expertise in setting up shop online.

I explored the Elance Web site and was immediately impressed with the bid system, the way projects were presented by buyers and responded to by providers. It seemed fair and honest for all parties.

What I needed was a Web design, some reworking of the existing logo, copyrighting and the creation of a personal and sensitive donation letter.

The team I assembled consists of three professionals —Michelle (Wisconsin), Rashida (Ohio) and Beth Ann (West Virginia). We collaborate through conference calls. I come away feeling relaxed and confident that the work is getting done.

Michelle composed the donation letter, Rashida handles the copyrighting and Beth Ann works on the Web site. The best part of bringing them together is knowing that we are all on the same page. Two of the ladies are also moms, which means that they can work from home and still be there for their kids.

I invited them into my world to see what I see, feel what I feel and share my passion for building something good and lasting for the young people I deal with.

My advice, from a buyer's perspective, is to know your business —inside out. Be clear about your goals, then give the jobs to capable people who will save you a whole lot of money and headaches.

Doug Hollie, Retired
Seattle Seahawks Defensive End

U.S. and Canadian-based people who provide Virtual Outsourcing services (either as Virtual Assistants or Virtual Consultants) tend to be individual men and (mostly) women who work from home. Overseas, there appears to be a higher percentage of men offering their support services than women and they sometimes work in small groups or collectives of people who share the same skill sets.

Better Than Telecommuting

At first blush, Virtual Outsourcing and telecommuting may seem very similar because in both instances, support staff performs work from their homes. But this is where the similarity ends. While telecommuting staff may have more freedom in regards to where they complete their work, they are still very much employees —and we know what THAT means for you the employer. Once again, the fact that Virtual Assistants and Virtual Consultants are always independent contractors is a source of huge fiscal, strategic and managerial benefits to those businesses that use them.

Be that as it may, we can look at telecommuting as the first toe in the water of trying something other than the traditional "everyone works under one roof" approach to business. Telecommuting really didn't first kick in until the mid 1990s because it requires the low-cost communications infrastructure that only the Internet could provide. There are a number of reasons why telecommuting has continued to grow as a trend in larger companies. The ability to work from home is considered a highly attractive employee benefit by many. No more fighting traffic for (in some cases) several hours a day, spending money on gas and car maintenance, and having to dress up just to do one's work. In addition to having more productive employees[19] (i.e., those not exhausted from the wasted hours of long commutes[20]), telecommuting also allows companies to expand their workforce without having to provide additional physical office space. With the appropriate quality assurance systems in place, managing a telecommuting workforce can be considerably easier.[21] They are more focused on the job at hand (remember, no nasty distractions from office mates or pointy-haired bosses —young kids are another story). Productivity-robbing office politics and endless meetings are greatly diminished as well.

An increasingly important ancillary benefit to telecommuting (and likewise, Virtual Outsourcing) is its mitigating impact on global warming.[22] Hydrocarbon emissions due to commuting are a major source of the greenhouse gases affecting our planet's climate. There is sweet irony in the fact that the "greenest" thing you can do for your company is incorporate Virtual Outsourcing.

Lifestyles of the Virtually Talented

The emergence of the remote employee is just the beginning of a much more significant sociological trend in the way people work and interact with each other in a business environment. In her book *The Popcorn Report: The Future of Your Company, Your World, Your Life,* trend master Faith Popcorn popularized the notion of "cocooning" as a growing trend where people attempt to protect and insulate themselves from an increasingly frenetic and perceivably dangerous world. September 11 added fuel to that fire in that it caused millions of people to suddenly (and for many, the first time) consider that there are more important things in life than spending most of their waking hours at some distant office, doing things they may not enjoy doing, working with people who often aggravate them or having to endure long commutes to and from such a place. As a result, having a closer connection with family in physical, temporal and emotional terms has become a priority for many.[23] Sometimes becoming a VA means having flexibility to do things that others simply couldn't even dream about...

Have Laptop and RV —Will Travel

My motto is "Anything is possible!" In fact, some people say that my family and I have reinvented the American dream.

So, why did we choose to sell our home in California and all the furnishings and possessions attached to it? Quite simply, we wanted to find a richer quality of life and a better location that would offer those things.

"The times...they were a-changing" in the Bay Area and not, in our opinion, for the better.

Lifestyles there were just getting too crazy. Most important, we were not happy with the cost of living and existing school system for our kids. We wanted a family life that was going to be profitable, enjoyable and more compatible with the kind of wholesome values we wanted to impart to our daughters.

My niche is marketing coordination in the real estate business —listings, virtual tours, product enhancement. I started my VA business in 2001, before our one-year road trip. Yes, after leaving California, we spent one year living out of our RV.

Wherever we stopped, we found RV communities to be open and accepting worlds unto themselves. Each new motorized arrival (and its inhabitants) was warmly welcomed into the fold, regardless of its year, make or model.

Older RVers, especially in Florida, sang the praises of this lifestyle and actually supported us for taking our trips while we were young and healthy.

The absolute hardest part of living in transition was dealing with Internet connections, or the lack of them, especially when faced with crucial timelines.

Today, however, many RV parks have a wireless Internet connection, many truck stop/travel centers have Wi-Fi, Verizon Aircards and DataStorm mobile satellite systems have upgraded their services.

We're no longer in our RV, though. The adventure led us to a new home in Idaho. We've lived one dream and plan on starting a new one! One of the reasons we chose our area of Idaho is because the people are so great, so genuine. We feel secure and supported by neighbors who still come to our door to introduce themselves and welcome us to the community.

Our children have never been in a neighborhood where they could just knock on a playmate's door and spend the afternoon together. The local school system, in particular, has restored my faith in public education.

Our full-time RV days our behind us, for now. The best part of this experience was that it gave us the ability to have the life we want, not one that we had to have. We've moved to a place that we love, where we can enjoy seeing our children grow and prosper.

Because of my VA business, we were able to choose this place independent of needing to find local employment. We would never have been able to do this if we hadn't taken our show on the road and made it work for us!

Amber Drake
Peripatetic VA

And for some, becoming a Virtual Assistant means a way to bootstrap from just scraping by to thriving…

It Just Keeps Getting Better and Better

Each year my children would ask, "Is Santa going to bring presents this year?" And each year I would faithfully answer, "Only if you believe." Sometimes, believing that good things will happen is all you have.

After experiencing a cross-country trek to accommodate my husband's new job and to refresh a troubled marriage, surviving a corporate work story that ripped the rug out from under me, and grabbing any job I could find (including mowing neighbors' lawns), I gave new meaning to the expression "overcoming obstacles." My story is a decathlon of perseverance and survival!

We moved far from our Toronto home; in fact, as far away as the Canadian countryside would allow —5,000 miles from the east to the west coast. Leaving family and friends behind was wrenching; saying goodbye to my parents was like cutting off a limb.

The marriage failed after just one year in our new surroundings. I was at a low ebb, trying to remain positive for the children and provide for them, at any cost. It's what any parent would do. I went to school and became a certified marketing specialist, taking advantage of every opportunity to find any sort of administrative work that I could do at home, preferably, to be there for the kids.

I worked part-time as an on-call secretary for the local school board. I worked for neighbors, looking over their business books. I had a bunch of small, part-time jobs that I'd run to at irregular times. It paid the rent. When I finally landed a solid job with a computer sales and service company, I was grateful for the stability it offered and, of course, for the steady income. Then, suddenly, that changed, too. One day, the president of the company just picked himself up and walked out the door and away from the business forever, leaving us all without paychecks.

I couldn't afford to crumble. I became the "Jackie of All Trades," pulling the business together as best as I could, while remembering an unusual term I saw on the Internet —Virtual Assistant. People with this funny sounding job title were able to make lucrative incomes using very specific skills —and do it from the comfort of their homes.

Administrative support and Web design were my specialties. I decided to give the virtual world a spin. Luckily, the customers left behind in the corporate debacle I had just witnessed, followed me and soon became my first clients.

There is something to be said, in a very big way, for the value of ethics, personally and professionally. I volunteered to complete these clients' projects, free of charge. It just seemed to be the right thing to do. Positive word spread and soon I was getting steady work. My life actually improved for the better the day my boss walked out on all of us! I just didn't see it then. My business has experienced a total upswing in the past year, practically tripling my yearly income. Today, I have a three-month waiting list for new clients.

The best example of how my job as a Virtual Assistant has changed my life will culminate in a grand vacation in January. I have booked a family cruise to the Caribbean! It will be our first real trip together. For me, it is a milestone. A dream come true!

My advice to anyone who is contemplating the benefits of becoming a Virtual Assistant is, JUST DO IT! Yes, it's scary at first, but take control of your own life! When you look back, you'll be pleasantly surprised and gratified.

I know just how that will feel when I'm sitting on a tropical beach, sipping a tall island drink and tapping the keys of my laptop, in time to the sound of crystal clear waves creeping to shore....and back again.

Tawnya Sutherland
VA Poster Child

And for others, it is a way to express and receive payment for their talents that otherwise just would not be possible in a traditional work environment...

My Glass Is Always Half-Full

When you know you have a strong life force, talent and skills, there is always something you can do. It's just a matter of finding it. I have to be doing something beneficial or I don't feel that I am contributing to my home, my family or the community, in general.

These goals were compromised when symptoms of my illness began to appear. I could have chalked up my persistent fatigue to the cumulative effect of the daily, hour-and-a-half commute to work (each way) or the energy I gave to my job or the stress of executing it. We all go through physical and mental slumps.

This feeling was different and it was increasing. Eventually, I began to downscale the kinds of work I could comfortably do. My last job was being a receptionist. Answering phones and taking messages was not grueling work.

Seven years and five doctors later, I was diagnosed with multiple sclerosis (MS). I knew then that work —as I had known it —was no longer a possibility for me.

My husband was completely supportive of whatever changes and decisions we would need to make. It was his suggestion that I stop working, stay home and "administer" the home front. I love sewing and cross-stitching, but the charm of this humble, busywork soon paled. I had a vast administrative and managerial background, and I wanted to find work that would offer my skills to clients and also accommodate my abilities and my adjusted lifestyle.

I methodically approached my own options in the same way I usually approach new projects —by writing everything down. I'm a list maker, a note jotter, a sticky note fiend! I literally made a list of all my strong points and went online to research work-at-home options. It wasn't long before I stumbled upon the category, "Virtual Assistance." At last! I had struck gold! I could do this! Over the next year, I researched the nitty-gritty of establishing my own business as a VA.

I started my business in March of 2003; by fall, it was pretty much going at full speed. Most of my clients are local (Canada), with one steady client in the States. Most of their needs are not time-sensitive. So, if I need to take a break, I can relax on the couch in my office and return to work, refreshed. I provide general administrative work, bookkeeping, Web design (which I often subcontract out), mailings, and Internet research, which I most enjoy.

The benefits of working in the virtual world are multifold. It is one of the "safer" jobs with regard to investment capital, which is relatively minimal. I'm more productive, focused and I adhere better to self-imposed schedules. When I lay out my day, the work flow is tighter since I don't expect distractions. The biggest distraction in my day is letting the dog out…and letting the dog in.

Word of mouth and professional networking have been big pluses for my business. I can't see myself working for someone else, again. I would feel smothered!

I believe good will is also necessary in a business such as mine. I have a time clock on my computer, which helps in billing clients. But, if I take a break, so does the time clock. I simply stop it and then resume counting hours when I come back to the computer.

Hopefully, my story will resonate with people who are disabled or unable to continue to work in traditional office environments. Being a VA is one of the most important decisions I've ever made.

Lori Padgett
Virtual Assistant

Working from home as a virtually outsourced independent contractor is a way for talented people to have their cocoon cake and eat it too. Working on their terms, their schedule, doing the kinds of things for which they receive greatest satisfaction, for the kind of people they truly enjoy helping —all within an environment that is safe, secure and emotionally most important to them —their home.[24]

We've looked at why more and more people want to work from home and have seen that the Internet is the "how." Now let's cover the major trends that dictate "who" is likely to offer their skills to businesses as virtually outsourced talent.

Who Are These "Virtual People"?

Remember, large companies are aggressively using outsourcing and offshoring as strategic means to stay competitive in an increasingly global economy.[25] These activities inevitably result in substantial downsizing of these organizations, which releases tens of thousands of skilled workers (many are now white-collar) back into the "looking for work" ranks.[26] A growingly significant portion of these people see this change of affairs as an opportunity to start their own business, often as consultants or independent contractors.

This is just one segment of the supply side of the Virtual Outsourcing equation. Based upon a study published in 2005, there are approximately 65 million female workers in the U.S. Of these, about 55 million are still in their childbearing years and 73 percent of those (about 40 million) are in white-collar jobs.[27]

> " Working from home as a virtually outsourced independent contractor is a way for talented people to have their cocoon cake and eat it too. "

Many highly talented women quit at the top of their career so they can participate in one of life's truly magnificent joys —having children! And, six to eight months after that little bundle of joy comes into the world, spending nearly every waking hour (assuming there is any other kind at this stage) talking baby-talk, changing poopy diapers and cleaning spit off of every surface other than the ceiling, these women are ready to get back to the real world —and the sooner the better!

They long for real adult conversation, which went by the wayside with their husbands long ago because they are just as tired (or pretend to be) as the moms. At this point, they're itching to get back into the fray, mix it up, make a difference (in business) and maybe even start earning some money to help pay for junior's $10,000/year preschool. This "talented as hell but stuck with kids" group of females is part of a growing demographic who realize that virtually outsourcing their skills is a way to "have it all." It allows them to spend as much time as they want with their growing family, continue to develop and express their talents in the context of interesting people and projects, while getting paid well to do so.

Three Reasons to Go Virtual

I was pregnant with triplets, as big as a house, talking to just about anyone who would listen about my departure from my job as a high-powered, high-profiled executive in project management for an enormous health insurance company.

Perhaps, unlike others who make a conscious decision to work virtually, the situation to start a small, home-based business was essentially forced upon me! More than anything, things seemed to happen by chance. When I first learned that I was pregnant with three babies, we were told that there was a high chance of miscarriage. By my fourth month, I was still pregnant, living in a shoebox-sized house, telling my husband that they're not all going to fit into the Toyota Celica or Ford Probe. And what was I going to do about work? The worst part was that my husband was self-employed, so I carried our health insurance.

I have degrees in bio-chemistry and physics and a master's in business and health administration. Most of my work was in hospital administration and insurance. But, there I was, out in the cold, looking down the road with tripling expenses, and shrinking our income by one-third. We didn't live large, we weren't particularly wasteful; we had a comfortable lifestyle. Big adjustments were on the horizon.

My kids came. When things began getting a little easier and I had more free moments to spare, I needed something to do. I was getting bored and frustrated with making my trip to the mailbox the highlight of my day.

I practically jumped on the postman so I could converse with someone on an adult level! I even befriended the garbage collectors. I gave them donuts to make up for the weight of my diaper-laden trash.

Finally, a friend of mine who was an executive of an advertising agency came to my rescue with projects for me to do, in small increments at first. This, I liked —enough to start my own little business. Before long, this felt really good. It was the best way to go.

Things continued to get better. A steady increase in interesting and challenging projects began to arrive from more corporate clients. I began marketing my services and built systems for invoicing and tracking client payments. As my list of clients grew I became more comfortable and confident in my new role..

Like me, there are tons of highly educated, qualified professional women who embrace this option, especially when the welfare of children are involved — or when they just want to step away from years of corporate craziness. Women are generally the ones who warm to working this way, possibly because we can "multitask" better than men! One of the hardest parts of making this adjustment, however, is training yourself to think and speak a new lingo, one that sets limits.

If you're sitting in an executive staff meeting, you're not likely to say, "By not letting me leave now, you are asking me to choose between staying here or letting my children get off a school bus with no one there to meet them. I will be available to you any other time. But right now, I have to go." This is the hardest script to learn, and harder still, to say when corporate America owns you. The longer you're in the corporate world, the harder it is to break the pattern for yourself and your family.

The thought of working at a corporate job ever again is so distasteful to me now. What I do think is needed in the virtual world are solid business models for anyone who is thinking about changing their work choices and patterns.

People who are intelligent, self-confident and hard working approach virtual employment more readily, perhaps because of their individual goals and personality traits. But what can we do for those who are just as skilled, but lack the particular perseverance of those that take the plunge sooner? What part of obtaining a business degree, a master's or an MBA talks about working virtually or managing a virtual employee? These are vital areas that need to be explored.

To those who are still teetering on the brink of the virtual world, my best advice is to just try it. Don't be afraid of it. If it fails, there are always other options, in or out of corporate America.

Cindy Harnish
Proud Mother of Triplets
Executive Virtual Assistant

This trend of highly skilled corporate females entering into the ranks of Virtual Assistants or Virtual Consultants is likely to increase. As of this writing, 59 percent of U.S. college students being awarded undergraduate degrees are women, 60 percent of those earning their master's are women and 48 percent of those earning doctorates are women. Perhaps even more importantly, nearly 56 percent of all U.S. students entering college are women.[28] And, until medical science figures out how men can take over the birthing of babies, this source of highly skilled virtual talent is only going to become more significant over time.

Not Going Gently Into That Good Night

There are approximately 25 million baby boomers who will be entering retirement age by 2008.[29] This demographic cohort has been described as the most healthy, affluent and restless of any generation that has ever come before them. While many of them may have prepared financially to spend their waning days sitting in the shade and sipping mint juleps, most still have way too much life left in them. Now that they have made it this far, they want to continue to enjoy life and still make their contribution —continue to "give" before they "go." Even if they don't have to work for financial reasons, many continue to do so because it provides meaning and fulfillment in their lives.[30] And these people bring with them something that no other generation can —a very full lifetime of invaluable, real-world work experience and hard-won accumulation of bankable skills.

Working (albeit part-time) as virtually outsourced independent contractors is an ideal situation for these individuals. While they still want the sizzle that comes with applying their skills in exciting and rewarding ways, they no longer want to put up with the grease —crushing deadlines, office politics, idiot bosses, loathsome clients. As a Virtual Assistant or Virtual Consultant, they can pick and choose the types of projects to work on and the people they want to serve. This is later-in-life career fulfillment, but strictly on their terms. And, they are typically not out to make a financial killing at it. What they do and who they do it for are more important than the financial reward. What all this means to you as a business owner is that there is a huge wellspring of very reasonably priced, incredibly talented people who have the skills and experience that you otherwise could never hope to tapping into.

Seasoned Virtual Talent

Older doesn't necessarily mean wiser. However, it does mean that some of us have more experience and professional sophistication than our younger counterparts, and, quite often, that means better. Virtual Assistance is today's word for freelancing; and since I've continued to do it for the past 20 years, it's hard for me to consider myself anything but semi-retired.

Years ago, it wasn't nice to tell people that you had a home office. It sounded too professional! Yet, as a freelancer (like William Shakespeare and other lesser known authors), I work from my humble abode. Internet technology whips by at a dizzying speed, but I'm holding on for the ride. I continue to successfully tap the freelance job market online and find projects that utilize my skills and keep me in the game.

Not only are actual writing assignments secured in cyberspace, but the finished product can also create the illusion of time and place. I guess, in a way, I was freelancing virtually when I wrote on topics and places that I'd never experienced firsthand. I didn't go to New Jersey or Hawaii to write travel brochures, but you'd never know it!

I've spent the majority of my adult life working as a commercial copywriter of direct marketing materials for some of the largest firms in Chicago, including Leo Burnett, Young and Rubicam and Stone and Adler. For 16 years, I used to go "downtown" to work in the rarified and frenzied environments of advertising agencies, whose names and reputations are known throughout the world.

I've written technical copy without knowing how a piece of factory equipment or machinery actually works, yet this very fact enabled me to carefully write instructions and/or questions pertaining to its use in layman's terms. Surely, there are hordes of consumers who could benefit from any number of products designed for home use, if they could only understand the written directions. One of my direct mailing pieces won the Direct Marketing Association's highest, most prestigious award, The Golden Mailbox, showering kudos on the ad agency and me. At the time, the product brought in $20 million in sales, which would probably equate to about $80 million today.

If I had to use just one word to describe my skill, it would be versatility. In most cases, a good writer with sharp research abilities and an eye for the unusual can write about almost anything. I don't consciously follow a formula, but explore and digest topics the old fashioned way —I read, ask questions, find background information, learn how something works, why it is important and why people need to know about it.

Unless you own a company or are the company, I strongly advise people who have traditional, corporate jobs to be darn sure they have a sideline business to fall back on. For 10 years of my career, I wrote copy for television ads and commercials. Ad agencies are insanely competitive and jobs like mine are not generally known for their longevity. In fact, when an agency loses a client, most staff associated with the ad campaign are generally laid off, almost without exception.

Successful freelancing can undoubtedly keep one afloat for years. The Internet has bridged the gap for many freelancers like myself, making it possible to share skills across the country or around the globe, for anywhere from one hour to an unlimited period of time.

We don't move backward. Our past and present freelance experiences can only enhance our performances in the virtual world, prompting us to come of age in our specialized, competitive fields. As for age and wisdom, I offer this old story, which I believe sums it all up. A young, 20-year-old actor just out of film school meets a revered, veteran actor, known for decades from his performances in hundreds of films and plays. The young kid walks up to the actor and asks, "What have you done?" The old actor looks at the kid and says, "You first."

Stan Holden, Semi-retired
Virtual Copywriter

Let's see now. So far we've covered how downsizers, biological clock watchers and frisky baby boomers all feed the rapidly growing population of potential virtual talent that can make a huge difference to your business. As large a base as this is, there is still more to the supply side of Virtual Outsourcing.

Good For The Country – Good For You

The U.S. military has a problem. One that has plagued them since our armed forces went to an all volunteer model. They are having real issues in recruiting and retaining high-quality, married, enlisted and officer personnel. The main reason for this is that the "trailing spouses" of these valuable, dedicated military men and women find it nearly impossible to find and keep a good job, no matter how skilled. When you're relocating on a fairly regular basis, as most military personnel are, it's impossible for the spouse to keep a regular job. This means that their standard of living and ability to purchase decent housing becomes difficult at best. And when you're in a career that keeps you struggling financially, in addition to potentially putting your life on the line, well let's just say that's a prime reason to say, "No, thank you" at the next re-up. Fortunately, the military's very innovative solution to this particular issue also means a plethora of additional virtual talent from which your business can benefit.

Staffcentrix, LLC (http://www.staffcentrix.com) is a virtual company (i.e., all their staff is virtual) located in Maryland and Connecticut. They pioneered the idea of training military spouses to have "portable" careers as professional Virtual Assistants. Think about this for a moment. Working as an independent VA, military trailing spouses can do their work no matter where they are relocated, since virtually every base has high-speed Internet. And better yet, they can now provide a good steady income (once they have built up their client base) from home, which allows them to raise their children as well.

Talk about a "Win, Win, Win!" The military wins because now with stable, higher incomes, dedicated military people have more incentives to stay in their chosen career. The military family wins because they can now afford a much better lifestyle and still raise the kids with a mom (or dad) always at home. And, you the business owner win because you now have access to even more highly dedicated (and often very appreciative) virtually outsourced talent.

Chris Durst and Michael Haaren, Esq. are co-founders and CEO/COO respectively of Staffcentrix, LLC. Chris is another one of the original pioneers of the Virtual Assistants movement back in the mid 1990s. She helped found the International Virtual Assistant Association (http://www.ivaa.org) and has written or co-authored several books on how to have a successful career as a Virtual Assistant.

Her business partner Mike is a service-disabled veteran whose military lineage goes all the way back to his great grandfather, the 15th Commandant of the Marine Corps. Mike is also a former Wall Street attorney with a great deal of entrepreneurial experience working in venture funding, corporate board building and international marketing. When Chris and Mike teamed up to form Staffcentrix, the *Portable Career & Virtual Assistant Training Program for Military Spouses*™ was a natural result. With his military background and legal experience, Mike was able to successfully navigate the often Byzantine corridors of the Pentagon to sell the idea of training military spouses as independent Virtual Assistants or MSVAs (Military Spouse Virtual Assistants).

As of this writing, over 1,500 active-duty military spouses have completed this training. And, there are a lot more where those came from with approximately 800,000 active-duty spouses currently in the U.S. military. Presently, there are at least 50 military bases that offer this training program, with more expected to make it available in the near future. By 2009, it is anticipated that at least 10,000 active-duty spouses will have completed the Virtual Assistant Training Program. This is still just a drop in the bucket of numbers that are possible from this one source alone. Even assuming that only 40 percent of those military spouses who apply are accepted into the program, that still means a potential for several hundred thousand dedicated Virtual Assistants.

While these potential numbers are large, it's important to remember that this program has a significant impact on a lot of lives and the families of each individual MSVA that takes advantage of it.

My Career Travels With Me

When you are the spouse of a military husband or wife—moving around and being mobile most of the time— you're on a self-perpetuating treadmill, always looking for new jobs and new career opportunities. When you decide to have children, employment options become even more compromised. Not only is your longevity on the job unpredictable, but that job must also allow you time to be a parent.

My husband is in the Air Force. Around the time I looked into starting my own business, we were stationed at Peterson Air Force Base in Colorado Springs. Our daughter was just a year old and I was home with her. Any parent will tell you that there comes a time when the joys of motherhood are tested to their limits! Being home alone with a baby can be a real struggle and even more frustrating if you have no outside interests or outlets. I definitely did not want to leave her with sitters, but I wanted something to do, something different.

Staffcentrix, a business known for training individuals to begin their own portable career as a Virtual Assistant, conducted a two-and-a-half day workshop at the base and completely turned my life around. The workshop gave us step-by-step information about finding out what we were good at, what our employable strengths were and a true nuts and bolts rundown of starting your own business. I decided that this was exactly what I wanted.

I quickly realized how Virtual Assistance can be an employer's dream come true as well as the answer to my prayers! There is an entire scope of talent in America's homes that has not been tapped appropriately. Women, especially, fall into this category. There are smart, vibrant moms everywhere, raising families, running households, handling minute-to-minute situations and organizing life for themselves and their families. In most cases, the skills that saw them through traditional, corporate jobs have been put on hold. They are very qualified and more than willing to work; they just need job flexibility. The skills I performed in a traditional office stay with me to this day. I never stayed home when we all knew the boss was on vacation for a week. I still had my job to do and that didn't change. Any worker who is responsible enough to hold things together when the boss is away has those necessary traits to create a career lifestyle. In the instant I made this comparison, I knew that I could do this in a business owned and operated by me!

These decisions require initiative, drive and curiosity, at best. If I didn't already know how to do something, I learned how. Ambition doesn't have to be looked upon as something negative and ego-gratifying, but inventive and lucrative. In my case, a family friend asked me to help with a spreadsheet assignment for a large company in Silicon Valley. This is an area of expertise for me, so I agreed. I was pleasantly surprised when I was asked to do the same task each month, not just sporadically. I was thrilled. I could meet deadlines with ease and make dinner in the same time frame. My business is in its third year and this client is still solid.

Employment in the virtual world is making a tremendous impact on economies all over the world, not just in the United States. It's a cleaner, more direct process. The meetings and fighting can take place in corporate conference rooms; but when the job is handed to a VA, it's ready to go. We are independent contractors, totally on our own. When I receive my work, managers can manage the things that actually need their attention while I do the things they shouldn't have to worry about.

Work is something my children share with me. Sometimes they sit with me, watch a video or color at the desk while I'm at the computer. The lesson they learn is that Mom is a viable contributor to our household, an equal partner. At the end of my day when I put my head on the pillow, I see my children being raised appropriately, I see my house in order, I see a business that is thriving and clients that are happy. I feel so alive, so accomplished.

Mary Hern
Military Spouse Virtual Assistant

It has been my personal experience in using the services of many different Virtual Assistants that the ones who are also military spouses just seem to be more dedicated than the typical VA (not to cast aspersions to any of the thousands of other hardworking and dedicated VAs). They also seem to be more appreciative of being able to do the work for you while maintaining the military lifestyle and raising a family. Think about this for a moment. Every time you hire a military spouse VA, you're not only helping your own company succeed, you're also helping a family who very much deserves our support, and you're helping the U.S. Military keep the best of the best to defend our country. It just doesn't get much better than that.

Keep in mind that education and skill levels of the trailing spouses tend to increase with rank. Not too surprisingly, spouses of officers tend to be more highly educated and have more real-world business experience than enlisted personnel spouses. At the high end of this scale are trailing spouses of the U.S. Diplomatic Corps whom Staffcentrix has just started training as well. Many of these people have completed at least four years of college and have postgraduate or advanced degrees. Many also have extensive business experience that is either highly strategic or requiring refined skills. This is the kind of virtually outsourced talent that you would use for higher level functions of your business (i.e., strategic planning, business process development, etc.) The fact that they may be completing this work for you from Istanbul (or some other overseas location) is largely irrelevant. With the Internet and the low cost of phone communications (thanks to voice transmission over the Internet), geography is simply not a factor.

Clearly, the trend toward working from home is not a passing fad. In fact, the number of skilled people in just the U.S. alone is likely to grow dramatically.[31] And then of course there is the huge pool of inexpensive overseas virtual talent as well. All of this means that you as a business owner have a cornucopia of any kind of virtual talent imaginable to choose from —if you know how to access it.

Here is a quick review of what we covered in this chapter.

Key Ideas and Chapter Review

- Virtual Outsourcing consists of two primary categories: Virtual Consultants[†] or project-based work and Virtual Assistants for ongoing support.

- Virtual outsourcing offers major financial and managerial benefits to all for-profit and nonprofit organizations;

- Both Virtual Consultants and Virtual Assistants tend to be highly specialized in the type of skills they can offer your business. In other words, you are most likely hiring a "master" rather than a Jack (or Jane) of all trades;

- "Virtual" in the context of Virtual Outsourcing doesn't mean "not real"; it simply means real people who are independent contractors that perform (typically) highly specialized job functions remotely;

- Virtual Outsourcing and enterprise outsourcing/offshoring are different. The first is much more intimate in that it consists of independent, skilled individuals (or small groups of them) performing work for small to midsized businesses from a distance, while enterprise outsourcing is big business contracting with other big businesses to handle major non-core business functions;

- The worldwide pool of virtually outsourced talent is large and growing rapidly thanks to very strong demographic and sociological trends, and the ubiquity of a high-speed Internet infrastructure that allows people to perform nearly any kind of work from nearly anywhere.

Now it's time to go into the step-by-step details of how you find, evaluate, hire and manage your virtually outsourced support, starting with the world of Virtual Consultants. Get ready to discover incredible "talent on demand" from anywhere in the world, often available to you in just minutes!

[†] In the following chapter the term "Service Provider" is used interchangeably with "Virtual Consultant"

Virtual Consultants

Nearly Instant, Affordable Talent for
Any Kind of Project You Can Imagine

One of the things I've learned is that many business people have trouble with the distinction between "a project" and "ongoing support." This is especially true for independent salespeople who generally have difficulty seeing their profession as a business rather than a job for which they are paid a commission. It's also true that anyone who runs a business will always have several projects in the wings just waiting for the time, talent and/or funds to complete them. So just to make sure we are clear about this, a "project" has a beginning, middle and end. Once it is completed, you may never need the person who did it for you again, regardless of how well they did it. Ongoing support, on the other hand, is a job function that is continually or periodically completed, usually by the same people. Now that we are clear about what we mean by "project," let's see how this distinction can impact your business in a very profound way.

A Highly Profitable Thought Experiment

Imagine having access to an almost unlimited supply of highly specialized talent in nearly every field of expertise you could think of. In addition, let's assume (for the moment) that these individuals have been objectively vetted by other business people for whom they have completed projects, so you can be reasonably certain they will get the job done on time and meet or exceed your quality standards. Oh, one more thing: imagine that many of these talented specialists are willing to do your project for far less than you can, well… imagine. In fact, they will aggressively bid against each other just for the privilege of doing your project!

> *successfully identifying high-impact projects for your business requires a certain level of strategic thinking.*

Excited yet? I hope so, because this is not an empty flight of fancy. As you will soon see, these resources are very real. So now it is time for you to do a little "project." With pen and paper in hand, take a moment right now (yes, right now!) to list several projects that, if completed, would make a big impact on your business.

(Five minutes later…)

Well, how did you do? Was it easy or difficult to come up with these projects? I've found that this exercise can be a challenge for the typical small business person. That's because they are so into "doing" their business, they literally cannot see the forest for the trees and, as a result, have trouble working "on" their business. Perhaps their day consists mainly of putting out fires rather than productive work that moves their business to higher levels of profitability. Or, they are so used to doing everything themselves, it's hard to imagine anyone else doing anything for them.

In any case, successfully identifying high-impact projects for your business requires a certain level of strategic thinking. That's because most business projects involve either creating strategy or completing the tactical steps that are required to implement a strategy. Here are some possible projects for your company that would definitely make a big impact on your bottom line:

- **Business Plan** – You've heard it all before; if you fail to plan, you are essentially planning to fail. Yet, according to a recent Wells Fargo/Gallup poll, 69 percent of all small businesses do not start with a written business plan.[32] The main reason for this is that the business owner either doesn't know how to do it or doesn't have the time. If you fit into this category, know that there are many, many Virtual Consultants who are skilled at helping businesses just like yours develop a well thought out, executable plan;

- **Marketing Plan** – Have you identified your target market, figured out how to uniquely answer the question, "What's in it for them?" Have you researched your main competitors, completed a SWOT (Strengths, Weaknesses, Opportunities & Threats) analysis, or otherwise created a comprehensive strategic marketing plan? If your answer was "no" to any of the above, then rest assured there are VCs available to you that do this every day and are exceptionally good at it;

- **Branding** – Differentiating your products or services via a unique brand is a powerful step within the strategic marketing process. It is also a critical component to creating a viable exit strategy when you decide to sell your business. Creating brands that resonate with your target market is a specialty that is easily found within the VC community;

- **Graphic Design** – Whether it's something as simple as your letterhead, or important as logo creation, having on-call access to a stable of exceptional graphic designers can be a big boon to any business that simply cannot afford to keep a designer on staff. Also, because graphic design is so style-centric, having access to hundreds of superb graphic designers who represent different styles is a huge advantage. I have used many different VC graphic designers for my businesses. The freedom to choose a designer that best fits my style requirements for a given project gives me design flexibility that even the "big boys" often don't have;

- **Research** – How many new opportunities would arise if you only knew "X"? Whether it's determining the size of a potential new market, psychographic or behavioral trends for a certain market segment, or what new things your top competitors are up to, good research can pay off in spades. However, few business owners have the time or expertise to do good, meaningful research. Thankfully, there are many people who do and they are just a few mouse-clicks away;

- **Packaging Design** – Great package design is both an art and science. In addition to "looking good," your product packaging needs to meet shipping specifications, be affordable, be easy to store and assemble, and meet various regulatory requirements. If you are creating new products monthly, chances are you have in-house staff for this. Most small to midsized businesses only occasionally need this kind of expertise. This is one of the many advantages of hiring a VC; you use them only when you need them;

- **Software Design** – One of the hallmarks of a good entrepreneur is always having great ideas. Likewise, one of the frustrations is figuring out how to implement them affordably. Recently, I had such an idea that required the services of a "world-class" software user interface designer. This is not a programmer per se; instead, this is a person (or team) who designs the look and feel of software that will be used by others. Using the resources I will be sharing with you shortly, I found such a person in just hours for about one-fifth the going price in my locality. And no, they were not working out of some DSL-connected hovel in a third world country. This particular designer, whose work took my breath away, happens to reside in Boise, Idaho. If you have any kind of software project whatsoever, finding the right people to do the job for less money than you could hope for, is frankly quite easy;

• **Trademark Filings** – If you need to brand your products, services or even the entire business, you will need the services of an intellectual property rights attorney. Most small business owners won't have one of these (or even a referral to one) in their pocket. Yet, you can have legal resources who specialize in filing trademarks bidding for your services in just minutes or hours, probably willing to do the work for less than what is charged in your area. For example, Peter Scherman is a client of mine in Virginia who is an inn consultant and broker licensed to do business in several East Coast states. While he had his brand identity since 1993, he felt it was important to protect both the name and logo by formally registering them with the U.S. Trademark office. He posted his request for an intellectual property rights attorney to do this job online (once again, using the resources I will be sharing with you shortly) and found a highly qualified and affordable attorney in the Boston area. That was several years ago and Peter has maintained a relationship with that attorney ever since. Now the average business owner might at first think twice about finding and hiring legal assistance this way. Most people understandably rely on referrals for legal or accounting help. Well, the great news about the process of finding a good legal or accounting Virtual Consultant is that *they are* referred by others, others who have used their services successfully;

• **Presentations** – Let's say you finally have a shot at making a pitch to that big prospective client you've been working on for months (or years). Are you suddenly going to turn yourself into a PowerPoint expert to help you communicate why they should be a client of your business? How clear and compelling you make your presentation can make or break the deal. Finding a VC who knows how to communicate complex ideas using PowerPoint or other types of media is easy. In fact, there are so many VCs who have this skill, the challenge often is picking the one with the *style* that best fits your needs. Not too long ago, I started (yet another) company that required a fair amount of "angel" investor startup capital. This meant creating the show (i.e., pitch) and taking it on the road to various angel investor groups. Even though I happen to know the in's and out's of PowerPoint fairly well, in this particular case, I didn't feel confident in my ability to create the professional look I was hoping to achieve when speaking to these investors. So I simply went online, posted my request and found an excellent PowerPoint expert who happened to live in Sacramento, CA. As a side note, in my travels of making my pitch to raise these funds, I had the opportunity to see others do the same. And I can honestly say (from my admittedly subjective and probably quite biased viewpoint) that my PowerPoint presentation was far more professional looking and compelling than the others;

- **Proposals** – If your business requires that you make a lot of proposals, chances are you have this down to a science. For many small to midsized business owners however, the need to make a formal written proposal happens infrequently. Once again, it's all about communication, and there are VCs who know how to do this well and probably for a lot less than what your time is worth. Imagine needing a highly professional proposal by next week and all you have to do is spend a few minutes on the phone with a proposal expert who works to craft a winning document while you're freed up to continue running the business. "Sweet!" you say. Well, that's just the beginning;

- **Business Processes** – Well-documented processes for every aspect of your business ensures standards of service, quality and scalability. Most small businesses don't operate that way. If anything, they allow their employees to develop ad hoc processes that only they know and end up taking with them when they leave. This is not only very inefficient, but downright dangerous to the continued growth of a company. Having formal, written business processes for every aspect of one's business is the first step to sustained growth and eventual salability when you are ready to retire. With these processes, it will be much easier to run your business with high standards and interchange the help needed to execute them. One of the reasons so many businesses don't have written processes is that creating them is beyond the ability or time constraints of their owners. Fortunately, there are VCs who are experts at documenting business processes and do this for a living. Once you find one, it's simply a matter of having them interview you and your key staff and, from that, they will create your process manual. You'll be amazed at how much more in control you'll feel with your business processes fully documented, tested and executed consistently;

- **IT Infrastructure Design and Troubleshooting** – Every business requires at least some level of information technology (IT) infrastructure. Whether it's a simple network connecting your office computers, or a sophisticated system that includes servers, network backup and storage, switching systems, VPNs, etc., there are VCs who can design and spec out your requirements for you. Keep in mind that while a VC specialist can design your IT infrastructure from anywhere, you'll need to have someone local to physically install it. OK, let's say you have a killer system installed and it's humming along until one day, well ... it isn't. As long as you still have Internet access working, a VC can likely do much of your system's trouble shooting from a distance. There are online tools that allow them (with your permission, of course) to get into your system, diagnose and fix many of the problems that could arise. So instead of waiting for an IT specialist "house call" (and possibly losing a ton of business and hair in the process), your Virtual Consultant IT guy (or gal) can be "there" in just minutes to fix the problem —and probably for a lot less than what a local person would charge you;

- **Web Site Design** – These days, Web site designers are almost as ubiquitous as real estate agents —everyone seems to know at least half a dozen of them. And, every business needs one if they plan on staying competitive. Figuring out who is good and who isn't can be a challenge, especially if you do it the old fashioned way of trial and error (which can be quite expensive and time-consuming). Why not get truly objective feedback from others who have already gone through the process. And, while you're deciding which one to use, explore samples of their work anonymously so you're not constantly being "sold" their services. The fact that there are literally thousands of VCs in the world who do an awesome job of Web design may at first be a bit intimidating. However, the Virtual Service Provider Marketplaces that you will soon have access to empower you to cull through them very quickly. You'll be taken back by the talent that's available and how quickly you can choose just the right one for your Web site design needs;

- **Copywriting** – Good copywriting is one of the most underutilized business marketing weapons. Words are power, and skillfully crafted words are incredibly powerful. Unfortunately, most business owners couldn't write good marketing copy to save their life, yet many of them attempt to do just that. Only it's not their life they are trying to save, it's their business. Good copywriting is very much an art that requires inherent skill finely honed by a lot of experience. You might be first tempted to think: "I can't afford someone like that even if I could find them." Or: "If someone is really that good, they are already too busy." Thanks to the Internet and the emergence of Virtual Service Provider Marketplaces, finding good copywriters is not hard, nor are they necessarily expensive. What is most definitely expensive is settling for crappy marketing copy in the first place. Here's an example of why these marketing mensches are available to your business. A friend of mine owns a successful business-coaching company out of Ottawa, Canada. He was looking for someone to write much of his direct response copy, the most powerful and expensive of all marketing copy because it demands instant results. His staff found someone in Chicago using the methods found in this book. This particular person had the talent and the experience. You see, he was retired but wanted a way to keep busy doing something he loved and make some extra money to supplement his pension (remember the earlier discussion of demographic trends).

The above is just a very short list of all the potential possibilities for incorporating Virtual Consultants to handle your business projects. Remember, the challenge for most small to midsized businesses is not finding the great VC talent, it's deciding what high-impact projects can be done.

If You Can Dream It...

Taken as a group, the range and scope of possible support specialties and skills that are available to you (i.e. the small-to-mid sized business person) are enormous. Here is just a partial list of support services that are available from one online Virtual Service Provider Marketplace (i.e. an online service that matches businesses that have specific projects to be completed with virtual consultants who have the skills and experience to do them):

Administrative Support

Bulk Mailing

Customer Response

Data Entry

Event Planning

Fact Checking

Mailing List Development

Office Management

Other - Administrative Support

Personal Assistant

Presentation Formatting

Research

Transcription

Travel Planning

Word Processing

Architecture & Engineering

Architecture

CAD

Civil & Structural

Contract Manufacturing

Electrical

Industrial Design

Interior Design

Mechanical

Other - Architecture & Engineering

Audio, Video & Multimedia

Animation

Commercials

Embedded Video/Audio

Music

Other - Multimedia Services

Photography & Editing

Podcasts

Radios Ads & Jingles

Videography & Editing

Viral Videos

Programming & Software

Application Development

Database Development

Enterprise Systems

Handhelds & PDAs

Network Administration

Other - Software & Technology

Project Management

Scripts & Utilities

Security

System Administration

Technical Support

Wireless

Sales & Marketing

Advertising

Branding

Business Plans

Competitive Analysis

E-mail & Direct Marketing

Grassroots Marketing

Lead Generation

Market Research & Surveys

Marketing & Sales Consulting

Marketing Collateral

Marketing Plans

Media Buying & Planning

Other - Sales & Marketing

Pricing

Product Research

Project Management

Promotions

Public Relations

Retailing

Sales Presentations

Search & Online Marketing

Telemarketing

Voice Talent

Design

3D Graphics

Banner Ads

Brochures

CD & DVD Covers

Card Design

Cartoon & Comics

Catalogs

Corporate Identity Kit

Digital Image Editing

Direct Mail

Displays & Signage

E-mails & Newsletters

Graphic Design

Illustration

Label & Package Design

Logos

Menu Design

Other - Design

Page & Book Design

Presentation Design

Print Ads

Report Design

Sketch Art

Stationery Design

Legal

Bankruptcy

Business & Corporate

Contracts

Criminal

Family

Immigration

Incorporation

Landlord & Tenant

Litigation

Tradeshows & Events

Training & Development

Business Skills

Business Software

Corporate Training

Diversity Training

Management Training

Media Training

Other - Training & Development

Policies & Manuals

Programming Languages

Sales Training

Technical Training

Website Development

Blogs

Ecommerce Website

Flash Animation

HTML E-mails

Online Forms & Database Integration

Other - Website Development

SEO & SEM

Simple Website

Usability Design

Web Design & Development

Web Programming

Website QA

Writing & Translation

Academic Writing

Article Writing

Children's Writing

Copywriting

Creative Writing

Editing & Proofreading

Ghost Writing

Grant Writing

Newsletters

Negligence	Other - Writing Services
Other - Legal	Press Releases
Patent, Copyright & Trademarks	Report Writing
Personal Injury	Resumes & Cover Letters
Real Estate	Sales Writing
Tax	Speeches
Wills, Trusts & Estates	Technical Writing
Management & Finance	Translation
Accounting & Bookkeeping	User Guides & Manuals
Billing & Collections	Web Content
Budgeting & Forecasting	eBooks & Blogs
Cost Analysis & Reduction	
Financial Planning	
Financial Reporting	
HR Policies & Plans	
Management Consulting	
Other - Management & Finance	
Outsourcing Consulting	
Process Improvement	
Stock Option Plans	
Supply Chain Management	

Here's how some small businesses have used these resources, starting with a self-admitted serial entrepreneur who was able to assemble an entire virtual team to develop, quite literally, his new "baby"…

Working With the Best of the Best

I have just what children —and their reluctant parents — need! Another toy!

Now, before you start rolling your eyes and begin to re-program parental controls on your computer, consider this: You will be able to design the toy yourself! Surprised you, huh?

I'm an entrepreneur at heart. I started my first business when I got out of college. It was a very industrial product —liners for shipments of hazardous material. It went well and we began working with companies around the world. Like most things, once you get the hang of it, and it goes well, you tend to keep doing it.

I guess it's that inquisitive, inventive part of me that needs to create just about anything. Fortunately, I've made it a career.

My latest project is certainly one of my most whimsical, and the way I'm gathering information about it is unique, too. What I've done, with the help of freelancers I hired from Elance, (the upper crust of online, freelance work Web sites) is to create a mammoth toy contest, open to the… er…well, world!

I've just always thought that awarding project bids to freelancers was an interesting, time and cost effective way of finding folks around the world with very specific, sought after skills.

What creative minds everywhere are vying for is the chance to win not only material prizes, but also the prestige of having created the world's first Starby —a fictional, alien space baby, measuring in at a miniscule seven inches in height.

At present, we have received over 600 graphic designs, from all over the world, depicting the particular image a Starby evokes in the minds of its creators. The secret will soon be revealed and a contest winner declared.

In the meantime, you should know that Starby has been rescued from the idyllic, azure waters off the island of Bermuda by marine biologist, Lisa Raven. The infant alien was removed from its eight-inch-long, walnut shaped rock …which gently vibrated in her hand. Lisa has temporarily named the little visitor Koova, after the whisper-soft sound it makes when it sleeps.

How do you like it, so far? The story, Web design, Starby blog, logo for the "government" agency that will process Starby (and its relatives?) and a manufacturer of plush toys are all freelance "artists" in their own rights. I've formed a wonderful team of productive, creative individuals, focused on propelling Starby to….uh…..stardom!

I've had the opportunity and good fortune to work with the best of the best all over the world! It's pretty cool.

Freelancers do their thing and love what they're doing. I don't ask for or realistically expect them to show up in my office in the morning. If they want to work at their computers in their PJs 'til three in the morning, that's fine with me.

As for having more time to devote to the business of business, my own personal downtimes are late afternoons. I can kick back a bit, without worrying about productivity or deadlines. My team is taking care of those things for me, when they aren't poking around for another Starby…or two….or three…..

Mark Richards
Serial Entrepreneur

Sometimes Virtual Outsourcing allows your business to quickly, easily and affordably expand its service offerings without having to add expensive onsite staffing and concomitant logistic support…

Being Bigger Without Getting Larger

"C'mon dude," I typed, "this is what I mean and this is what I'm looking for with this project." There was an instantaneous "silence" on my computer screen.

My primary service provider responded, "What is dude? What is this word?"

"It means a man, or a cool guy," I explained, humorously absorbing the lesson in this priceless moment. I had become so comfortable and completely satisfied with the work of the freelance Web experts I hire, across oceans and continents, that this exchange forced me to catch my breath and savor the interaction.

While "computer-ese" is a universal language, the use of one's own slang expressions, when communicating with someone in India or the Philippines, for example, can make for some very funny moments.

I started my own advertising business about two and a half years ago. As an art director and project manager, I wanted to do more of the marketing kinds of things the business requires and not concentrate heavily on Web development and/or business collateral.

In addition to the artsy demands of my clients, they also wanted results that required specific expertise in certain Web skills.

I found my "specialists" on the Elance Web site and I now have a team of Web savvy freelancers, producing very specific aspects of my jobs.

A lot of people asked a lot of questions about my decision to outsource parts of my business; the most common is, why don't I just hire someone in-house to pick up the slack? I found that here, in California especially, freelancers charge just as much as I charge my clients, if not more!

The second question is, if my clients know I am outsourcing parts of their projects, why wouldn't they just eliminate me as the middleman and use freelancers themselves. It's not about revealing a "best kept secret." Business people, including my clients, know that the option to subcontract always exists. The truth is that they can't or don't want to do certain things themselves, either!

About 90 percent of my work is outsourced to providers in Russia, India, the Philippines and Australia. Global time differences actually work very well for me. I can send my team members something at the end of the day, that evening or early the next morning and know that I will have a professionally executed product returned to me in a timely fashion.

There is also another plus involved when working with people in different countries: professional etiquette. Whenever a task is completed, it is always accompanied by a note of thanks from a team member for allowing them to do the work, including requests for repeat business. There is an element of respect in these communications, which is not often seen at home.

And, even though I probably work a few hours more than I should, my husband loves the fact that my decision to outsource frees me up to be able to work remotely, as long as I can log on —and today, that is just about anywhere.

Both my mother and father were successful, hardworking entrepreneurs, but continued to put in long hours in a physical office. Mom, especially, finds it strange that I am on the go and still working.

Although I have never met my service providers, they have enabled me to make more personal visits to my clients' offices and establish that face-to-face familiarity.

It brings me such joy when I walk into a presentation, reveal a perfectly cohesive project that reflects both my efforts and those of my freelancers, and the client absolutely loves it! That's when it all comes together.

Phillis Sylvester
Advertising Company Owner

There are tens of thousands of similar Virtual Outsourcing success stories being played out every year by businesses just like yours. And the only difference between you and them is that they're already using it to their distinct advantage.

Your One-Stop Talent Rental Shop

OK, let's assume for the moment that you now have some ideas of what kinds of high-impact projects could be done for your business if you only knew where to find the talent. Now imagine going into a store where each department consists of a large room with one-way glass so you could see in but no one on the inside could see out. And, each of these departments contained hundreds of people who all shared a specific skill or specialized talent. As you stroll down the aisles, you look for the room/department that holds the kind of talent you need for your next project. Once you identified the right room (i.e., specialty), you simply slip a sheet of paper with the description of your project into a slot in the door. Waiting perhaps just a few minutes, you notice that responses to your project request start flying back out that same slot, each one essentially a competitive bid to do your project from different people in that room. After reviewing the bids, you find the one that seems to best fit your needs and budget and take it to the checkout counter. Only this checkout counter is a bit different from other stores. That's because you don't actually pay for the talent you have just chosen. Instead, you simply make a promise that you *will* pay the store, once your project is done.

Now, how different would your business be if a store like this actually existed within your community, where you could "check out" talent like you would a DVD at a movie rental store. What kinds of possibilities would be available to you and your business if you had access to such a one-stop "talent rental shop"? Too fantastic to be true? Hardly. In fact there are "talent rental shops" like this (only much better) that you don't even have to drive to because they're just a few mouse-clicks away.

Instead of "talent rental shop," this category of service has the more formal sounding name of "Virtual Service Provider Marketplace" (VSPM). A VSPM typically consists of a vast number of people with available skills and talents in different categories (i.e., Virtual Consultants), and provides a controlled, competitive bidding framework by which any individual or firm may hire this talent on a project-by-project basis. Thanks to the Web and ubiquity of the Internet, several companies have created highly sophisticated, yet easy to use VSPMs that allow you to shop for Virtual Consultants with complete anonymity. A good way to think of these companies is that they are the "eBays" of virtual talent where you post your project, and VCs from around the world bid against each other for the opportunity of doing your job.

As someone posting a project for bid, you have huge advantages using these VSPMs to look for Virtual Consultants:

- *It's free* – With few exceptions (which will be covered later), it costs nothing to post your project for bid on a VSPM, whether you end up using any of the respondents or not;

- *You remain anonymous* – Your anonymity is completely protected, even up to and including project completion if you so choose;

> " A good way to think of these companies is that they are the "eBays" of virtual talent where you post your project, and VCs from around the world bid against each other for the opportunity of doing your job. "

- *You know who is bidding* – Most of the better VSPMs provide ample information about each bidder (including their name, contact information, Web site, previous work, performance history, etc.) that will help you quickly decide which one to choose (if any) to do your project;

- *You are not obligated to choose any of the bids* – If you don't like any of the bids, or even if you do but are not ready to start the project, you don't have to commit to any of them;

- *You have access to hundreds of thousands of people* – Several of the larger VSPMs have hundreds of thousands of VCs that together cover nearly every skill category you can imagine using in your business. The vast majority of these people would never otherwise be available to you without the large-scale aggregating effect of these VSPMs;

- *Your financial information is never revealed to any of the bidders* – When your project is completed, you pay the VSPM (usually by credit card) who then in turn pays the Virtual Consultant who did the work.

And this is just the beginning of the many unique benefits of using VSPMs to shop for Virtual Consultant specialists to do your next project. As you'll soon see, it's fast, easy and systemically designed to help you receive the best bid possible from the most qualified of specialists.

As Easy As *1-2-3-4-5!*

Once you have a project in mind and have become an approved buyer of services for one or more VSPMs (not to worry, I'll explain this), there is just a simple five-step process to take your project from idea to completion:

1. *You post your project* – Each VSPM will present you a series of on-line forms that allow you to describe your project specifications with enough detail and supporting documentation (which can be uploaded to the system) so that service providers (i.e., Virtual Consultants) will have a clear idea as to what you want and therefore be equipped to give you their best bid;

2. *Service providers bid* – Depending on the nature and complexity of your project, you could start seeing bids come in within minutes. Each bid includes important information about the respective service provider, including their bid amount, comments to your posting, how many times they have completed other projects (within the VSPM), how past users of their services rated them, samples of their work, etc;

3. *You choose a service provider* – Using the information provided in the bids, you can quickly cull through the bidders who appear to be the best fit for your project. Using the VSPM's built-in messaging system, you can ask additional questions of any bidder, or even ask them to modify their bid while still remaining anonymous. By "awarding" a bid, you effectively have chosen a provider to do your project and have obligated yourself to pay the bid amount once the project is complete;

4. *Service provider completes project* – The more sophisticated VSPMs provide a built-in online "workspace" for each project in process. This is essentially a private intranet that allows you and your chosen service provider to communicate, collaborate and manage the entire project process through to completion;

5. *You pay for project and rate the service provider* – Once your project is completed, you pay the VSPM (usually by credit card) who then in turn pays the service provider most of the entire bid amount (VSPMs

will usually keep between five and 10 percent of the total bid for themselves). After payment is made, you are then allowed to rate the service provider's performance with respect to completing your project. As you might suspect, this rating means everything to the service provider because it's the first thing potential buyers look at.

That's basically all there is to it. Don't worry, I'll cover each of these five steps in greater detail and share many of my hard-won tips and tricks developed by using these services for my own businesses over several years and dozens of projects.

The Top VSPMs

While the Virtual Service Provider Marketplace industry continues to grow and add new players, in my experience there are currently just two that stand out for small to midsized businesses: Elance.com (http://www.elance.com) and Guru.com (http://www.guru.com). You will find a more comprehensive list of VSPMs at http://www.virtualoutsourcing.org. Both companies operate in a similar fashion. They each maintain a large database of skilled service providers from around the world and utilize sophisticated online systems that allow you to access them through an anonymous, competitive bidding environment. Their business models are rather straightforward as well. Each retains a small percentage of the amount paid to the service providers on completed projects.

The most lucrative part of their respective business models however, is the ongoing payments they receive from a large portion of their service provider base. This is definitely a win, win, win situation. The VSPMs win because they have a potentially huge monthly revenue stream coming in from the hundreds of thousands of service providers who want to be on their system. The service providers win because the VSPMs are the only practical way to have access to the world's largest business market place (i.e., you!) and pay a fraction of what it would cost to advertise to have direct access to it. And best of all, you win because you don't have to pay a dime to use these services that give you access to affordable talent that you otherwise wouldn't have a prayer of accessing. Without question, the emergence of VSPMs represent one of the most innovative uses of the Internet to effectively and seamlessly bring highly skilled talent and the businesses that use them together, regardless of their respective geographies.

Of the two VSPMs mentioned above, Elance is the oldest (if you consider being founded in 1998 as "old") and has the more impressive pedigree of senior management and venture capital backing, including lead investor Kleiner Perkins Caufield & Byers, one of the largest and most successful venture capital names in Silicon Valley.

The Best Kept Secret In Business

Elance states that there were 28,000 unique companies which posted a total of 76,000 project requests, of which 39,000 were completed and paid for, representing roughly $21 million in awarded projects (in the year prior to this book being written). The disparity between the number of posted projects and those that were actually awarded and paid for may at first glance seem high. However, when you consider that many business owners post the same projects with more than one VSPM, or are just testing the waters of what talent might be available, this difference is not so great.

> *many of the business people that do use them don't like to talk about it because they view these virtual resources as their "competitive edge."*

Twenty-eight thousand may seem like a lot of businesses using this resource. Actually, it's just a drop in the bucket compared to the estimated 26,000,000 or so small to midsized businesses in the U.S. alone.[33] In fact, during an interview with Fabio Rosati, CEO of Elance, he indicated that a recent study showed that less than half of one percent of all these domestic businesses even knew they existed. This makes Elance and other VSPMs like it the best kept secret in business. So secret in fact, many of the business people that do use them don't like to talk about it because they view these virtual resources as their "competitive edge."

Made in the USA (mostly)

As of this writing, Elance has about 300,000 independent service providers available covering 11 major categories and 165 subcategories of specialty services. While it is true that Elance and other similar VSPMs attract service providers from all over the world, the majority of them are from the U.S. The following table is a geographical breakdown of that portion of their service providers who were actively responding to project posts in the past year:

United States	29,178	57.65%
India	6,656	13.15%
United Kingdom	3,658	7.23%
Canada	2,753	5.44%
Australia	1,023	2.02%
Pakistan	750	1.48%
Romania	484	0.96%
Russian Federation	414	0.82%
Germany	323	0.64%
Ukraine	275	0.54%
Philippines	262	0.52%
Hungary	249	0.49%
New Zealand	245	0.48%
China	201	0.40%
Netherlands	201	0.40%
France	198	0.39%
Ireland	196	0.39%
South Africa	196	0.39%
Argentina	190	0.38%
Singapore	187	0.37%
Italy	184	0.36%
Spain	165	0.33%
Poland	157	0.31%
Indonesia	155	0.31%
Malaysia	141	0.28%
Switzerland	137	0.27%
Brazil	130	0.26%
Turkey	118	0.23%
Mexico	114	0.22%
Sweden	112	0.22%
Belgium	110	0.22%
Israel	109	0.21%
Aruba	106	0.21%
Japan	106	0.21%
Nigeria	100	0.20%
Bangladesh	95	0.19%
Bulgaria	91	0.18%
United Arab Emirates	89	0.18%
Egypt	86	0.17%
Denmark	84	0.17%
Greece	73	0.14%
Hong Kong	68	0.13%

Thailand	64	0.13%
Yugoslavia	63	0.12%
Belarus	61	0.12%
Czech Republic	58	0.11%
Armenia	54	0.11%
Austria	50	0.10%
Portugal	50	0.10%
Norway	46	0.09%
TOTAL:	**50,613**	

Great Idea to Breakthrough Resource

My first project was posted on Elance in December of 2000. I needed to find someone to edit a book I had just written about the Internet. Within 24 hours of posting this project, I received several dozen bids. By the end of the third day, nearly 100 had come in. I was frankly astounded at all the incredible talent that showed up, and for prices I just couldn't believe. The person I chose gave a bid of $250 to edit my rather dense, 256-page book. And, she was rated a straight "5" across the board (the highest possible) from all the businesses who hired her previously through Elance.

When that project was completed (which didn't take long, by the way) I was a different kind of business person. For the first time, I truly understood the power of Virtual Outsourcing and remember saying (to my Virtual Assistant, of course), "Wow! —what other things can we outsource?!" From that point on, I looked at my business quite differently, as you will when you really "get" that there is effectively an unlimited supply of highly skilled talent at awesome prices that can do just about any kind of project you can imagine. Running and strategically growing my business shifted from, "How am I going to get things done?" to the much more powerful, "What projects can I virtually outsource that will have a huge impact on my business?"

I have used Elance many, many times and have gained enormous insight into how to work with this and other VSPMs most effectively while avoiding the "gotcha's" and pitfalls. For several years, I was frankly quite happy using Elance exclusively, mainly because no other VSPM service of its size or sophistication showed up on the radar screen. That is, until Guru.com came on the scene in 2004.

Your Own Support Guru a Mouse-Click Away

Like many highly innovative successful startups, Guru.com had a rather modest beginning. It started its life in 1998 as SOFTMoonlighter.com in the basement of its founder, Inder Guglani, providing primarily outsourced information technology services. Between 1998 and 2004, it went through a number of iterations. In July, 2003, Guglani purchased Guru.com's employer membership base and domain name. Nine months later, the new Guru.com Web site was launched that reflects it current services and business model. It wasn't until he renamed his company Guru.com and made substantial improvements to the online infrastructure of his VSPM that it caught my eye.

> " *As a business owner, I'm concerned about one thing when posting a project, who can do the best job for the least amount of money.* "

In the last full 12 calendar months, Guru.com states that there were over 55,000 posted project requests, of which over 20,000 were from unique companies. Of those projects that were posted, over 20,000 were completed.

While Guru is not as large as Elance in terms of numbers of completed projects, its online project transaction platform is very similar to Elance's. However, Elance is not sitting on its digital laurels. They have just been awarded what appears to be a broad U.S. Patent for the VSPM business process[34]. How this patent will affect their competitors is not yet clear, but it is likely to cement its position as the dominant VSPM player.

Technically speaking, Elance and Guru are direct competitors. However, the reality is that the biggest barrier they have to growing their respective businesses is not an oversupply of competitive VSPMs —it is clearly the simple lack of awareness by small to midsized business that these resources exist. The more these kinds of services proliferate, the better it is for you the business owner. You see, from your perspective, it doesn't have to be an either/or choice as to which VSPM to use…

Two VSPMs Are Better Than One

Since both services are so similar in the way they operate (post project, receive bids, choose provider, get work done, pay and rate provider), I post my projects to both services. This strategy gives me access to a much larger base of potential talent for my business, since their provider databases are obviously not the same, even if they do have some overlap. As a result, I have created a very easy, yet highly effective process for using both (or any number of similar services) simultaneously. So which service do I end up using most? Actually, it's currently about 50/50. As a business owner, I'm concerned about one thing when posting a project, who can do the best job for the least amount of money.

Whether I choose someone from Elance.com or Guru.com is unimportant, only that I choose the right provider to do the job. By taking this approach of posting to both, I feel as though I'm nearly doubling my chances of finding the best provider.

Before You Post Your First Project

Several things have to be done before you can post your first project. First, you must register and become approved as a buyer of services with (I recommend both) Elance.com and Guru.com. The reason VSPMs typically require this is that they want to make sure you can pay for the services once a project is completed. I suggest you do this right now. (Go ahead, I'll wait…) While registering at each site takes only a few minutes, the approval process may take a day or more. As you can imagine, these services are a bit touchy about having deadbeat buyers posting projects within their systems.

The next step is to choose a project that will have a positive impact on your business, (and here is the important part), yet is "simple." By simple I mean a project that is easily defined and requires only one person (i.e., skill or specialty) to complete it. Having your new logo designed is an example of a "simple" project —despite the fact that many expensive advertising companies manage to make it an exceedingly complex and costly process! On the other hand, having a Web site designed is potentially a very complex process involving designers, programmers and copywriters. It also requires a great deal of planning on your part before you even start searching for the right people to do the job.

Keep your first project uncomplicated so you can fully appreciate the power of using these services to complete important work easily and very affordably. Once you have several completed projects under your belt, you'll be confident enough to tackle the more complex projects that require several different postings for the different components necessary to complete them.

Describing Your Project —The RFP

The ability to effectively communicate exactly what you want done for your project is perhaps one of the most challenging aspects of using a VSPM. The formal name for this process is creating a "Request For Proposal" (RFP). Getting this right is important. The more ambiguous you are in defining your project specifications, the more likely you will see fewer bids and increase your risk of not seeing satisfactory results. For most business owners, writing project specifications is not a strong suit. Not to worry though because I have created a template that will help you write your project specification like a pro. And in so doing, the service providers will more likely reward your efforts with great bids.

The following is an outline you can use to describe your project in an explicit and unambiguous way:

1. **Project Name** – Give your project a short, descriptive title.

2. **Description** – This is where you describe your project in detail. The following structure will help organize your project specifications and make it more clear to potential bidders. Use this to outline this part of your project. This way you can post your project into as many VSPMs as you want via "cut and paste":

   a. *Overview* - A brief overview of your project so a potential bidder has the big picture before launching into the details.

   b. *Project Specifics* - The specifics of your project. If appropriate, use bullet points or numbers to break your description up into logical parts. Your project specifics should include the following:

   - *Deliverables* – A very specific description of what you will receive when the project is completed, including any pertinent specifications.

   - *Format* – In what form you want the deliverables. For example, if you are having graphic design done, be sure to request that the final design be in either Adobe Illustrator or Photoshop file format —this will make it easy for anyone to use and apply this artwork in the future.

   - *Uploads* – Most VSPMs allow you to upload files (within limits) as part of your project posting. Typically you will do this if they contain either supporting material or examples of what you are looking for. Be sure to cover the details of any uploaded files here.

   c. *Bid Requirements* – This is where you detail what needs to be included with bids from any service provider who chooses to respond to your project posting, such as:

   - Intellectual Property Rights – Includes a statement that this project is a "work for hire" and that you will own all resulting work products and that the provider warrants that they have the ability to legally assign those rights. (NOTE: Since I am not an attorney, you should check with yours to make sure this language is sufficient to protect your intellectual property rights.)

- Miscellaneous – Required commencement and completion dates and, when appropriate, samples of their previous work, number of revisions included, etc. Having them specify number of revisions is especially important for any creative projects. You will find that many graphic designers found on VSPMs will give you unlimited revisions until you are fully satisfied. Try getting that kind of deal with your local advertising firm!

3. **Budget** – In most cases, you do not want to disclose your budget, otherwise you establish a bidding "floor" that may in fact be much higher than what some highly qualified bidders are willing to do your project for. Fortunately, most VSPMs allow you to post your project without disclosing your budget.

4. **Time To Bid** – For less complex projects, use the minimum time to bid. This creates a sense of urgency, which works in your favor.

5. **Scope of Service Providers** – This is where you indicate which "class" of service providers can bid on your project. In most cases, it's fine to open your project up to the broadest range of providers possible (but always within the service category that best fits your project). This will also tend to lower the minimum required bid. For example, as of this writing, Elance requires a $500 minimum bid if you post your project to their "Select" providers exclusively. Unless your project is quite large or highly complex, this is not usually necessary. And, by making your project available to their entire database of providers, the minimum required bid is only $50.

If you use the above template to outline your project, you are well on your way to successfully posting projects that result in incredible bids from highly qualified service providers. Here is an example of an actual project I posted on both Elance.com and Guru.com that generated nearly 100 bids before I shut the bidding off early:

TITLE: Character Illustration

OVERVIEW:

I am an international speaker about the Internet and target marketing. I want to create branding elements and the look/feel for my new project: "Yellow Penguin Marketing." The concept behind yellow penguin marketing is that it's all about differentiation (i.e., the way a yellow penguin would stand out among all the black and white ones).

PROJECT SPECIFICS:

I will need the following drawings done in Windows compatible Adobe Illustrator format:

a) An anthropomorphized yellow penguin character (cute but smart / clever "personality" and professionally drawn). NOTE: This primary branding element may eventually be drawn within several different contexts (i.e., shown doing and/or wearing certain things), but for now I just want one version that is engaging, clever and fun to look at. BTW, just to give you an idea as to what an actual yellow penguin looks like, go to: http://www.yellowpenguin.co.uk/index.html

b) Once this character design has been approved by me, then I want him to be drawn within the context of "standing out" among a group of typical black and white penguins. This will constitute the logo of "Yellow Penguin Marketing." This logo needs to include the title "Yellow Penguin Marketing" and use an appropriate logotype and include the UPS: "We Help You Stand Out From The Crowd" NOTE: this logo needs to work with or without the UPS phrase. One suggestion for the logo context is placing the yellow penguin character turning to face the viewer within a group of typical black and white penguins waddling away from the viewer --just a thought.

The overall look and feel needs to be very clean, professional, yet fun and engaging for my primary market --small business and entrepreneurs.

I will need to see examples of your previous work creating characters.

REQUIREMENTS FOR BIDDING ON THIS PROJECT:

1. Your bid needs to include the number of revisions you are willing to make before I'm satisfied with the final product.

2. Within the bid you need to let me know how much it would cost to draw the final yellow penguin character within different contexts (this is for possible future work).

3. I will need to own all copyrights to the work products produced for this project and have written assurance from you that you have the right to assign all the copyrights of your work product.

The above outline was first written out in Word. Using "cut and paste," I was then able to easily post to both Elance.com and Guru.com. For this particular project, the winning bidder came from Elance.com (a very strong runner-up bid however came from Guru.com). Instead of an individual, this particular virtual service provider happened to be a design group from Argentina. Their bid response below may not have been crafted using the most perfect English prose, but what they had to offer came over loud and clear:

> Bid Amount: $139.00 (for initial character illustration)
>
> Thank you for taking the time to review our bid. At ******* we pride ourselves on providing our clients with exceptional design and development services as well as quality assured client services. We took a look at your project description and definitely we can design the EYE-CATCHING ILLUSTRATION you are looking for (our bid is per character creation, $90 of each additional pose, $150 for situational ilustration). Our designs are 100 % original and customized to your needs and style preferences .
>
> This is how it works. First you will answer a questionnaire that we will send you. Then you will receive
>
> 1) A Minimum of 2 Original Drafts for your ILLUSTRATION. Our bid entitles you to UNLIMITED CONCEPTS, we will work until we get the design you are looking for !
>
> 2) Unlimited revisions, to 1 Draft. We will refine your ILLUSTRATION until it is you are 100 % satisfied!
>
> 3) Final files will be provided in print ready format. Turn around time for final ILLUSTRATION design is normally 10/15 days.
>
> Please feel free to view our BIGGEST ONLINE PORTFOLIO, there you will find our kind, quality and wide range of styles. Also please take a look at our profile that certifies our commitment on satisfying our customers in 110%. If you have any additional questions, comments or suggestions, feel free to contact us via the Private Message Board and I will respond promptly. We work for customer satisfaction, so you will have to be 110% satisfied to be invoiced, NOT UP FRONT MONEY IS REQUIRED TO START YOUR PROJECT.

First of all, I couldn't have had this project completed locally for even 10 times the bid amount of $139.00. While pricing was important to me, getting the character right was more so because it represented the look and feel of the branding for a whole new business. Their offer to give me unlimited revisions until I was completely satisfied was very attractive. Also, according to Elance, this bidder had completed over 1200 previous projects awarded through Elance, with an astounding average previous user rating of 4.9 out of a possible 5.0 (more on this later). And finally, their design portfolio, fully viewable online, indicated a wide range of graphic design styles, which meant they could probably achieve the style I was looking for, even though I didn't really have a clear idea as to the look I wanted.

It took about seven total revisions before I approved the final design. The initial concepts were hand sketches which they faxed over to me. And these folks were fast! It typically took only an hour or two to incorporate and fax back any changes I requested. More often than not, they were waiting for my comments so they could continue moving forward with the project.

One last thing, you will notice in the above project description that I expressed what I wanted in "emotional" terms. If you are like me and find yourself to be graphically challenged, then describing how people will react emotionally to the design is a powerful way to give your designer direction without telling them exactly how to do it. This frees them up to do their best work, yet gives them a specific goal of how their work should affect the viewer. It also keeps you focused on the primary purpose of design, the impact it has on people.

The above represents just one of many, many projects I had successfully completed through either Elance.com or Guru.com. Later in this chapter, you'll see rather unique examples of projects completed for other business people just like yourself. Now, once you have adequately described your project in an outline, you're ready to post it.

Posting Your Project

The project posting forms on most VSPM Web sites tend to be quite similar to each other and are easily completed in just a few minutes (assuming you had previously outlined your project). There are a few things to keep in mind when posting that will help you receive the best possible bids. As mentioned earlier, each VSPM has a list of skill sets or specialty service categories. During the posting process, it is critical that you identify the category that best fits your project (i.e., "Graphic Design" if you want a logo created). The reason this is so important is that the only service providers within the system who will see your project will be the ones in your chosen category. Choose the wrong category and you are not likely to receive any bids at all. Remember, to encourage the most competitive bids, avoid disclosing your budget. Also, unless your project is quite large or complex, make sure you post your project to the widest scope of service providers within each VSPM so your minimum bid (as required by the VSPM you happen to be posting to) is reasonable.

Once you have completed the online forms, reviewed them for accuracy and then hit the "SUBMIT" button, a number of things start working for you right away. First, all service providers within your project's category will immediately receive an e-mail notice of your new project RFP. Then, depending upon the size or complexity of your project, you could start seeing bids come back in literally just minutes. Most VSPMs allow you to be notified by e-mail when bids come in; however, you might want to turn this feature off if you expect many responses to your post.

When you post your first project and start seeing bids flying in, you're going to think it's Christmas in July. That's because for the first time, you'll really "get" that there are people all over the world who represent a potential and highly affordable solution to your business problems. This is not rocket science, yet the visceral kick you get from seeing those first bids come in can be quite a high. Now, if you do receive an abundance of bids for your first project, you might start thinking that this is too much of a good thing ("How the hell am I going to pick the right service provider out of all these bids!?"). Once again, don't worry because you are about to learn a very effective protocol to cull through even hundreds of bids to find the best one in no time.

Choosing Your Project's Winning Bid

A key strategy to finding your best bid is to quickly find and separate your "most likely" bids from the others and then just focus on those. Most VSPMs let you identify your "favorite" bids for later review. Here are three steps to help you identify these "most likelys":

1. **High Ratings** – Stick with bidders who have very high average ratings from previous users and who have completed at least five projects in the last six months. Most VSPMs allow users to rate service providers on a range of characteristics, including quality and timeliness of work completed and overall satisfaction. Ratings typically range from 0 (the lowest) to 5 (the highest). Look for ratings of 4.5 or higher. You also want to make sure that this average rating has depth to it, meaning it is spread over a large number of projects. For example, someone who has a 5.0 rating but completed only one job is not as attractive as a 4.5 rated provider who has completed 30 projects.

There are exceptions to this rule. For example, if you see samples of a new provider's work who happens to be exactly what you are looking for, then by all means consider them;

2. **Bidder Comments** – Read the response from each of the highly rated providers you have identified. Make sure that their comments reflect that they really did read and understand your proposal and have addressed it accordingly. Some service providers will use a boiler-plate response just to get their bid in quickly. These are the ones you want to avoid because they didn't even take the time to specifically address your project RFP;

3. **Bid Amount** – Ideally you had an internal budget in mind when you posted your project. Therefore, it is a simple matter of selecting those providers whose bids are at or below this figure.

Any provider whose bids meet the three criteria above should go into your "most likely" category. Once you have identified this smaller group from which to choose your winning bidder, you can review each one in more depth. This includes reading rating comments of previous users and reviewing samples of the service provider's work.

A Question of Style

Any project you post on a VSPM will typically fall into one of two categories: process-based or creative. A process-based project is one where the results will look about the same no matter who does the work (assuming they have the requisite skills and experience). Developing a spreadsheet equivalent of an existing paper form used in your business is a good example of a process-based project. Creative projects cannot by definition be completed by a strict step-by-step process. Graphic design, copywriting and page layout are examples of creative projects. A key distinction between a process-based project and a creative one is that with creative projects, the results will almost always be different depending upon who does the work. And that difference can be summed up in one word —style. Anyone who does creative work for a living usually has their own style, unless of course their job is to mimic others' styles.

If your project requires any kind of creative work to be completed, then the style of the service provider is an important factor to consider. A potential big mistake when choosing a creative type of service provider is to expect that they can change their style. Just as you would never expect Van Gogh to paint like

Matisse, don't ask a creative type service provider to change their style. You won't like the results and they won't enjoy doing the work.

Of course, the easiest way to determine someone's creative style is to look at examples of their work. Most VSPMs give you the ability to review the portfolios of service providers before you hire them. There were so many great designers that responded to my "Yellow Penguin" project that I first culled most of them by looking at their work. If their style didn't have the look and feel I was trying to achieve, they were dismissed immediately. By using this approach and the three steps mentioned earlier, I was able to whittle down nearly one hundred bids into about three or four really good candidates in very short order.

When In Doubt —Contact Them

Sometimes you may need to contact one or more of the final candidates before making your choice. This is usually to ask for further qualification of their bid, or to address any last concerns you may have. Now remember, up until this point you are still anonymous to all the bidders. VSPMs typically allow you to contact them through a message board on their Web site in a way your anonymity is preserved. This can be very useful to help make that final choice. I sometimes even call them (forfeiting my anonymous status in the process) because that may be the only way to fully communicate the finer details of my project. The beauty of this whole process is that you have all these options available to you.

Awarding Your Project

A "winning" bid does not necessarily mean the lowest price. It is one that best meets all of your project and service provider criteria for a price that is at or below what you originally had budgeted. The act of awarding a project to a service provider is usually very straightforward, often involving no more than a click of your mouse. Some VSPMs require that the service provider acknowledge acceptance of the project after you have indicated that you chose their bid. After that, your project is good to go, well... maybe. If your project is large, strategically important to your business and/or has several well-defined progress milestones, then I advise having a formal written Project Plan Agreement between you and your chosen service provider. Fortunately, some VSPMs (most notably Guru.com) provide online templates that can be used to formally define the work to be done, nondisclosure terms, time-lines, payment structure, change order process, etc. For more complex or strategically sensitive projects, having a written agreement, in the words of Martha Stewart, "is a good thing!" Realistically, most of your projects will not fall into that category, so probably will not require that level of formalization (most of mine never did). I'll leave that choice to you; at least it's nice to know you have one.

One other thing to consider when you award your project is how you will pay for the services rendered. Some VSPMs provide an escrow service that will hold your payments until the work is done to your satisfaction. This is a very smart way to work with these services. It's also a great way to mitigate any disputes that might arise. For example, let's assume that the work completed is not up to the standards you were expecting and you couldn't work it out satisfactorily with the service provider directly. If you used an escrow service to hold your payments, they are then in a position to help you mediate or even arbitrate your dispute. At first, they will attempt to mediate (i.e., facilitate working it out through a three-way discussion). If that doesn't work, then it will go to arbitration, with VSPM being the appointed arbitrator.

According to Guru.com, only three percent of all their awarded projects go to mediation, and .5 percent to arbitration. In all the years I've used both Elance.com and Guru.com, I have used mediation once and never required arbitration. The very few times I was not entirely satisfied with the completed work, I was always able to work it out with the provider. There are easy ways to do this, which will I will share later in this chapter.

Getting the Work Done

Unless otherwise stated in the terms of your winning bid, the work on your project will typically start immediately. Many VSPMs provide a special online work area (essentially a private intranet) that facilitates communication and exchange of information and/or work in progress between you and your chosen service provider. The advantage of this is that it allows you to fully work with your service provider without disclosing your contact information. The disadvantage is that you must always log into the VSPM in order to communicate or receive work in progress. I personally have found that to be a bit cumbersome. My preferred way of working with service providers is to ask that they e-mail or call me when necessary so we have a more direct line of communication. If I trust someone enough to award my project, then maintaining my anonymity while the project is being completed is hardly necessary.

Reviewing and commenting on work in progress can be an important part of getting the job done to your satisfaction, especially if the project consists

> *" one of the huge advantages of hiring a service provider through a VSPM is that they are always highly motivated to make sure you are thrilled with their work. "*

of creative type work. You may end up going back and forth several times with your service provider during this phase as you both fine-tune the work product to be just the way you want it. This is why your bid request should explicitly ask for the number of revisions you are allowed for these kinds of projects. And make sure you ask for a sufficient number of revisions (which depends upon the nature of your project), otherwise it could cost you more than expected to get the results you want. Also, if your project had specific milestones, you want to make sure your provider consistently meets them. If milestones were not explicitly defined, then get a commitment from the service provider as to what phases will be completed by when —then hold them to it.

Remember, one of the huge advantages of hiring a service provider through a VSPM is that they are always highly motivated to make sure you are thrilled with their work. The basic principle here is that highly rated service providers want to stay that way. They will bust their rump to make sure you are very happy with the way the project was completed and its final results. The more projects they complete with high ratings, the more business they are likely to receive. Which brings us to…

Paying For Your Completed Project

Once your project is completed to your satisfaction, you make final payment to the service provider through the VSPM. It should be noted that most (but not all) VSPMs provide for making payments directly to them and they then forward it (less their percentage) to the provider who actually did the work. This approach has several advantages over paying the provider directly. First, it keeps your financial information (i.e., credit card number) secure by not having it revealed directly to the provider. Second, since your payments are made to a VSPM, which is a company rather than an individual, you will not have to generate a 1099 as part of your year-end tax preparation.

Some service providers may request that you make partial payments along the way, with the last payment made upon final delivery. This is fine for a highly rated service provider with many successfully completed projects under their belt. Likewise, avoid paying upfront fees to a new, un-rated provider. If pre or progress payment is asked for, it is a good idea to use an escrow service (if one is available) as mentioned earlier in this chapter to protect you should the final project results not meet your expectations.

At this point, you're probably dying to know, "What happens if I'm not satisfied with the completed work?" Well, fortunately you have several options available to you:

- *Work it out* – In more cases than not, just discussing why you're not satisfied with the results with your service provider will suggest a change in direction or approach that will give you what you want. If this doesn't work and it appears that this service provider just won't fill the bill no matter what they do, then you can;

- *Ask that the service provider cancel the project* – Simply ask them to cancel the project. The reason why most service providers will seriously consider your request, even after doing a fair amount of work, is that they know if they don't, your comments and rating of their work will be less than favorable. Even one poor rating can mean thousands of dollars in lost future projects. In all the years I've used VSPMs to hire Virtual Consultants for projects, I have only had to ask about three of them to cancel their project. Please don't interpret this approach as a license to "threaten" the service provider with low ratings if they don't happen to agree with you. As you will see below, this thinly veiled form of extortion can backfire on you badly.

  It can occasionally happen that a service provider feels they delivered exactly according to your project specifications and feel that you are being unreasonable to ask them to cancel the project. In those rare cases where you cannot reach mutually agreeable terms directly, you can;

- *Go to mediation or arbitration* – As mentioned earlier, some VSPMs offer to help you resolve disputes with your service providers through mediation and arbitration. By using these services, you are effectively asking a third party to help you resolve the issue at hand. This can be a useful approach since it tends to buffer any emotional or reactionary exchanges between you and your service provider and creates a well-structured approach to solving seemingly intractable issues.

The fact of the matter is, your chances of having a successful completion to your project and/or mitigating issues surrounding its completion are much higher by using a VSPM to find your required talent rather than finding them by any other means. These systems were specifically designed from both a technological and social engineering standpoint to maximize successful project outcomes.

Rating Your Service Provider

After final payment is made, you will be asked to rate your provider and submit any comments about their work that you think are appropriate. This is where you want to be honest and fair. If they did a great job for you (which will probably be the case in most instances), show them your appreciation by giving a great rating and glowing comments. If they did less then great, reflect that in your rating as well. Keep one thing in mind though, if you give a less than favorable rating, make sure you explain why in your comments.

These ratings are not to be taken lightly; your input can have a big effect on someone's livelihood. And, there is another aspect of this rating process that you need to consider. Your service provider is not the only one being rated. Most VSPMs allow the service providers to rate the people who hire them for a job. This means you will be rated as well. If you were difficult to deal with, communicated poorly or made overt attempts to take advantage of your service provider, it will all come out in their rating and comments about you. "So what?" you might ask. Well, it's a big "So what!" If you have managed to garner consistently poor ratings from service providers who have previously worked with you, these will be seen as a warning to all potential bidders for any future projects you may decide to post. This means the quantity and quality of bids will likely be less, thus hurting your ability to take full advantage of outsourcing projects to Virtual Consultants through these VSPMs. In fact, the best providers will probably choose to ignore your bids entirely. Treat these service providers with respect and common courtesy, and they will repay you in kind.

Keep in mind that it is in the interest of every VSPM to maintain the highest levels of ethical and reasonable behavior among both its service providers and employers (i.e., project posters). In speaking to Elance and Guru, they both made it clear they will not hesitate to remove a service provider or business owner who does not meet these standards. In the parlance of the project transaction process, it helps to minimize the "business-to-business transactional friction."

The process for defining and posting your project, choosing and working with the service provider who gets it done, and then paying and rating them is fairly straightforward. However, as with any endeavor, there are certain tips, tricks and strategies that can help you realize the greatest benefit from using these VSPMs. The following insights are a result of my experience over the years in posting projects, working with VSPM service providers and seeing projects to completion.

Tricks of the Virtual Consultant Trade

Every now and then you are going to post a project where either you do not receive any bids, or the ones you do receive are not particularly attractive. There are several things you can do should this happen:

- *Post under another category* – You may have posted your project under a category that was inappropriate for the kind of talent required by your project. Try another category that may be a better fit;

- *Refine your project description* – Review your written project description and ask yourself, "Will anyone reading this have enough information to fully understand what my project requires?" Consider rewriting it or providing additional supporting documentation that will help clarify your project requirements. Also, check to see if your project is too complex. That is, if it requires more than one kind of specialized talent to complete it. If so, consider breaking your project up into several pieces which you post separately;

- *Get help* – When all else fails, just ask for help. Some VSPMs provide complimentary project posting assistance. This is particularly useful if you are having trouble with your first few project postings.

Posting projects in a way that results in consistently good bids takes a bit of practice. However, as you will soon experience for yourself, the time and effort expended at refining this skill is significantly less than what it takes to hire, train and manage good employees. And don't forget the amount of money you will save by completing your project this way.

For some types of projects, you may not be aware of the need to ask for the final work product in a format that will give you the most value and flexibility. For example:

- *Graphic design* – If your project consists of having graphic design work done using a computer, it is important to specify the format of the final images. The reason is that there are two basic categories of computer graphic image formats – "raster" and "vector."

Raster images consist of pixels which are essentially tiny individual squares that make up a larger image. The main limitation of raster images is that they don't scale well. If you try to enlarge a raster image beyond a certain point, it becomes fuzzy looking (sometimes referred to as "pixilated"). This inability to maintain image quality at different scales limits what you can do with the image.

Vector images, on the other hand, consist of mathematical formulas that allow certain programs to scale them to any size without loss of quality. Whenever practical, you will want your final image format to be vector-based. The industry standard for vector images is Adobe Illustrator. Unless your graphic designer tells you otherwise, insist on receiving the final design files in Adobe Illustrator format. They can then be used by nearly every printer or professional page layout person for nearly any purpose. This will give you the most flexibility of all.

If for aesthetic reasons your designer insists that a raster image is the only way to achieve the look you want (which is true in some cases), then ask for the final format in Adobe Photoshop which is widely regarded to be the industry standard for raster image design. Don't worry if you're not familiar with the above mentioned programs or formats. Just ask for them within your graphic design project description because your printer or page layout person will be glad you did when it comes time to use them;

- *Programming* – Finding talented people to create custom computer applications is easy using most VSPMs. If you do plan on having a custom application created, make sure you specify that you receive the "source code" and that it's well documented so other programmers can quickly understand what was done and why. Also, be sure to reach an agreement with your programmer as to how long they will support their work once completed. A "debugging" period should be specified in the final bid. All software has bugs and this approach will help you minimize the cost of fixing them.

  If you have no experience at all with computer programming, it may be wise to first hire an appropriately skilled service provider (system's analyst or user interface designer) to fully spec out your custom software project so that your RFP more accurately describes what you want. Taking this approach for custom software development projects could save you a small fortune of re-work costs;

- *Multimedia* – Let's say you need a PowerPoint or Flash presentation. There are lots of folks available through the VSPMs capable of doing great work. First, make sure they understand who the target audience is and the purpose of the message you are trying to get across using multimedia. This is so the final look and feel is consistent with its intended audience. Also, make sure that your chosen service provider warrants that they have the right to assign all the copyrights to you for any artwork or coding they use to create your presentation. Finally, insist on receiving all original files used to complete your project. This is especially true with Flash since you cannot easily modify any Flash presentation without the original Flash files used to create the final presentation;

- *Research* – "Research" can be such a nebulous thing, so the more precisely you can describe what you want, the better the results are likely to be. When the research is completed, you ideally want it in a format that is easy to use and transfer to other programs. If the search result is pure data, then in most cases an Excel spreadsheet should do the trick;

- *Writing* – This one is easy; simply request that the final copy is in a well-formatted, industry-standard Microsoft Word document. The only exception to this is if your industry uses another standard (e.g., WordPerfect for the legal industry).

Finally, don't make the mistake of re-hiring a service provider outside of the VSPM you used to find them, even after they have previously completed an absolutely brilliant job for you. This is because the moment you do, they are no longer accountable to or affected by the user rating system which is the heart of the best VSPMs. Sometimes buyers of services think they will get a better deal this way. Instead, it's just an invitation to headaches because you lose all your leverage as a buyer of virtually outsourced services. No competitive bidding and no threat of poor ratings if the job is not done up to par.

Naturally, the more projects you post and see through to completion, the better you will become at it. More importantly, you will also be more comfortable in utilizing Virtual Consultants as an integral and strategic part of running and growing your business.

There appears to be no limit as to how creatively other business owners have used VSPMs to solve important problems and access opportunities that otherwise would not be available to them. Here are several real-world "case stories" from different business owners achieving just such results.

Our first case story illustrates an interesting phenomenon among virtual service providers. In addition to responding to bids posted on VSPMs, they may also run other businesses that use VSPMs to outsource non-core projects for their clients, effectively wearing both hats in the virtual consulting equation...

Business Owner by Day / Provider by Night

I wear two hats and it suits me just fine! I own an advertising agency which contracts out services when we need to and, on the flip side, I am also a free-lance author and regularly provide my own specialized services. In freelance cyber lingo, that makes me a "buyer/provider" hybrid!

I began exploring the concept of outsourcing specialty projects when one of my advertising clients needed a sophisticated database tool for their marketing needs. We wanted the job, but didn't really know how to do what they were asking. I was advised to check out Elance, one of the most sophisticated freelance Web sites on the Internet, and found a company in India that had experience in this particular area. I ended up saving money for my client, while expediting the delivery of the product. To them, I was a hero!

Outsourcing labor has allowed employers to find the right people with the specific specialties required. You can be "bigger" than you are and more successful than you are. It is definitely a symbiotic relationship, for the good. For me, it was an all around positive experience. Yet, there are those people who still ask me why I'm employing people who live halfway around the world instead of hiring the guy who lives down the block.

It's simply a matter of economics. I'd love to work with the guy down the block if he can meet my price, my schedule and understand the needs of the project. For me, the best providers have been from other countries.

One of the best features of a long-distance relationship with overseas providers is that if you make a request at 6 p.m. your time, you'll have it in your inbox the next morning. I've found time differences to be fun and not a bother. We never interrupt each other's middle ground. It just feels more efficient.

Almost 15 years ago, employers almost always hired locally. Today, the tool is electronic communication; transportation barriers don't exist anymore and location no longer matters. Because the guy down the street is local, doesn't necessarily make him the best candidate for the job —especially when he doesn't return phone calls and people in India do!

My response to these folks is that the world has changed and will continue to change. You can bemoan the fact or alter your thinking and business operations to fit it.

As a ghost writer, I tend to write for people who have a public presence; those who are suitably visible to market their own material. I don't have a big name or a publisher. Frankly, I probably wouldn't get the project done if I were doing it for myself! Business people don't have the time or the inclination to write a book because they are out in the field selling whatever it is they end up writing about!

One important piece of advice to buyers who advertise on freelance work sites is to make sure that your expectations are crystal clear when you present a project for bidding. Providers, in turn, must be willing to prove themselves. All parties extend a certain amount of trust when they use such sites, which allow participants to read "reviews" of both buyers and providers. You are no less safe working with the guy down the street, who can take your money and run as easily as someone online!

Jeff Haden
Advertising Company Owner (by day)
Virtual Consultant / Ghost Writer (by night)

Not all Virtual Consultants are self-employed. Sometimes they work a normal nine to five for others during the day, while easily earning significant extra income completing Virtual Outsourcing projects in the evening ...

Straddling the Virtual Fence

I feel as if I'm nestled in a semi-secure place at this point in my life. There's a duality about what I do for a living and how I do it that places me in two worlds. In the very near future, I know that I will have to choose one or the other, mostly because it is becoming physically impossible to maintain the busy pace of doing both. I don't want to blow my own horn, but I give 100 percent to what I do and then some. I am realizing that what started out as some curious poking online for a little extra work to augment my income, has dramatically presented me with an incredibly busy, full-blown second job. I have a full-time job designing custom signs and when I come home from that job, I freelance as an illustrator and graphic designer. I retire to my "dungeon" after the kids go to bed and spend the greater part of the night and sometimes the very early hours of the next morning, turning out projects. There are just too many hours spent at work and then working from home.

When I graduated from the Art Academy of Cincinnati, I have to admit that I was a little bit jealous of friends who went on to begin their own businesses and ply their creativity in a more direct way. I found my current job then and I made it a career. I always saw myself as trying new things, drawing things in a different way, even when I was creating signs for others. Now that I've gotten my chance to show my skills, I am in a very real quandary. I've had a lot more success freelancing than I ever anticipated. My freelance income now matches that of my full-time job. Over the years, I have become the one guy in the store who knows computers. I wear many hats at my current job. I get cold feet when I think about having to tell my boss that I'm leaving, although I have taken "baby steps" in preparing for that eventuality. I've drafted a letter to him, but I still have no idea how or when I will present it. I'm still a little timid about making that choice. I see the results of my creativity paying off as a freelancer, but will I ever be at the point where I can do it exclusively?

I'm a novice, really, to the online bidding-for-jobs process, which I looked into just a few months ago. As a "bottom feeder" on the site, I was amazed and gratified by the jobs that came my way in a rather short period of time. Before I knew it, I had already blown past my humble financial goal and I'm still working on jobs from buyers on the Elance work site and from the Elance agency, itself. That was a big surprise! They told me that they could send me four or five jobs a week and pay me twice the amount, per job, that I was getting from buyers —and the best part is that I didn't have to compete with anybody else.

If I wasn't married with kids, one of whom is my four-year-old autistic son, I would have taken the leap a long time ago. I guess it's part of human nature to hold on to what we know we have. It's the fear of the unknown that usually strikes at those big decisions in life. In this business, you can never be that sure that a customer is really going to call you back. I realize that it takes hard work, but I have landed some really good jobs that forced me to advance my talents and learn new things. When the client is happy, it's an acknowledgment that I'm good at what I do and that something I've actually worked on is out there in the world.

Greg Essert
Graphic Designer

As any experienced business person knows, ideas are a dime a dozen unless you can put them into practice. Here is a case where an idea triggered by watching a TV commercial became the germ of a very successful business. And, if it were not for the ability to quickly bring it to fruition with the use of a VSPM, it just might have gone onto the crowded shelf of "someday I'll get to it"—instead of becoming a growing business with 18 territories ...

Tools of the Trade

For the last 10 years, I owned a real estate investment company that managed company and client owned real estate portfolios. Maintenance and construction is a natural component of managing real estate, but having to deal with unreliable contractors was frustrating. I began hiring my own construction staff to overcome the reliability issues and developed some good systems for handling large quantities of smaller jobs.

We began getting requests from homeowners asking us to do work at their homes and I realized that there was a large unfilled need for our services. I had been playing with the word "handyman" for some time and happened to see something on television that was "on demand," and "Handyman on Demand" struck me as the perfect way to describe what we could do.

I let the idea blossom in my head. I had heard about the Elance Web site, where buyers list projects and freelance specialists with diverse skills bid on them. I think I was luckier than most people because my first experience was so immediately positive. I listed the project on Elance and within 24 hours I had a name and logo for my business, thanks to the excellent Web design services of a company in Malaysia. The freelancers on the job were great, to the point where I thought to myself, "This is too easy." So, to test my theory, I asked them to try a few different things, a second or third time. We ended up deciding on the original presentation, which validated their skill even more. The concept stood up to scrutiny. This was a pleasant development at the time, coinciding with the fact that I was slowly coming to a boil over the quality, or lack of it, of the in-house construction and maintenance people. I decided that if I was going to be unsatisfied with the work they did, I might as well bring in my own employees and at least have more control over that part of the business.

I can comfortably say that Handyman On Demand is virtually thriving beyond our expectations. Between our domestic and international staff, we currently employ almost 100 people and provide maintenance and light construction services to commercial and residential customers throughout Southern California. We outsource our accounting to a firm in Calcutta, our software development to a firm outside of Mumbai, our graphics design to a firm in Malaysia, and our marketing to a firm in Florida.

We've reached the point where we feel these associates are truly part of our organization. They have taken on departmental functions. We constantly use instant messaging in the course of a workday so that a person or team is a legitimate presence right there with us. These are genuine, sincere work partners who want to maintain good, solid relationships with their American employers. We use three Indian contractors. Aside from saving money for us, they come to the table with a better work ethic, a great attitude and superior skills.

I actually thought about visiting Calcutta and Mumbai to give a face and personal touch to the operation. They present themselves as strong, cohesive organizations; but there's always a concern about the work practices of people you don't know well. Right now all we can do is evaluate performance; which has been outstanding. In general, the Indian population we deal with is highly educated, enabling it to create an Internet platform and compete on a global scale. Combined with drive and ambition, they are building a happy future, in which they are committed to mining every nugget. For them, it's the gold rush!

Some people are still uncomfortable dealing in the virtual world. A shift in focus requires the biggest leap. I come from a very traditional accounting background. People worked in cubicles and had file cabinets that held lots of paper. Making the transition from a paper process to a paperless one was the biggest obstacle for me to overcome. I had to rethink every accounting principle I ever learned. It's a big stretch, much like the explosion of computer technology in the 80s. Outsourcing will get easier as we learn how to interface effectively. Look at hiring a contractor using the same criteria you would if you were hiring someone who was sitting next to you. But, be aware that very often the results are not the same —they are better.

Lee Clements
Chairman of the Board
Handyman On Demand Ventures, Inc.

OK, we covered quite a bit of territory within this chapter —most of which was a practical methodology to using Virtual Consultants within your business. If you follow the approach laid out here, you will be able to start successfully posting your projects immediately.

Here is a quick refresher to help you remember the main concepts…

Key Ideas and Chapter Review

- Virtual Consultants are typically used for project-based work (a job function that has a beginning, middle and end). No matter how brilliantly they did their job, you may or may not use them again depending upon your needs;

- The easiest way to find, evaluate and hire highly talented and affordable Virtual Consultants is through Virtual Service Provider Marketplaces (VSPMs), which bring together talent (i.e., Virtual Consultants) and those that need to use it (i.e., businesses) in an anonymous, competitive, transaction bidding environment;

- Currently, Elance.com and Guru.com are the two largest general purpose VSPMs that offer access to talent in nearly every business project category imaginable;

- Within the context of talent found on VSPMs, the terms "Virtual Consultant" and "Service Provider" are synonymous;

- Most business projects tend to be strategic or tactical in nature (i.e., growth related) rather than operational (i.e., support of day-to-day functioning);

- Most VSPMs are free for businesses to use (i.e., post projects to) and offer access to qualified talent from around the world typically at prices that are far less than if hired locally;

- The biggest challenge for businesses to realizing the full potential of hiring talent through VSPMs is *a)* determining appropriate projects that can be outsourced, and *b)* adequately describing those projects within a posting so potential bidders have a clear picture of what is wanted;

- Another term for a posted project is a Request For Proposal (RFP);

- A practical strategy to effectively using VSPMs is to outline your project with a Word processor (using the template mentioned earlier) and then post the project description into several VSPMs in order to realize the widest possible range of service provider prospects;

- Resulting bids from posting projects on VSPMs provide a great deal of information about each bidder, including objective previous user feedback that empowers you to quickly determine the best service provider for your project;

- When your project is completed, in most cases you pay the VSPM who in turn pays the respective service provider who did the actual work. This helps keep your financial information secure and unambiguously documents the fact that you paid for the completed work;

- In the unlikely event that the completed project does not meet your expectations, there are several steps you can take. In addition to re-discussing the project with your service provider or asking them to voluntarily cancel it, some VSPMs provide mediation and arbitration services that are very useful in the event you ever have an intractable dispute with your service provider;

- Upon completion of a project, you get to rate the performance of the service provider. And, the service provider gets to rate you on how easy (or not) it was to work with you. The higher your rating as a user of these services, the better the bids you are likely to see for any future posted projects;

- There are nuances to posting projects in a way that will maximize the benefits you see from the completed project with the minimum amount of effort on your part —learn them.

Exciting and revolutionary as it is, using highly talented and affordable Virtual Consultants to execute your business projects is just half of the Virtual Outsourcing equation. In the next chapter, we will explore how you can run and grow your business using ongoing "virtual" support (i.e., Virtual Assistants) that, for the most part, you will never meet, have to provide office space for, train or manage —and that's just for starters…

Virtual Assistants 5

Assistance from a Distance

Completing strategically vital projects brilliantly and affordably is certainly an important part of growing your business. But let's face it, as a small to midsized business owner, you spend most of your time in the day-to-day grind of just making sure your business runs smoothly. This is where you need ongoing support that you can depend upon day in, day out. Traditionally, that meant bringing in employees to handle your support issues, which as we saw earlier, can create a whole new set of issues.

Virtual Assistants and Virtual Support Organizations (VSOs) are the other half of the Virtual Outsourcing solution for business. They both provide ongoing support, just like an employee would, except they do it from a distance —that is, from offsite using the Internet, phone and fax to deliver their support services. Where VAs tend to work as independent contractor individuals (or small affiliated groups of them), VSOs are companies that provide specialized outsourced support functions to small or midsized businesses. And like individual VAs, they often never meet the clients they service. *NOTE: Most of the focus in this chapter will be on the use of individual VAs.*

When first hearing of this "Assistance from a Distance" notion, many business owners and managers immediately start thinking of all the reasons why it won't work. This is a rather common human trait. Many people would rather be certain of their misery rather than risk the misery of uncertainty associated with trying something new. And, these reasons can typically be lumped into two basic categories:

- *Control* – "How can I be sure the work will get done, on time and correctly? How do I know that a VA I've just hired won't just slough off because no one is watching over them? How do I know I can trust someone that I've never met in person to do important support work for my company? How can I be certain that a VA won't compromise my company's proprietary information? No one can do it as well as I can! I need to be right there with them to make sure it gets done right! I need my staff in the office in case something urgent comes up. Who will I bounce ideas off of if my staff is invisible?" And so on;

- *Integration* – "I wouldn't know where to start in hiring a VA for ongoing support. Every job function in my company requires the person doing the job to be onsite. Even if I could find great VAs to do some of our work, I don't want to lose the onsite people that we already spent a fortune training! I just don't see how we can train someone to do our work when we never even get to meet them in person. Won't using VAs make our annual company picnics, well... sparsely attended?" And so on.

Do any of these sound familiar? Perhaps you're thinking along these lines this very moment. You're not alone here —most employers show the same initial resistance when they first hear about using Virtual Assistants within their business. At this point, I don't expect the heavens to open up and bathe you with ethereal light and angelic chorale sounds as you gaze up in slack-jawed wonder at this marvelous new way of running your business. All I ask is that you be open to the possibility that there might actually be something here —something that could have a huge, positive impact on your business, career and life. So take a deep breath, and with an adventurer's hat firmly on your head, let's set out to see how we can address the above issues.

Control is a big one for most small to midsized business owners and managers mainly because the vast majority have built their companies from the ground up and wholeheartedly subscribe to the bromide: "If you want the job done right, you've got to do it yourself (or at least stand over the shoulders of the ones doing it)!" As we will see in the next chapter, this attitude is the number one reason why small, semi-successful businesses rarely turn into highly successful businesses. It may not seem like it now, but eventually you'll see how this kind of control is more of a millstone than an enabler. We'll also see how you can easily mitigate any trepidation about the use of VAs and the matter of control.

Concerns surrounding the integration of VAs into your day-to-day operations usually stem from just not being familiar with the context of what kinds of support are possible from a distance. It never seems to fail that when I speak to business audiences around the world, they're simply blown away by how many of their non-core competencies can be virtually outsourced to highly talented, independent VAs. Once you know "how" it is done, the "what" (i.e., job functions) becomes much easier to envision. VAs can provide a very wide range of general support functions as well as highly specialized ones within specific industries.

Here are just a few ways VAs can support your business, no matter what it is:

- *Bookkeeping* – I used to have a local bookkeeper for my businesses. It was difficult for her to keep me up-to-date on the financial picture because she insisted on using traditional PC-based financial software. That all changed when I hired a bookkeeper who lives about 1500 miles away and uses a Web-based accounting software such as QuickBooks Online. This approach to my bookkeeping allows me 24/7 access to my financial books and reports from any Web browser no matter where I happen to be on this planet. It also means that security surrounding my business finances is higher because my bookkeeper is the only support person within my organization who really knows how much money my businesses earn for me. While she has the ability to cut checks and transfer funds from one account to the other as needed, only I have the ability to sign checks or otherwise withdraw funds.

- *Scheduling / Setting Appointments* – Scheduling and setting appointments can be a time-consuming, thankless task that anyone but you should be doing. In most instances, it doesn't require on-site staff to handle scheduling or setting up your appointments, just someone with good communication skills with access to e-mail, phone and fax. Also, with the growing use of online calendaring systems, modifying and tracking scheduled activities is a breeze.

- *Call / E-mail Screening* – If you spend most of your productive hours meeting with people, it pays to have someone handle your calls and e-mails as they come in. In addition to greatly increasing your productivity, your business image is perceived to be highly professional because, through the efforts of your VA, people receive immediate responses to both phone and e-mail inquiries. By the way, as you will see in the next chapter, there are online services, which I refer to as "Virtual PBX's" that allow you to integrate phone communications with any number of virtual staff in a completely seamless and highly sophisticated way —all without adding a single extra phone line;

- *Marketing Plan Execution* – After you have hired a Virtual Consultant marketing specialist to help develop your killer marketing plan, you will need one or more people to execute it consistently. Here are some of the ways you can use VAs to help you do just that:

  - *Advertising* – Successful advertising requires a relatively complex mix of appropriate creative (i.e., design, layout and copy), positioning (i.e., media where it will be placed) and tracking abilities. There are VAs with advertising backgrounds who can handle every aspect of your advertising campaigns from literally anywhere. Chances are these VAs will manage the process for you while subcontracting out (to other VAs of course) the various functions of putting your ads together. You will find that the practice of VAs using other VAs to get work done is fairly common; in fact, there are whole networks of VAs that work this way.

  - *Newsletters* – A custom newsletter designed to specifically deliver high-value information to your prospective and existing customer base can be a powerful way to generate new business. Few small to midsized businesses bother to go this route though because of the time and effort it takes —if you try to do it all yourself. Having your own custom newsletter can be an affordable reality if you use a VA who specializes in creating and distributing them. Each month, your newsletter can be created and distributed to your customers without you having to lift a finger.

- *Surveys* – Getting objective feedback from your clients is an important part of the marketing process. There are highly affordable online survey systems that allow you (or better yet, your VA) to quickly and easily create, distribute and analyze any kind of survey you can dream up.

- *Event Planning* – Let's say you want to put on a free public seminar that will give your business great exposure and help you be perceived as "the expert" in your field. Setting these up so they run without a glitch is not for the feint of heart or inexperienced. Fortunately, there are VAs who have extensive experience doing just this and love nothing more than to see your event become a huge success (so they can do more of them for you).

- *Brochures* – Like advertising, creating effective brochures requires several skill sets, including design, page layout and copywriting. While there are myriads of VAs who have experience designing brochures, you may want to hire an experienced VC copywriter to do the copy first. I'm a firm believer that great copy is the most important element in any marketing medium, and everything else (design, layout, packaging, etc.) is there to support the written message.

- *Copy Editing* – Any kind of marketing strategy invariably requires copy of some kind. And, the last person you want to edit that copy is the copywriter. Their job is to communicate and compel via words; the editor's job (in this case) is to make sure the spelling and punctuation is correct to avoid embarrassing mistakes that would otherwise reduce the power of the copy. This can easily be done with the help of a VA from anywhere. For example, my VA editor (whom I've never met) lives somewhere in the Midwest and I only pay her for a few hours a month to edit my articles. In addition to being fast, her services are quite reasonably priced.

- *Drip Marketing* – Drip marketing consists of one or more "campaigns," each of which comprise a series of prewritten messages that are sent over a period of time.

The idea is to automate the process of staying in touch with prospective and current customers using periodic communications that are perceived to be highly valuable by the intended recipient. Most typically used in e-mail marketing, you can also have drip "snail mail" (i.e., postcard) marketing as well. To successfully set up, consistently execute and track drip marketing campaigns takes experience and focus. There are VAs who specialize in this kind of marketing (I know, because I use one for my business). Since most of the systems used today to execute drip messaging are Web-based, a VA that even lives on another continent could run them for you.

- *Direct Mail* – Despite the increased use of the Internet for marketing purposes, direct mail continues to be a viable strategy for many businesses. To be effective, direct mail campaigns need to be well targeted, compelling from a creative standpoint, continually tested and tracked for results. This requires a specialized set of skills better left to the experts (as any business person will attest to who has attempted to do it themselves). The good news is that every aspect of executing direct mail campaigns can be done remotely —hence by a suitably experienced VA.

  Many businesses see their marketing efforts sputter after early success. This is primarily because as the marketing strategies start to generate business, focus often shifts from continuing to execute the plan faithfully to just trying to handle the business it generates. By utilizing VAs to outsource the implementation of your marketing plans, you know it will always be executed according to specs, no matter how much new business it generates.

- *Quality Assurance* – Manufacturing industries typically have quality assurance down to an absolute science (e.g., ISO 9000 certifications). Yet, it seems that many service-based companies still have a long way to go before they achieve consistent, high quality standards of service. This is where a VA can be of immense help. Once you have specifically defined in writing the parameters of your quality service standards, it shouldn't be too difficult for a VA to remotely qualify and document your organization's ability (or inability) to maintain these standards.

- **CRM** – Customer Relationship Management (CRM) is an extremely important function for any company that hopes to grow. Its primary function is to help you plan, execute and track the sales process, from first contact all the way through to closing the deal and staying in touch afterward. There are a number of software applications that are specifically designed to help organizations with this function. The most exciting of these are Web-based. This means that one or more VAs can run your entire CRM program remotely and generate whatever kind of reports you want;

- **Sales** – If your company uses telephone sales (inbound or outbound) or telemarketing, then this is a natural for VAs who specialize in this kind of work. Using a combination of Web-based call tracking applications and the "Virtual PBXs" described in the next chapter, you have everything you need to virtually outsource your phone sales operation;

- **Customer Service** – There are a number of different ways to deliver customer service, including the phone, e-mail and online chat —all of which can be used remotely. Here is an interesting possibility that makes your company look just like the "big boys," yet with no onsite staff whatsoever. There are inexpensive Web-based customer support chat systems that allow you to designate and manage as many remote customer service reps as you want. These systems log all conversations and time spent between your reps and customers. Imagine hiring VAs in different time zones around the globe to act as your dedicated customer service staff with each one covering a different part of the day. This means that you could offer 24/7 customer service even if you were a company consisting of just one person —you! Now before you choke on the idea of hiring a bunch of VAs around the world just to man your online chat customer support lines, consider this: These chat systems typically log the exact amount of time each rep spends chatting with a customer. Since VAs typically have a number of different clients they work for, it's not out of the realm of possibility that you could negotiate a "per chat minute" fee, rather than pay them whether they chat with your customers or not;

- *Tech Support* – For some companies, tech support is one of the most costly impacts to their bottom line —especially if the tech support staff is in-house. With the advent of Web-based tools that allow your tech support staff to remotely diagnose and fix problems, VAs trained on your systems can handle this function for you. Combine this capability with an online trouble ticket system and post service survey, and you have a powerful way to provide highly scalable, superior and affordable tech support;

- *Copywriting* – As mentioned earlier, publishing a newsletter (whether e-mail or paper-based) requires ongoing writing that can easily be outsourced to one or more VA copywriters. Other possibilities include direct response copy, packaging copy, technical writing, ongoing narrative reports, etc. If you examine all the possible areas where one or more copywriters could apply their craft, you will likely find there are many more than you realize;

An important thing to remember about copywriters is that they all have their niche. Some are great direct response copywriters for direct mail or e-mail campaigns, but couldn't author a good article to save their life. Likewise, a story writer is not likely to do well composing compelling direct response ad copy or precise technical manuals. Just like any other creative endeavor, hire according to the needed outcome —which is easy to do when it's virtual;

- *Graphic Design* – In addition to advertising, you may have other ongoing graphic design needs. Fore example, a marketing director for a large regional Midwest sales organization hired a California VA (whom he has never met) to continually produce new marketing-based graphic design work (post cards, flyers, etc.) for the use of their sales associates. He used to have an in-house designer, but she was too costly to maintain onsite just for that function. Since then he has been consistently receiving better quality and a broader range of designs for less money while completely eliminating his management headaches;

- *Project Management* – Effectively managing projects is a fairly specialized skill set that few small business owners have or can afford to hire onto their staff. If your operations include ongoing project-based work (especially if it is service related), it can likely be run remotely via one of the many Web-based project management applications and the use of a VA with suitable experience;

- *Human Resources* – In the "good old days," the primary function of HR was hiring, firing and organizing company functions. Now it is much more about managing employee benefits and CYA with respect to regulatory compliance, avoiding workplace grievance and wrongful termination suits. Most small to mid-sized businesses simply don't have the number of employees or budget to warrant hiring a full-time HR administrator. Fortunately, there are VAs and VSOs with significant HR experience who can set up and administrate much of what you need. And, since you only pay for what you use, this kind of high-level administration is much more affordable than if you brought someone in-house;

- *Financial Management* – Not many small businesses can afford to have their own CFO. Yet the importance of the CFO's function for nearly any business cannot be overstated. They can help you strategically plan, create budgets, manage cash flow and help arrange bank financing in ways necessary for the assured growth of your company. If you utilize the online accounting systems mentioned earlier, it's easy to see how a "virtual" CFO could remotely manage and keep you up-to-date on every aspect of your company's financial health;

The thought may have occurred to you by now that some of the most important functions within your organizational chart (Marketing Director, HR, CFO, etc.) can be effectively outsourced. In the next chapter, you'll get a chance to see just how much of the rest of that chart can be virtually outsourced as well;

- *Billing and Accounts Receivable* – If your business generates a large number of invoices and/or maintains a sizable receivables account, someone needs to manage that—often aggressively. Once again, by utilizing a Web-based accounting system, you can hire a receivables VA specialist who keeps track of this vital part of your business and hunts down your nar-do-well, over-30-days-late customers;

- *Web Site Maintenance* – Nearly every business today can benefit from having a Web site. And, to remain effective, it needs to be periodically updated and maintained. This can be a rather tedious, thankless job that often just doesn't get done, or if so, poorly at

> *" Anything that doesn't absolutely require close geographical proximity to your business to be performed can likely be outsourced to a Virtual Assistant or Virtual Support Organization. "*

best. Clearly a VA could handle this for you from anywhere in the world in a way that totally frees you up to continue doing what you do best. For example, I have a Canadian VA keep my speaking schedule up-to-date on all of my Web sites in addition to posting it on several other event scheduling sites to help maximize my exposure. While these updates are important to my business, this is the sum total of what she does for me. I don't have to worry about it because I know it will get done like clockwork and for relatively little cost;

- **Search Engine Positioning** – If your Web site is responsible for generating a significant portion of your sales, then search engine positioning is a critical function that must be performed continually. There are currently two primary ways to drive traffic to your Web site via search engines:

  - *"Organic" Search Engine Optimization (SEO)* – This is where a search engine specialist tweaks your site so that when potential customers search using certain words or phrases, your site comes up near the top of the list. Due to the dynamic and ever changing nature of search engines, this kind of skill is highly specialized and requires the efforts of someone who does just this for a living.

    There are companies who have whole teams of people (typically wearing wizard hats) who spend most of their waking hours trying to figure out the latest and greatest SEO positioning strategy. Because of this, I tend to avoid hiring VAs for this particular kind of search engine positioning. It is simply not possible for them to be on top of this "black art" if they do any other kind of work.

    If you go this route, keep several things in mind. Not all SEO firms are reputable. Some will make promises and guarantees that they can't possibly keep, yet gladly take your money with a smile. And, the ones that are honest and very good at what they do tend to be expensive.

Expect to pay thousands to set up and maintain your SEO efforts.

- *"Pay-Per-Click" Search Engine Advertising (PPC)* – PPC is a way you can very quickly, effectively and affordably drive traffic to your site. In theory, you only pay the search engines when people actually land on your site by clicking on their search results. It's a very powerful way to know precisely how much it costs you to drive Web traffic. While it requires a specialist to set up and constantly maintain your PPC campaigns, this process is nowhere near as formidable or expensive as SEO mentioned above. In fact, this is an ideal job for a VA pay-per-click specialist who can set up, manage and tweak your PPC accounts from afar.

  In summary, if you plan on utilizing PPC search engine advertising to drive business to your site, consider using a VA that specializes in this as their primary business. Otherwise, hire a reputable SEO firm to "organically" (i.e., naturally) have your site come up near the top of search results;

- *Research* – Independent writers, analysts, consultants and marketing specialists are just some examples of people who typically need to do ongoing research. Effective research is one of those tasks that you either love doing or consider a drudgery, looked upon with fear and loathing. Since I squarely fit into the latter category, I'll let you in on a little secret. I virtually outsourced nearly every aspect of the rather considerable amount of research that was required to complete this book.

  If your research needs are extensive and ongoing, you may want to consider hiring a VA research specialist to manage the whole process. This means that they will take responsibility for producing your research results, even if they subcontract out some of that work to others. This way you are working with one individual who really understands your research needs, yet are freed up to use other resources to get the job done in the most effective and affordable way.

The above list of possible VA functions is hardly comprehensive. It is designed to just help you start thinking about the possibilities of using VAs for certain types of functions within your business.

Here is a good general rule to remember when considering VAs for your business: Anything that doesn't absolutely require close geographical proximity to your business to be performed can likely be outsourced to a Virtual Assistant or Virtual Support Organization. As you continue to consider the various ways in which your business can be virtually supported, more ideas of what can be outsourced will come your way.

Here are several case stories of business owners who have done just that...

Brandy, You're a Fine Girl

I have been doing financial planning for almost 20 years, beginning as a door-to-door agent, then getting into retirement planning and ultimately having clients coming into an office. As businesses become more sophisticated, so too should the methods used to solve administrative demands. Life insurance and investing never used to be viewed as a real business. But as the industry matured, then literally exploded, agents and business owners alike couldn't possibly do it all. Using a Virtual Assistant has been one of the best decisions a small business owner like myself could make. For me, it has been a wonderfully smooth ride. My solution can be summed up in one word: Brandy.

Prior to going the virtual route, I hired a full-time, onsite assistant. A common concern for employers is not being able to keep in-house staff busy all the time; this is exactly what I experienced, so that decision was short lived. Some businesses need onsite employees, but the specificity of my needs taught me a different lesson.

Enter Brandy. What I needed upfront was to have a database entered using specific software that would mine and catalog client information. The particular program was time-consuming and very detailed. Finding Brandy and giving her this assignment as an offsite VA allowed me to step away from the burden of that task. What followed was a re-hauling of my data system, my mailing system and my plan to follow-up by phone with the fifty people who attended my last seminar. I gave these jobs to Brandy and I was instantly surprised to find that I was effectively paying fees for just the specific tasks in question. I have to say that I was brave enough to step out of an old mindset and spend the money I needed to get the job done in an efficient, timely and professional fashion. The common denominator is that thinking has to change to allow businesses, big and small, to make time and cost effective decisions. Anything else doesn't make sense —or cents!

Big companies (like Amway, for example) allow people to work the hours they need to work from home to meet quotas. Businesses don't have to provide workspace or benefits, and people working from home are productive on their own schedules. Computers and telecommuting have proved that amazing things can be done. Brandy has educated me as to just how amazing these capabilities are!

Small business owners in particular should take a lesson from this old business guideline to assess "strengths, threats, weaknesses and opportunities" and address these questions anew. "Where am I weak? What threatens my business? What opportunities can make it grow? What can I do to help?" If we don't ask such questions, we'll never be aware of suitable solutions we may have never even considered. The concept of Virtual Assistance may be foreign to many small entrepreneurs, yet they should take time to examine what it is that they absolutely hate to do and, more important, what is costing them extra money. Don't leave it to big business to tell you what to do when you are capable of making the very same decisions for your own smaller, successful enterprises.

Sherry McNee
Financial Planner

The range of businesses that can be supported through the use of Virtual Assistants effectively has no limits. There also appears to be no limits to the praise and gratitude business owners often have for the virtual support staff that help them succeed...

A Virtual Feast

Like many young girls, my love affair with cooking began in the form of a small oven with the amazing baking power of a high wattage light bulb. From baking pies in my Susie Homemaker oven, to volunteering to sweep the floors at a local restaurant (so I could longingly watch the cooks), my craze for all things culinary just kept growing—right along with me. I'm sure it comes as no surprise to learn that over time I managed to turn this passion into a very fulfilling career.

Now that I'm a professional teaching chef, and owner of Kids Culinary Adventures, I spend the majority of my time in the field doing what I love! This wouldn't be possible though, if I hadn't brought a VA into the mix. During one of our first conversations, she made it known that she wanted to pick up my "accent"- not the verbal one, but my personality, my rhythm, my voice, so that she could represent me in all she would be doing. I knew then that she was going to be a welcomed addition to Kids Culinary Adventures. My business is an extension of who I am, and she readily embraced that. This would prove to be the first of many times that this skilled professional would know what I needed before I did.

Thankfully, this is the 21st century and Virtual Assistance is here to stay. My VA is a key ingredient in my recipe to success and brings a vast skill set to the table. I really don't know what I'd do without her! My VA is industrious, self-motivated, and totally capable of removing stress from the aspects of my business I choose not to deal with directly. She does almost everything, bookkeeping, marketing, customer/vendor relations, copy writing, desktop publishing – she is Kids Culinary Adventures. When we do come across something that's not in her realm of expertise, she has a great network of professionals she seamlessly integrates into the project to assure that my business receives the highest quality of service.

Whether she's upgrading my media contact list from 10 places to over 300, or helping me analyze my financials, my VA provides unsurpassed service and dedication. I know that I am not my dear VA's only client, but she makes me feel as if I am, and all from 2300 miles away! I highly recommend retaining a VA to any entrepreneur with a full plate; it has been one of the best business decisions I ever made.

Gayle Gaggero, Chef / Owner
Kids Culinary Adventures

Even the most staid of businesses have started benefiting from incorporating Virtual Assistants into their operations…

Insuring Better Business

I'm a guy who is constantly on the go —it's the nature of the business. I am a partner for New York Life. I recruit and develop agent and financial service professionals. I am out and about so often that it doesn't make sense to have someone in my office —a secretary or someone to answer phones. Based on an associate's recommendation, I have now contracted with a capable, professional VA who completes 20 hours of solicitation phone calls each month to contacts, licensed insurance agents and people to whom I was sending direct mail pieces before. The beauty of this arrangement is that my VA then simply e-mails me the results of these calls, with particular contact information and a brief description of what services they may be interested in.

This is a new thing for me. Prior to hiring my VA, I was doing it all myself. It was just too much! I couldn't get to the tasks as much as I would have liked and/ or was necessary. I have been using Virtual Assistance for just three months now and what a big difference it has been for me in terms of freeing up extra time. I can't see myself returning to the way I handled this before. It has been very smooth and very effective. In fact, I see the possibility of increasing the use of Virtual Assistance in the near future.

The trust factor is intact in my relationship with my VA. She is very professional and dependable. In fact, I think that a VA conducting business from a home-based office is more likely to be in a good, relaxed, comfortable mood, particularly when she is making solicitation calls to business contacts. In my case, she can do this on her own schedule, rather than perform on my schedule in an office where the atmosphere may not be as pleasing to her, which could affect the quality of the calls.

Larger corporations are outsourcing all kinds of work, today. Managers can still manage, without actually seeing someone face-to-face. I've never met my VA. With e-mail and voicemail and other technology, you're still connected. I can only offer my own experience using Virtual Assistance as advice to others who are considering this option. Think like a business owner and not an employee. Delegate something you can or have been doing yourself to a capable VA and learn how to better utilize the precious time you now have in new, more productive ways.

Vince Spaniolo, Partner
New York Life Insurance

Now that you have some idea of how a wide range of business functions can be virtually outsourced, let's take a much closer look at the distinctions between traditional onsite staff and their virtual counterparts.

VAs vs. Employees

One of my favorite times speaking to business audiences is when I compare VAs and employees (think "revenge of the managers"). The distinctions are so dramatic that I am compelled to first ask if there are any employee support staff in the audience. If so, I apologize ahead of time, explaining that by the time I'm done, they may feel a bit more uncertain about their job than when they first came in. In fact, during one speech, an assistant to a high performance salesperson suggested to her boss that they attend, not knowing ahead of time that the subject of VAs would even be discussed. By the end of the meeting, she was visibly concerned and wondered if she even had a job anymore! I'm much better now at managing the expectations of any employees who happen to be in my audiences. I let them know that there is still a place for them (perhaps with even more responsibility and pay), *if* they help their employer incorporate the benefits of Virtual Outsourcing.

	Employees	**Virtual Assistants**
Hard Costs	**More than you might expect!** If you currently have employees, you know they cost a lot more than the hourly wages you agreed to pay. Other costs include taxes, insurance, benefits, perks, training, office space, equipment, etc. As mentioned previously, these costs add considerably to the actual wages you pay. And these are just the "hard" costs, the ones you can identify within your P&L. However, this is just the tip of the iceberg…	**You pay only for what you use.** VAs are independent contractors, which means the fee you pay for their services is the only thing you pay —period. I encourage business people to pay VAs by the results of their work rather than by the hour (more on this later). If you do pay by the hour, it can range from less than $10/hr for VAs located in developing countries to $25 - $45/hr domestically, and up from there for highly specialized VA work.[35]
Soft Costs	**Do you really want to know?** Soft costs are those things that impact your bottom line, but can't be specifically identified as a line item in your P&L. For example: Time you spend managing, dispute resolution (i.e., office politics), surfing the Net when they should be working, unnecessary meetings, mollifying employee entitlement demands, time spent dangling from ropes and other high places (team building) when they should be working, etc. While it can be hard to accurately estimate the impact of these soft costs on your business's productivity, a recent survey by America Online and Salary.com indicates that U.S. employers pay about $759 billion for unproductive hours spent by their employees.[36]	**Few, if any.** If you follow the procedures I've laid out in the latter part of this chapter on how to hire VAs, you'll find that you will have few if any "soft" costs associated with using them. Because the good ones are specialists and have a clear idea of what needs to be done, you won't need to manage them. Also, issues related to organizational politics, employee entitlement mentality and motivation just don't exist —mainly because VAs are never onsite. And, they are independent contractors who understand what it takes to run a profitable business. They also are intimately aware that their success is tied to how they can help you become more successful.

	Employees	Virtual Assistants
Logistics	**They need a place to do their work.** Whether you own a home-based business or run a 10,000 square-foot operation, you will need to provide office space, desks, chairs, computers, software, office equipment, phone, computer lines and more. These are all substantial capital expenditures that someone (i.e., you) has to pay for. And, if any of it breaks down or needs upgrading, that falls on your shoulders, too.	**They already have a place.** VAs typically work from their home, own and maintain their own equipment, software, telecommunications lines, etc. If something breaks or needs upgrading, they pay for it. The reason they are willing to absorb these capital expenditures is that they get to work in their own environment, dressed the way they want to, and free to do the work in the manner and time frame that best suits their schedule.
Flexibility	**"You want me to work when?!"** Some business owners wince just thinking about asking a staff member to change their schedule or work extra hours to finish a critical project. If you think that's unpleasant, just imagine telling them you only need them for two hours this week instead of their regular 40. Remember, by definition, you are their meal ticket and any request you make that threatens it will likely provoke an unpleasant reaction.	**"No problem!"** Since VAs work with any number of different clients (in addition to you), they can be much more flexible with respect to the number of hours they work and when they get done (many VAs are night-owls and often work late into the evenings). The key is to build this kind of flexibility right into your independent contractor agreement. In any case, you will find VAs to typically be very accommodating in this regard.
Hiring	**As easy as 1-2-3 —wrong!** When your business is growing by leaps and bounds, you are constantly looking for more help. And of course we all know how easy it is to find good employees. As mentioned earlier, the hiring process is a very time-consuming, thankless job that most small to midsized business owners are just not well equipped to do. One of the biggest mistakes we can make is hiring someone who is just like us, which happens more often than not because we can "relate" to them. Instead, we should be hiring talent that is complementary to our own. The problem is we may not like their personality, the way they dress or how they talk —even though	**Measured in hours, not days or weeks.** As you will soon see later in this chapter, finding, evaluating and hiring a highly qualified VAs is an easy, straightforward process and can sometimes take just a few hours to complete. There are many reasons for this. First of all, if you stick to hiring only VAs who are specialists, it becomes much easier to find people with the skill set you need, rather than risk hiring a generalist that needs additional training. Second (and perhaps most importantly), since you never get to meet them in person or even know what they look like, all those judgments on how they look, dress and sound don't even enter into the equation. They

	Employees	Virtual Assistants
Hiring *(Continued)*	**As easy as 1-2-3 —wrong!** they may have the skills and integrity for the job. The cold, hard truth is we typically will not even consider a person's capabilities until they pass the "I like them!" test first. That's what happens when you have to "live" with your staff in the work environment.	**Measured in hours, not days or weeks.** could have purple hair, tattoos and piercings all over their body. You could care less —*because you never have to see or live with them in the office.* This means your focus during the hiring process is mostly on whether they can do the job capably, consistently, affordably and in a trustworthy manner.
Firing	**Ouch...** When things slow down or your business goes into a slump, you might be looking to cut your biggest expense, your staffing costs. We already covered the horrors that can befall the hapless business owner who is not careful about how they let employees go. However, even if you do everything right, it still is expensive. There are severance costs and whatever bundle you spent on getting that person trained, all of which goes down the drain when you say, "bye, bye."	**Quick as a phone call or e-mail.** Unless your VA independent contractor agreement states otherwise, you can usually terminate your relationship with a simple phone call or e-mail. No threats, lawsuits, calls from the state employment department, COBRA filings, IRA transfers, payroll system adjustments, changing of locks, cleaning out of desks, or security officer escorts through your lobby. Just a simple "I no longer need your help at this time. Thank you!"
Management	**Stand over their shoulder.** As mentioned earlier, the very nature of the employer/employee dynamic means that having onsite employees is going to be management intensive. This includes keeping them motivated and on track, resolving disputes, handling demands and complaints, finding people to replace those that go MIA, etc. In other words, it's a full-time job.	**It just gets done.** If you follow the procedures and protocols I lay out in full detail later in this chapter, you will effectively eliminate any need for managing your VAs. This is primarily because for each VA you hire, you will have a written description of the work objective (i.e., measurable end result) and a written process that describes exactly what needs to be done. And remember, these are independent contractors who tie their own success with yours.

	Employees	Virtual Assistants
Training	**Seems like it never ends!**	**It never even has to start.**
	According to the American Society for Training & Development, training represents nearly three percent of the total wage cost of having employees for large companies.[37] For small to midsized firms, those costs can go much higher. One of the primary reasons for this is that few employees in small companies are hired as "specialists" (where as the best VAs are specialists). In particular, if you are a small business, it is difficult and expensive to maintain a comprehensive employee training program. So guess who ends up doing it most of the time —you!	If you hire VA specialists to handle specific job functions within your organization, they are already well trained. (In fact, they could probably teach you a thing or two!) Granted, they may need to initially familiarize themselves with the nuances of the way things get done in your business. However, they can usually get up to speed very quickly, with little input from you.
Talent Pool	**A small pond.**	**The ocean.**
	As a small business owner, you simply cannot afford to hire many (if any) people from outside your geographical area. The average cost to relocate a new employee from outside your area is over $52,000.[38] This means your pool of available talent is restricted to your local geographical area with a radius equal to a reasonable commute.	By definition, a VA can do their work from anywhere that has a high speed Internet connection. This means that the entire world is your oyster in terms of finding and using talent. It also means that you can take advantage of different time zones (24/7 customer support for example) and "geographical wage arbitrage," the difference in pay scales depending upon the VA's location.
Focus	**Like a guy trying to multitask.**	**Like a guy on a mission.**
	When you have onsite employees, the temptation to interrupt them (or they you) can be overwhelming. And every interruption is a break in focus. In fact, studies have shown that every interruption robs at least 25 minutes of productivity from a day's work.[39] Multiply this by the average number of interruptions in a day and you get an idea as to how much this costs you.	You will find that once you are comfortable working with VAs, there are very few interruptions. That's because, as stated above, they just get the job done. Also, the main form of communication with VAs is e-mail, which is non-interruptive (if set up for manual download). This approach allows you and your VAs to focus on what each of you do best respectively.

	Employees	Virtual Assistants
Experience	**You are their world.**	**They are your world.**
	When you hire an employee, they work exclusively for you. This means that what they learn about their job is limited by, well... you! You are the sum total of their current experience in what they do. They may have brought previous experience with them when hired, but the *growth* of their experience and expertise is now limited to what they pick up on your job or from you.	As independent contractors, VAs work for more than one person or company. This means that their experience and skills are constantly growing because they have contact with so many different people and ways of doing the same thing. The better ones are literally getting smarter every day. Now take a guess as to who is the beneficiary of all this extra experience and creative insight in the ways your job can get done.

Given the above comparison, it should be clear as to why I apologize to any onsite staff that happen to be in my audiences before I go into the distinction between employees and VAs. The differences (and respective benefits) are so stark, it can be quite upsetting to those who have not been forewarned. Now let's take a look at what might get in the way of you taking full advantage of all these benefits.

Almost Ready For Prime Time

If there's a fly in the ointment of Virtual Assistants, it's that there are simply not enough of them to service even a small fraction of the small to midsized businesses that could use them. To the best of my knowledge, there have been no rigorous studies by independent research companies completed on the current size of the VA industry. However, I can give you a purely unscientific yet educated guess of its size, based upon my extensive involvement with the industry. Currently, in the U.S. alone, there are probably no more than 5,000 or so home-based support workers that refer to themselves as Virtual Assistants. Without a doubt, there are many more individuals who provide similar ongoing "remote support" for businesses, but don't call themselves Virtual Assistants because they never heard the term before. All together, worldwide there are probably no more than 15,000 – 20,000 VAs.

Unlike the VSPMs mentioned in the previous chapter, this industry has had a difficult time in scaling up rapidly to meet the expected demand. The primary reasons for this include:

- **Fractionalization** – Small, loosely organized groups and associations of VAs seem to be forming every day. Unfortunately, they all have different agendas and ideas as to what even constitutes being a VA. Typically poorly capitalized and with limited management capacity (run mostly by volunteers), none of these groups are poised to lead the industry to grow as it should. Instead of looking for ways to combine their efforts, they often spend their energies competing with each other for the attention of potential new members;

- **Lack of Standards** – If different groups of VAs cannot agree on the definition of "VA," they certainly will have different notions about what constitutes "best practices" and standards. Exacerbating this further is the fact that no one VA organization could possibly hope to set standards and best practices for all the vertical market VA service specialties;

- **Lack of Scalable Training** – Other than the previously mentioned *Portable Career & Virtual Assistant Training Program for Military Spouses*™ created by the Staffcentrix organization, there is no scalable training program available to train people on how to become successful Virtual Assistants. While this problem is addressed head-on in the final chapter (The Future of Virtual Outsourcing), there are other related concerns. Whether scaled or not, generalized VA training will only go so far. That's because to be consistently successful as a VA, one needs to specialize, rather than run ragged trying to be everything to everyone. Specialization requires specialized training AND a way to pass down hard-won, real-world experience from masters to beginners. This is not a trivial issue, but one I do believe can be adequately ameliorated through the formation of vertical market-specific VA "guilds" covered in the next section;

- **The Virtual E-myth** – Speak to any VA who is a member within one of the many current VA groups and they will most likely refer to themselves (proudly) as an "entrepreneur." And indeed, they probably are —and that's a problem, a big one at least with respect to the growth of the industry.

  It is well known that only a small percentage of the working population has sufficient entrepreneurial talent to market their services successfully. There are many more people who could act as a viable

Virtual Assistant "Technician" (the "doers" in the parlance of Michael Gerber's E-myth), if they didn't have to market themselves. Until recently, this was a major stumbling block to most of the people who have the ability to offer viable VA services. They either didn't know how to obtain clients or outright failed when they tried. A potential breakthrough in solving this problem is the emergence of "Virtual Staffing Agencies" mentioned in the next section.

Despite the above barriers to fully scalable growth, the VA industry is destined to become a major force and human resource alternative for supporting small to midsized businesses. So, as a business owner, what do you do between now and the time this growth happens? The answer is very simple —*use it now*. Typically only 10 percent of the people reading this book will take immediate action to implement Virtual Outsourcing in any of its several forms. This means "snooze you lose" and first movers get the pick of the crop. Now, here is where you can start your search for ongoing virtual talent.

Where to Find Virtual Assistants

There are no highly systemized Virtual Service Provider Marketplaces (VSPMs) for VAs —not yet anyway. The main reason for this is that VAs perform ongoing support work whereas VCs do project-based work. The latter facilitates the ability to objectively rate the performance of service providers on a per-project basis. No one has yet figured out how to objectively rate the performance of VAs in a similar manner. When you have someone doing work for you on an ongoing basis, you may be reluctant to give objective feedback about their work performance. Here's why. First, you may not want other businesses to use their services for either competitive reasons or fear that your VA will become too busy. Second, their performance may be less than stellar and you don't want to make it worse by giving them a rating below "excellent," thereby risking having them feel their work is not fully appreciated. Also, working with a VC for project-based work often creates less of an emotional connection between you and the person completing your project, as opposed to a VA who has worked for you over the past year.

It's much easier to say what you really feel about the performance of someone you probably will never work with again once the project is completed, than someone for whom you may have developed some kind of working relationship. All in all, it's the ongoing nature of VA support that makes it very difficult to receive objective feedback about their services in a systemized way similar to that of a VSPM.

While there are no formal VSPMs just for Virtual Assistants, you can still use a VSPM like Elance.com and Guru.com to find VAs. In fact, that's just the first of at least five major source categories you can tap into to find highly qualified VAs:

1. **VSPMs** – Even though Elance.com and Guru.com primarily facilitate project-based work, they can also be used to hire VAs. This involves changing your project description into a *job* description. So instead of asking for a bid on a completed project, you ask prospective service providers to bid on how much they will charge per hour and the number of hours they think it will take to complete a specific support process. The beauty of this approach is that it allows you to still benefit from the objective feedback ratings offered through VSPMs. The reasoning goes that if a project-based service provider has maintained consistently high ratings as a project-based VC, then they are likely to maintain that level of excellence while providing ongoing work as a VA. Also, given that each of the larger VSPMs have hundreds of thousands of available service providers within their ranks, they currently represent the largest single source category for finding viable VA support.

   Here is an example of how one entrepreneur used a VSPM in a very clever way to find ongoing support for his own business, and in the process started offering their services to others in his industry, for a profit…

If It's Broken, Fix It

Once you realize that an idea doesn't remain an idea forever, go to work on it and get it done! I'm not one to dillydally over trying things, especially if it's going to save me money and give me the best results possible. If it makes sense, I run with it. For me, traditional ways of running my business were not working —or at least, key parts of it. Why then wouldn't I consider doing things another way? Many people have the impression that virtually outsourcing means relinquishing control and the responsibility of direct management. It doesn't. In fact, you feel as if you have more control since you are hiring point people with top-notch, niche talents to perform very specific jobs. The days of observing a roomful of onsite, full-time employees who are bored or whose skills are ill-used, some or most of the time, is over. In the virtual world, I have the ultimate control at the end of an assigned project; I just don't want to be involved in the process.

Successful experiences using VAs are, in my opinion, a direct result of being extremely specific in communicating exactly what you need and expect from them, right down to intricate nuances of graphic illustration and deadlines. To wit, my experience in nailing down an exact cartoon logo for one of my other businesses, JungleGrips.com, a site which displays and sells arm and hand exercise equipment. I had visited five or six local ad agencies whose designs were middle of the road and unexciting. I advertised online for a graphic artist who could supply the following: a cartoon-type gorilla with large, popping muscles, wearing the kind of body-building attire you see on guys competing on stage. His hands would be holding a barbell loaded with weights, curving under the strain of them. As a last detail, I wanted what could only be described as a "shit-eating grin" on his face. And, the image needed to be animated. I got a bid from a provider in Barcelona, Spain, insisting that he could easily accomplish this. He nailed it on the first try and offered unlimited revisions and options, if I desired. His fee was unbelievably reasonable.

When you find outsourced talent that focuses on the task and produces the best end result at the best price, you can bet that you've embarked on a long and prosperous working relationship. Once you find 'em, you've got 'em! Talent pools in just about every business category feature the best of the best! This project smoothly moved from an idea, to print, to Web site, to animation in two weeks! And, Jungle Grips is mostly outsourced. It has no real location.

As for my real estate business, the outsourcing principle is the same and ongoing. Line up your business needs and decide what can be done internally and what you should outsource. I use VAs from 15 different time zones for Web site development (Canada and Russia), marketing management (Nashville, Tennessee), administrative support, online research of real estate market stats, some telemarketing (in accordance with permissible standards) and more. One of the most specific and ingenious ways I use VA services is in the creation of "call lists" of expired real estate listings. Acquiring this information and visiting these locations are my specialty. I found this particular VA eight time zones away by first posting a project on Elance.com. This person did such an amazing and consistent job in creating these lists, we converted this project into an ongoing job function. And, because these same lists are quite valuable in markets outside of my own, I've now created yet another virtual business selling this service to other real estate people.

If I had to summarize my experience with Virtual Outsourcing, I would conclude that it's clearly better than working with local talent. You can try to pull out a desired level of work from someone who is just not able to give it to you, or you can fix the problem by expanding your talent pool and finding the right person for the job.

Rick Parlante
Entrepreneur

2. **VA Associations** – The International Virtual Assistant Association (http://www.ivaa.org) is the best known and currently largest Virtual Assistant association. As a business owner, you can go to the IVAA Web site and post an RFP (Request For Proposal that describes your specific support request) which will then be forwarded to the IVAA membership for possible response by one or more members. It should be noted that this approach is nowhere as efficient, orderly or anonymous as when you post a project on a VSPM. That's because this and other organizations like it don't have the budgets or staff to build and maintain sophisticated online job-matching platforms.

    IVAA was founded by Chris Durst and Michael Haaren of Staffcentrix (mentioned earlier) and was incorporated as a nonprofit organization in 1999. It received its formal 501(c)3 nonprofit designation in February, 2001, with all of 28 members. As of this writing, it has just over 700 members, not as many as one would expect for such a strong, emerging industry.

    While these types of VA associations exist for the purpose of supporting and growing the VA industry, their failure to attract much larger memberships is due to two primary issues. First, these kinds of organizations typically don't focus on supporting a specific industry which otherwise could benefit from rapid word-of-mouth growth. Many members often try to be all things to all businesses and, as a result, often struggle. Second, many of the more successful VAs simply don't have the time to participate in organizing activities or support groups that will not directly benefit their own business. Both of these points are mitigated in the next VA source category;

3. **Vertical Market-Specific VA Communities** – These are online communities consisting of VAs who specialize in supporting a specific industry and business people within that industry. These communities allow business owners and managers within a specific industry to safely explore the possibility of finding and hiring VAs who have experience in and specialize in supporting their kind of business. VAs within these types of communities typically have a much deeper understanding of the specific vertical market industry they support than VAs who do general business support. As a result, business people (within the respective industry) are typically much more comfortable hiring VAs who already understand their business so thoroughly. Likewise, VAs who belong to these communities find it much easier to connect with business owners who need their services. It's a powerful, industry-specific, symbiotic relationship of VAs and the business people who could use their services.

Currently, REVA Network (http://www.revanetwork.com) is the first such community, created specifically to support the residential real estate sales industry. It was founded in October of 2003 by myself and four other individuals who are VAs specializing in real estate support. As of this writing, it has over 1,500 VA members and nearly 1,000 real estate sales professional members.

Recently, it evolved from a simple online community to a much more sophisticated group of VA "guilds." Each guild represents a different real estate support subspecialty such as Transaction Coordination, Lead Management, Online Marketing, etc. The real estate industry is so complex that no individual VA could ever hope to be an expert in all aspects of its support. Within each guild there are Apprentice, Journeyman and Master VA members. Apprentices must work under the supervision of either a Journeyman or Master for a specific period of time before moving up in the ranks.

The more experienced VAs (i.e., Journeymen and Masters) typically have more business than they could handle by themselves. By mentoring Apprentices who are eager to learn and build their own base of clients, these more experienced VAs have a way to scale their client base by outsourcing some of the work to the Apprentices. In fact, it is quite common for VAs to use other VAs either for overflow work or scaling up their business. By wrapping this process within the context of a guild system, it becomes a very natural way for new members to learn from the best, and for the more experienced ones to take on more business. Each guild also has their own set of bylaws that dictate codes of professional conduct and best practices for its respective subspecialty. This approach also makes prospective employers of their services (i.e., real estate salespeople) much more comfortable because it is clear they will be hiring someone who really knows their stuff.

I truly believe that these industry-specific communities are the wave of the future for VAs since they solve so many of the problems associated with scaling up large groups of qualified VAs. REVA Network could easily become the template by which other such communities are formed;

4. **VA Portals** – These are simply Web sites that offer business people access to various loose associations of VAs, usually without any specific industry specialization. These are typically run by VAs who are interested in promoting the VA industry to the general business community at large. You will probably see this source of VAs become more prevalent and sophisticated as the VA industry continues to grow. However, currently it represents a minor and rather scattered approach to finding a VA for your business.

One significant exception to this is Staffcentrix (http://www.staffcentrix.com), which is run by Chris Durst and Michael Haaren mentioned earlier. In addition to training these groups of trailing spouses, the Staffcentrix Web site allows business people to post RFPs for specific support requests that will then be forwarded on to their database of trained military or diplomatic corps spouses;

5. **Virtual Staffing Agencies** – This appears to be a potentially scalable emerging source of VA support. While at first glance, the virtual staffing model looks very similar to traditional temp agencies in that you hire the agency and not the workers they provide, there are important differences:

   a. Since the support staff you hire are by definition virtual, they don't work onsite and you never meet them in person. This significantly reduces personality-related issues that can often crop up when a temp shows up onsite to work side by side with you or your other staff;

b. Instead of being employees of the agency, these Virtual Assistants maintain an independent contractor relationship with the agency that places them;

c. Due to the "virtual" nature of the work provided, virtual staffing agencies have the flexibility to fill permanent, long-term support positions even if you only need just a few hours of support a month. For example, I used an agency to fill a permanent proofreading position for my online newsletter, which typically requires less than two billing hours a month.

d. It's quick and easy. You can have your Virtual Assistant "on the job" often just a few hours after making a call to the agency with your requirements. And, once again, because the staffer is never physically present, you will not be caught in the revolving door of hiring temps that just don't "fit in" with you or your staff.

The reason this is an emerging source is that there currently appears to be only one such company that is sizable enough to scale its services: Team Double-Click^{sm} (http://www.teamdou bleclick.com). Founded in 2000 by CEO Gayle Buske, Team Double-Click^{sm} is itself a prime example of a truly virtual company. A quick look at their Web site contact page reveals that their key personnel are located all over the map. And, they use many of the online virtual support tools referenced in the next chapter to work as a cohesive, focused team despite their wide geographic dispersion.

According to Ms. Buske, Team Double-Click^{sm} currently has 12,500 in their pool of available Virtual Assistants from all over the world (most residing in North America) and are adding several hundred more per week. Of these, approximately 200 are currently placed and providing virtual support to over 300 businesses.

When you hire Team Double-Click^{sm}, you sign a contract with the agency, not the individual VAs they supply. They manage the pre-screening and support needs matching process prior to assigning you a VA. They also provide you with a Client Services Representative (CSR) who runs interference between you and your VA(s) and arranges for additional support when needed. For general administrative types of work, this approach can be a quick way to find reasonably screened and priced VA support.

After using this service myself several times, I find the Virtual Staffing Agency concept to be an attractive way to hire virtual talent. A simple phone call or e-mail is all it takes to find, screen and assign the support I need. And for business owners who don't want to take the time to go through the VA hiring process outlined later in this chapter, it could very well be the easiest way to get started using Virtual Assistants.

The following are several case stories of different types of businesses that used this agency to hire their virtual support. This first one shows just how quickly a business can scale up their virtual support when needed…

Virtual Support Just a Phone Call Away

I have nothing but positive things to say about the advantages of Virtual Outsourcing and about Team Double-Click℠, a Virtual Staffing Agency. American businesses —from big corporations to small, entrepreneurial entities —are either dipping their toes in the waters of virtual paradise or careening into the surf, arms waving and flapping! The concept is that dramatically different from the traditional brick and mortar corporate business model.

Our biggest battle, as a large, competitive real estate company, was winning over our corporate management team at the beginning of our research into Virtual Outsourcing. This management team is now part of our e-team and an integral part of our decisions and assignments in the virtual world. Thanks to the steadfastness and superior skills of the people at the Virtual Staffing Agency in preparing background materials, screening contractors, helping to write documentation and providing managerial training and support, the shift to hiring VAs for some very key operations was relatively seamless.

Our whole approach is about customer service. We have 3000 agents and 65 offices. With our virtual Customer Service Representatives we've been able to extend our hours of operation from 9 a.m. to 5 p.m. Monday to Friday to 8 a.m. to 11 p.m. 360 days per year. Since we've been using VAs, our volume of phone communication has grown tremendously. We get all kinds of real estate leads, telephone calls and Web-based requests. Therefore we need customer support people who are knowledgeable and versed in communicating a human touch, a "lights on at home" and "we care" image when they answer calls or send a personalized welcome e-mail as a response to an Internet inquiry. Some of our own managers even tested the call-in lines and found the exact responses we were looking for from our VAs.

The benefits of using VAs for phone support, database management, lead qualification/routing and a host of other tasks are multifold, including reduced and/or eliminated costs in salaries, taxes, insurance and onsite employee benefits. And most importantly, happy buyers, sellers and renters! Managers also enjoy the streamlined simplicity of deferring to the virtual agency to route increased staff for phone support to us; managers simply make a phone call and request extra VAs. Costs are reduced in finding those individuals who are experts in their respective business fields and contracting them to perform very specific, niche services from home-based offices. This guarantees the most effective and efficient use of virtual talent when the productivity of independent contractors is not distracted or compromised by the need to multitask at every phase of a project.

In an onsite office environment, an employee can do only so much to accomplish as many tasks as possible. Ultimately, that individual's viability as a multitasker decreases because one simply cannot give 100 percent attention and support to each and every diverse task as the need arises. Management, in turn, has been forced to rethink traditional meeting formats, for example, and other key activities. If your VA is involved in a meeting via a conference call, or waiting to receive faxed or e-mailed meeting notes to properly document them, managers are more apt to tighten their agendas, focus and condense the content of meetings. The realization that your VA is billing you by the hour steps up management's performance, as well.

I'm continually impressed by the quality of our VAs. One incident involved the case of a dropped phone call in customer service. When questioned about it, the VA explained that just as the call was coming in and she was preparing to answer it, the volunteer fire department in her town was heading out to an emergency situation. She thought it was best to not answer the call, thus sparing the customer from the ear-splitting scream of sirens in the background! In reality, this showed excellent judgment on her part.

Bob Borger
VP, Director eTeam
Prudential Douglas Elliman

No matter what business you're in, there will always be ways that it can be supported virtually. In this case, we have someone in the rather unique business of coaching beauty pageant contestants. Her virtual support allows her to focus on helping her clients look their beautiful best while others take care of the drab details of running the business...

Minding the Beautiful

I am not your typical beauty pageant coach. Most coaches are former beauty pageant winners who are reluctant to give up the whole pageant experience. Subsequently, what they pass on is only what has worked for them, what they know or consider to be advantageous. I am not a beauty queen. For 20 years, I was a Human Resources Director for a Fortune 500 company. What started out as a hobby, has since blossomed into a full-blown, nationally competitive business. I coach pageant contestants in personal development, self-confidence, public speaking skills and gleaning publicity for their community service for organizations of their choice.

There are actually beauty pageant boutiques that cater exclusively to avid contestants, regaling them in appropriate apparel and accessories. A friend of mine owned one such establishment and asked me if I would meet with a particular client of hers who showed impressive potential but whose interview skills were sorely lacking. I worked with her; she won and won big. I was slowly drawn into the concept of coaching and proceeded to take on more clients. I became more and more fascinated by the prospect of turning this activity into a bona fide business. It just happened to be pageant coaching in my case, but it could be anything for anyone. I could never do corporate America again. I wondered how I actually did it for so long and how people are still doing it! I don't understand it anymore. But, the one thing that I have been able to transfer from my corporate experience to running my own business is the degree of professionalism I offer and the level of expertise I bring to my work.

As my business grew, so did the administrative details. I found that I was doing everything myself. I did it all —answered the phones, e-mailed, scheduled, sent our brochures and marketed the business. I was working all the time! And I wasn't spending the kind of time with my family that I predicted a home-based business would afford me.

I started searching for Virtual Assistance agencies, per se, but came up rather dry. Then I found out about Team Double-Click℠ with its great services and competitive prices. It is a seamless solution for small entrepreneurs like me.

An interesting side effect of using remote administration assistance is that people, especially potential clients, are suddenly so impressed that I have an "assistant!" This fact has literally boosted by credibility as an expert in my field!

One of the more specific advantages is in the scheduling of appointments. Before using VA services, I was spending way too much time on the phone scheduling appointments, as well as answering phones, responding to messages, creating and replying to e-mails, putting brochures and marketing materials in the mail and getting sidetracked (in person or on the phone, mostly) by chit chat and general questions like, "What do you think of my gown…my makeup artist…my photos?" I was losing precious and potentially profitable time. I was fried. My fatigue and frantic pace interfered with my ability to be the best coach I could be. It finally inspired a major mind shift which freed me from dwelling on the administrative aspects of my business so I could focus on marketing and growing my business. The administrative tasks are now absorbed by my VAs.

Some of the most important words I've ever heard were offered by a respected marketing specialist: "Your ability to experience personal development will be a direct reflection of your ability to grow your business." I continue to use this message in approaching the needs of my students and my own personal and professional goals.

Valerie Hayes
Professional Pageant Coach

Not all small businesses are service related. Here's a fellow who just closed a deal with Wal-Mart to sell his candy, which is unique in that it has scripture quotes on the wrappers. This is a tough gig for a one-man show, unless you have your virtual road crew to help make it all happen…

Business Is Sweet

A year ago, I launched a new business, "Heartfelt Candies." I had learned quite a bit up to this time about the confectionary business and about functioning as an entrepreneur. However, one of the hardest lessons I learned was about letting go; it just didn't seem compatible with who I am or what my personality traits dictated. The truth was staring me in the face. I couldn't avoid it any longer. The message was that I couldn't and can't do it all by myself. I fell prey to the thought that if I just got the business up to a certain speed, I could bring others on board to help. The problem with that theory is that while you contemplate that eventuality, the administrative needs of your business swallow you whole. You feel as if you're on a treadmill and have forgotten where the "off" switch is. Yet, you continue to spread yourself thinner and thinner. Your energy wanes and your attention to your beloved business loses its acuity.

The next step was a huge segue for me: investigating the concept of Virtual Assistance. My experience with Team Double-Click℠ has sold me on this concentrated, expertly administered, time and cost effective way of running a business. Once I had taken the leap, I sang its praises to everyone I knew. It gave me a virtual, full-time staff at part-time prices. It was the ideal way for me to address marketing issues, mailings, answering phones, order tracking and more. Most recently, I hired one full-time VA to represent me in the field to meet with manufacturers and address the nuts and bolts of production. Another VA has become my personal assistant and also researches product development presentations for our Web site.

The biggest concern for me in using Virtual Assistants was the issue of trust, working with people I had never met and placing core business tasks in their hands. I have not been disappointed. I'm a hands-on kind of guy who likes to have a lot of sticks in the fire at the same time. My biggest challenge was accepting the fact that I couldn't play the game by myself. I was pleasantly surprised when each member of the team I built solidly contributed to the strength of the whole operation. Even when I took family vacations before, I was always fretting about my absence from the business because I, as the chief decision-making entity, could not be contacted. No matter how many Disney characters did their best to distract me and my kids, I never really checked into the Magic Kingdom. Even in this fantasy place, I managed to remain in a state of anxious speculation as to what was happening with my business when I wasn't there.

Today, no matter where I am, I have the complete peace of mind knowing that my Virtual Assistants are taking care of every aspect of my newly named business, "Heart and Soul Candies," which are now being sold in retail establishments across the country. You can't put a price on this kind of satisfaction.

Bill McGee, CEO
Heart and Soul Candies

Some small business owners provide products and services that are by their nature, highly creative. And it is not unheard of for creative types to struggle with the more mundane details of running a business. Here is a case where a clothing designer has virtually outsourced the fulfillment of her design orders, customer service and accounts receivable functions...

Designing a Dream Business

I thought about it one day and decided it was time to go to Asia. I'm actually an architect by trade. I had my own practice in California for many years and at one point I decided I needed a little sabbatical. I was a foreign exchange student in Asia when I was 16, and I hadn't been back since. I wanted to visit Thailand and Bali, too.

I completely fell in love with Bali. It is an absolutely fabulous, magical place. They have so many wonderful natural materials and the craftspeople are extraordinary. For a designer, it's one big candy store. So, I quietly sold everything at home, got on a plane and prayed that I'd meet some nice people on the other side of the world. I was shedding a lifestyle, not just material goods. Some say it was a brave decision; to me it was simply buying a plane ticket and embracing the prospect of having a great experience. If you've got something going and you want to do business in a better way, you have a responsibility to yourself to try it. If it turns out to be a bad experience, chalk it up to just that. Nothing we do is wasted. I'm a single woman in my 40s, so why was I living the life of a married woman with kids? I had the freedom to change my lifestyle and the ability to explore a heightened business goal.

I began to toy with income ideas that would let me stay in Bali for more than just a month or two. I needed to support myself after the big move. How do you make a living in paradise —aside from cutting open coconuts all day?

The local employment market was certainly glutted with coconut openers. I thought about crafting furniture. Hmmm —too heavy and it would need to be warehoused. Jewelry? A lighter product, but too expensive. I've always liked sweaters. Sweaters in Bali? This would be like selling surfboards in Alaska. Then again, maybe this could be a good thing. Nobody else was doing it. I'd have the market to myself. Today, I buy exotic yarns from all over the world and design custom-made, partially machine-knit, hand-embellished sweaters in Bali. Each piece is an original. The creative part of the business is thriving.

The administrative part is beautifully intact, too, because it is being handled by my trusty, knowledgeable, hard-working VA in Minnesota. I know that I could not function without Cheri. She is an essential piece of the puzzle, an integral liaison with a huge amount of responsibility in the States. I am so secure in this relationship with Cheri, that I actually feel as if I have a whole company behind me who is supportive of my goals. She is the lead person, making sure my merchandise reaches its destination in the States. I air ship bundles of orders to her and she makes arrangements for ground deliveries, as well as assuming all administrative details of the business.

My business is deliberately small and I would like to keep it that way to reflect my simpler lifestyle. Cheri and I have never met, but the business is growing because she is an important part of the growth. This is the only way to go, for businesses large and small that virtually outsource parts or most of their operations. It keeps labor and other costs in check while it streamlines the way a business can run. It also allows me to live my dream of creating to my heart's content while avoiding the inevitable nightmares of trying to manage the day-to-day business details myself.

Alejandra Cisneros
Designer

You can see an updated list of online resources to help you find VAs for your business by going to http://www.virtualoutsourcing.org, which is a Web site I created to specifically assist business owners in putting into practice the ideas and concepts found in this book. Other than the VSPMs mentioned above, the other categories of sources for available VAs are currently not large enough to support even a small fraction of U.S. businesses that may want to hire a VA. And, this state of affairs is not likely to change until major adult learning organizations get on board and start offering comprehensive online VA training and certification programs. This represents a huge opportunity for these companies because of the growing demand for VA support by the millions of small to midsized businesses and the millions of workers who are tired of commuting and working in dead-end, unsatisfying jobs. Once this kind of training is in place, the number of available VAs who could support your business will soar.

Now that you have some ideas about where to look for your perfect VA, let's explore how to go about vetting and hiring them…

The VA Hiring Process

One of the keys to successfully hiring the best VA for your purposes is to be very clear about what those "purposes" are. The more explicit you are about what you want your VA to do, the better. Ideally, before talking to any prospective VAs, you will have a comprehensive, written process in hand that precisely spells out what you want done, how it is to be done (if appropriate), and the desired measurable outcome once it is done. A formal, written business process is much more detailed than a "job description," which tends to be more of an overview of what you want done.

> *the most effective VAs tend to be specialists and will not stray too far from offering services within their specialty.*

Having written business processes for each operational function within your business is a smart idea, whether you hire VAs or have onsite employees doing the work. This approach allows you to standardize the way your business runs and makes it much easier to "plug and play" support as needed. Formal, written business processes are like computer code that dictates how your business operates day to day. By having your support people consistently follow the "code," you'll see consistent results. It also allows you to manage by objective, rather than by coddling or coercion —saving you a great deal of time and damage to your remaining hair follicles. As mentioned in Chapter 4, you can hire a Virtual Consultant business process specialist who can help you develop your company's processes if you don't already have them in place.

Another good reason to have a written process for the intended VA job function is that you will have a much better idea as to what kinds of special skills or experience are required to do the job most effectively. This will help you narrow down the field of prospective VAs from which to choose. That is because the most effective VAs tend to be specialists and will not stray too far from offering services within their specialty. So, it simply becomes a matter of matching prospective VAs and their specialties to the requirements of the job (i.e., business process). *NOTE: The following sections on the hiring process assume you will be contacting individual VA candidates directly and not using a Virtual Staffing Agency that would typically handle most of these steps for you.*

Initial Contact

OK, so let's assume you're really clear about what you want your first VA to do and you've identified several VA prospects to start interviewing. DO NOT pick up the phone to start calling them, at least not yet. Your first contact should be by e-mail. Most VAs will be very comfortable with this approach since that's how they handle the majority of their communications with their current business clients. And, how they respond to your initial questions in writing will tell you a great deal about them. It also will allow you to start evaluating them on the basis of their answers (i.e., objectively) rather than how they "sound" on the phone (subjectively). A person's phone manner can be very deceiving. Someone who sounds great (charismatic, confident, engaging, etc.) on the phone could be a disaster on the job, and likewise someone who is more reserved (which many VAs tend to be) may do brilliant work. Using e-mail for the initial interview process can help eliminate the hazards of making inappropriate judgments based solely on how someone sounds.

The following is an e-mail script you can use or adapt to for the purposes of making first contact with a prospective VA:

Hi [first name],

My company is seeking the services of a professional Virtual Assistant with experience in the following areas of expertise [list them here]. We found your listing on the [Web site name] Web site and it appears that you may have the proficiency we are looking for.

The work we need done on an ongoing basis is as follows: [either comprehensively describe here or mention attached job description/written business process]. Please take the time to review it carefully before answering the questions below:

1. Why do you feel you have the required expertise and experience to handle our support needs as described above?

2. Why do you feel you are the best VA available to do this work for us?

3. What assurances can you give us that any tasks we hire you to perform will continue without interruption or degradation of quality or timeliness if you go on vacation or suddenly become incapacitated?

4. What assurances can you give us that you will not take on more business than you can reasonably handle?

5. Given the above description of what we need done, are you willing to charge on the basis of achieving the end results rather than by the hour?

6. Within the last seven years, have you been involved in litigation (either as plaintiff or defendant) or had complaints lodged against you as a result of your work? If so, please give details.

7. Are you willing to allow us to do a background check on you and/or your company?

In addition to answering the above questions, please include the following with your responses:

- Your bio that includes any special training and/or certifications you have received relative to your VA work and a timeline showing when you started your VA business;

- The state/province in which your current business license/permit is filed;

- Sample of the Independent Contractor's Agreement you typically use;

- Samples of your work product that are similar to what we are asking to have done (NOTE: ask this only if it is appropriate to the work you are asking the VA to do);

- Contact information for three to six clients for whom you are currently doing the same or similar tasks as we are requesting. Please make sure that you have worked at least six months for each of these current references;

- Contact information for three to six previous clients for whom you have done the same or similar tasks as we are requesting. Please make sure that you have worked at least six months for each of these past client references.

If you need clarification for any of the above questions or documentation requests, just reply to this e-mail with your questions. Also, you can find out more about our company by going to our Web site at [Web site address].

We are looking forward to your response and the possibility of establishing an ongoing working relationship with you.

[your name]
[your contact information / e-mail signature]

Now let's dissect this first message to obtain a better understanding of why we asked what we did:

1. *Why do you feel you have the required expertise and experience to handle our support needs as described above?* – Their response to this will tell you

a) how well they understood exactly what it is you want done, and *b)* what specific experience and skills they have that relate to the job in question.

2. *Why do you feel you are the best VA available to do this work for us?* – The answer to this will give you a feel as to how competitive they see their own services and a sense of their self-image relative to the entire field of available VAs with the same expertise. Chances are this question will "throw" all but the most self-assured VAs simply because service people typically don't take the time to think about how they are (or could be) the "best" at what they do.

3. *What assurances can you give us that any tasks we hire you to perform will continue without interruption or degradation of quality or timeliness if you go on vacation or suddenly become incapacitated?* – This question is crucial because their response will tell you how well they have thought through possible exigencies that are bound to crop up in any service business.

4. *What assurances can you give us that you will not take on more business than you can reasonably handle?* – Related to #3, their answer to this question will give you an idea as to how experienced the responding VA is and how they handle overflow situations. It is not uncommon for new or inexperienced VAs to take in more work than they can reasonably cope with; thus, at some point, things start to fall through the cracks. Most experienced VAs, however, have developed networks or alliances with other VAs that act as an overflow buffer and will help them complete extra work when needed.

5. *Given the above description of what we need done, are you willing to charge on the basis of achieving the end results rather than by the hour?* – Ideally, they will be willing to charge by the results of their work, rather than by the hour. The last thing you want to do is spend time pondering over their last invoice as you wonder how efficiently they spent their time doing your work. When you arrange for payment by results, you know exactly how much your support function is costing you and it motivates the VA to perform it in a timely manner.

6. *Within the last seven years, have you been involved in litigation (either as plaintiff or defendant) or had complaints lodged against you as a result*

of your work? If so, please give details. – The purpose of this question should be fairly obvious. The last thing you want to do is hire a VA who has been sued for their work product or someone who is litigious (i.e., has a propensity to sue the people who hire them). Also, if you follow through with question #7 below, it will help determine how truthful they are.

7. *Are you willing to allow us to do a background check on you and/or your company?* – Clearly, a negative response on this question is a warning flag. If they say yes, and they are a serious candidate for an important support position for your company, doing a background check is not a bad idea. There are many such companies today that do this kind of research for a reasonable price. If you have never used this kind of service, they can be easily found via an online Google search.

The documentation they send back with their responses to your questions is important for the following reasons:

- *Your bio that includes any special training and/or certifications you have received relative to your VA work and a timeline showing when you started your VA business* – VAs are not employees, so they will not have resumes, hence the request for their professional bio. How extensive and well put together their bio is can tell you a great deal about their professionalism, training and experience. While a sloppy bio does not necessarily indicate they are not qualified, it does give you an idea as to what their work product may look like if it involves any kind of written communication.

- *The state/province in which your current business license/permit is filed* – If they don't have a business license, that could be a warning flag that they're not running their VA support business like a business and/or there could be issues with their independent contractor status. NOTE: Since most VAs work from home, don't be surprised if they balk in providing you a copy of their business license. That's because it indicates their business/home address. This is information they may feel uncomfortable revealing until they are reasonably sure they will be working with you.

- *Sample of the Independent Contractor's Agreement you typically use* – Not having one usually indicates lack of experience or sloppy business practices. While I am going to suggest that you use your own agreement, it's always helpful to see what they consider important by examining the one they offer their current clients.

- *Samples of your work product that are similar to what we are asking to have done* – This is only appropriate if their work product is tangible, and especially important if its "presentation" (i.e., look and feel) significantly matters to you.

- *Contact information for three to six clients for whom you are currently doing the same or similar tasks as we are requesting. Please make sure that you have worked at least six months for each of these current references* – Remember, VAs are not employees, so you're less restricted in the kinds of questions you can ask, and the people who use VAs feel less reserved about being truly candid. No matter how good a VA looks on paper (or sounds on the phone), it is crucial that you contact current and former clients for candid feedback.

- *Contact information for three to six previous clients for whom you did the same or similar tasks as we are requesting. Please make sure that you have worked at least six months for each of these past client references* – What you're looking for here is why they are no longer using this VA. Some VAs are great at starting new client relationships, but then eventually drop the ball or underperform until the client just lets them go.

How a prospective VA responds to the above initial inquiry e-mail will tell you volumes about them, their integrity and their ability to consistently and affordably complete your requested support function in the manner and timeliness required. Using this e-mail request approach, you will be able to quickly narrow down your list of likely prospects to the top two or three candidates. Be sure to do a full due diligence by contacting the list of current and previous clients only for those VAs who appear to otherwise meet your needs. This will keep you focused and save a great deal of effort.

Keep in mind that up until now, you have spent very little time in the hiring process (especially if you created a template of the above suggested e-mail script). The next step is to talk to your top candidates on the phone.

Phone Interview

The purpose of the phone interview is to get a deeper sense of who your VA candidates are and, if appropriate, to negotiate final terms of what you want done and how much it will cost you. It is also the closest you will likely ever come to meeting the VA you ultimately hire. Even though most of your business communications with a VA are by e-mail, you may have occasion to speak to them over the phone. No matter how talented and dependable they are, if you just can't stand the way they sound over the phone, it will likely become a problem for you sooner or later. Better to find this out before you hire them rather than after.

Two keys to having a successful interview are *a)* being fully prepared with questions that arose after reviewing their written response and contacting their current and previous clients, and *b)* letting them do most of the talking. Here is an example of a general script you can use after you and the VA have exchanged initial pleasantries of greeting each other on the phone:

- [other clarification questions you need to ask as a result of their e-mail response and/or contacting their clients]

- Now that you've had an opportunity to review the support process we need to have done, what other clarifications or specifics about it can I provide for you?

- Do you have any suggestions for completing what we need done in a more effective manner than the way it was described?

- Are you anticipating any initial setup before you can start? If so, what will it entail and how much will it cost?

- Why do you require a retainer? And, what happens to the unused balance, if any, at the end of each month? [ask this only if they insist on having a retainer]

- Why are you excited about taking me/my company on as a client?

- What is the range of hours during the day that I can contact you?

- Are their any restrictions as to when or how I can contact you in the event of an emergency?

- How often do you invoice and what "net" terms do you typically require?

- Do you have any concerns or objections if we use my own Independent Contractor's Agreement for our working relationship?

- How soon can you start?

Use the above questions only as a guide. They obviously will need to be modified given the unique circumstances for each VA you interview.

Guess Who Else Is Being Interviewed

When you are in the throes of interviewing a professional VA to provide support for your business, they (the better ones, anyway) are interviewing you as well. Remember, they are business people also. And the better ones are busy enough to be very picky about with whom they choose to work.

Some of my VA friends have shared with me how surprised a potential client is when they (the VA) turns *them* down. A truly professional VA will make sure there is a good fit in terms of skills, goals and personalities before they agree to take on a new client. So keep this in mind when you go through the interview process; they are evaluating you as much as you are evaluating them.

> *When you are in the throes of interviewing a professional VA to provide support for your business, they (the better ones, anyway) are interviewing you as well.*

Remember this important point: You are not hiring an employee —a VA is an independent contractor. There is nothing necessarily permanent about your business relationship with any VA you hire. You are not making a commitment to someone's livelihood, only to pay them for the work they complete (either by the results or by the hour), no more, no less. And, depending upon how you structure it in your agreement with them, you may be able to terminate the relationship with a simple phone call or e-mail.

The last step to formalizing the working relationship with your support VA is to have a written Independent Contractor's Agreement. As mentioned above, it is best if you use yours instead of the one a VA may provide. There are several reasons for this. First, since it is your agreement, you will know that it is written to specifically favor and protect you. Second, you will have a standard agreement that will work with all your VAs, instead of having a different form of agreement for each VA you hire. There are a number of places online you can find such agreements. You can also just go to my VirtualOutsourcing. org Web site and examine the template I provide there or explore the list of other online resources I've listed there as well. As always, however, be sure to have your attorney review and approve it before you use it.

Managing Your VA

The more thoroughly you have documented the written support process you want your VA to perform, the less time you will need to spend managing them.

VAs are used to working very autonomously and if what you want done is really spelled out, they will need little if any additional input from you to complete their job consistently. Once again, the most ideal arrangement is to pay them by the measurable results they produce (if feasible) rather than by the hour.

Here are some additional DO's and DON'Ts that, if you follow, will result in a most satisfying and trouble-free working arrangement (used with permission of Stacy Brice of AssistU.com):

DO:

- Value the relationship you have with your VAs;
- See your VA as an equal and a partner in your success;
- Articulate your needs and wants well to your VA;
- Maintain a trusting relationship with your VA;
- Stay centered, focused and organized so as to not distract your VA from their job of supporting your success.

DON'T:

- Fail to communicate with your VA when they request something from you;
- Attempt to micromanage your VA;
- Treat your VA like a low-level employee;
- Live in the "urgent" where everything is last minute and expect your VA to constantly put out fires that could have been avoided. (NOTE: VAs help you avoid urgency by taking care of what is important so it never becomes urgent.)

While finding, evaluating and hiring a VA can take more effort than using a VSPM to hire a VC to do project-based work, it's still far less involved and costly than hiring an employee. Depending upon the nature of the specific support function you want completed, it may only take a few hours to go from initial inquiry to having them signed on to do your job.

At this point, your head might be spinning just a bit; if so, it's quite understandable. The possibilities are so grand, yet this approach to staffing is completely different to what most business people are used to. Perhaps you are even thinking that this VA stuff may work well for other companies, but not yours. Well… that may be true, but chances are you would be selling yourself short. Here is an example of a very management-intensive company that tried going the traditional onsite employee route. After a few frustrating years, they made the transition to 100 percent virtual and have never looked back…

Virtual is a Process, Not an Event

If I had to choose just one word to describe what defines successful VAs, it would have to be character. In life and certainly in business, dependability and ethics play a huge role. Because we are on the brink, if not in the very hub, of exploring a completely new and more efficient way to run businesses, why would an individual's key professional (and personal) traits be evaluated any differently whether they're sitting in front of you or working in home offices, scattered across the country? It is possible to find and hire the best of the best, no matter where they are located.

Today, I speak from an accomplished, tried-and-true perspective after shifting all aspects of my business to virtual staff. But, it wasn't always this way. Because the natures of my businesses are so public and the clients are high-profiled professionals, I was in constant motion, seeing to every detail myself. When I hired onsite staff, I was then overrun with needing to physically manage them and supervise their tasks. Any employer could agree that this is one of the most stressful periods in the life of a business, especially if the owner needs to be free and flexible to move about in their communities, the country or even the world. This scenario, while not uncommon, weighs heavily on the financial success of a business, wastes precious time, ill-spent money and produces migraines worthy of a Richter scale rating!

I am the owner of a thriving, full-service event planning business, EzEvents. It prepares, markets and delivers all aspects of entrepreneurial meetings, gatherings and presentations. A division of EzEvents is Broker Agents Speaker's Bureau, Inc., which hosts and presents hundreds of well-known speakers in real estate, insurance and financial fields. Our clients are our number one priority and I make all efforts to insure that they are not only treated with care and consideration, but that their goals are met when they participate and share information in their areas of expertise.

Since 1990, I have planned events for Coldwell Banker (in 15 states), RE/MAX, Prudential, *The Wall Street Journal*, Unique Global Estates, *Unique Homes* magazine, Help-U-Sell, Century 21 and many others. My national marketing plan for Homes.com included organizing over 40 events a month, which generated tremendous sales. I've also authored over 50 trade articles. If I were in the hospitality industry, in the true sense of the word, I would be an upscale concierge with more knowledge and responsibility than anyone else —the person who really makes things happen! And therein lies the root of the same problem. Any high-caliber concierge doesn't go to the hotel's linen stash, grab an extra pillow and personally deliver it to the Presidential Suite! She finds that appropriate, qualified individual to do it on her behalf! Everyone's happy and well-utilized —the concierge is a heroine; the pillow-packing maid par excellence earns her keep (and a tip) and Mr. Big in the Presidential Suite is sleeping like a baby! It's a win-win situation all around.

Choosing to virtually outsource 100 percent of my operation was not a breeze though, mostly because we are trained and accustomed to staying glued to the traditional, brick and mortar business model. For some micromanagers who can't or don't know how to "let go," Virtual Outsourcing is the Trojan horse at the gate. You can politely open the door or be run down by its size, its strength and its shrewd approach to the task at hand.

I use VAs from all across the country and also in Canada and Mexico. Not only have I re-embraced the pleasures and advantages of personal, quality time, I am also providing work for a variety of skilled, niche-oriented contractors, many of whom are mothers, performing home-based administrative tasks for me while being present in their home for the needs of their children. They are earning proper salaries, enhancing their own qualities of life and getting the jobs done to my satisfaction.

Darlene Lyons, CEO
EzEvents, Inc.

Virtual Assistants are the important second part to the entire Virtual Outsourcing equation. They can be a hugely significant resource for supporting your business's success on an ongoing basis. We covered a lot in this chapter, so let's do a quick review of the key points…

Key Ideas and Chapter Review

- VAs provide ongoing "assistance from a distance" by performing well-documented business tasks or processes;

- Much of your business support can be outsourced to VAs whom you will never personally meet. Any kind of ongoing support you can imagine that does not specifically require close geographical proximity can probably be done by a VA;

- Many VAs are specialists in what they do which means you don't have to spend valuable time and resources training them;

- The difference between the benefits of using VAs versus traditional onsite employees is huge. Since VAs are independent contractors who do their work remotely and are only paid for what they do (no benefits, taxes, etc.), using them avoids most of the problems and costs associated with onsite staff;

- There are five major source categories you can use to find VAs for your business:

  1. VSPMs (Virtual Service Provider Marketplaces)
  2. VA Associations
  3. Vertical Market-Specific VA Communities
  4. VA Web Portals
  5. Virtual Staffing Agencies

- Currently, there are no highly scalable sources of VAs. However, VA Staffing Agencies and Vertical Market-Specific VA Communities show potential for significant future growth and scalability;

- Using a Virtual Staffing Agency is perhaps the easiest and quickest way to hire a VA;

- It is important to have a well-defined job description, or better yet, written business process before you start looking for a VA to do it;

- There are VAs and VCs who specialize in writing business processes if you need help getting that done;

- Use the comprehensive e-mail questionnaire found in this chapter as the first contact with any prospective VA whom you are considering to do your support work;

- Conduct a phone interview only with the most likely VA candidates, either using the script provided in this chapter or your own;

- When possible, use your own standard Independent Contractor Agreement when hiring a VA (there are many online resources for this kind of agreement);

- Once hired, managing VAs is very easy if you have them perform a well-documented job description or business process that has measurable results;

- VAs work best when left alone to do what they were hired to do, micromanaging them will only cause them to be less effective;

- It is in your best interest to treat VAs as "partners in your success" rather than just another employee you have hired to do a job.

Now let's take a look at how you can take what you learned about using Virtual Consultants and Virtual Assistants and smoothly integrate both aspects of Virtual Outsourcing into your existing business.

Virtual Outsourcing and Your Business
How to Smoothly Integrate VO with Your Current Staff

A t this point in our adventure into Virtual Outsourcing, it should be abundantly clear that this kind of support is highly affordable, quick and easy to find, and eliminates most of the headaches associated with onsite staffing. Yet, why is it that so many businesses seem to get stuck taking the first step of implementing Virtual Outsourcing?

The "C" Word

There are a number of reasons for this, but ultimately they all point to one thing —the need to be in "control." Now obviously, if you're going to run and grow a successful business, waking up every morning and saying, "Gee, I wonder how we are going to do things today," is not the way to do it. The more you have explicitly defined how everything is done, where your business is going and how it's going to get there, the more likely you are to see consistent results and be in control. Making sure things get done the way they are supposed to and on time, by delegating to the appropriate support staff, is in fact a necessary form of control.

However, many small and independent business owners confuse this concept of "control" with having to do everything themselves or standing over the shoulders of anyone doing something for them. If you fall into this category, then the thought of turning over a project or support function to someone you never meet can be initially scary indeed. In fact, it is the "virtual" nature of

Virtual Outsourcing (i.e., tasks being done remotely) that flies in the very face of the need to be in control.

This kind of "control" however is really more accurately described by another "C" word —chaos. If you attempt to do everything yourself, or delegate without really letting go, then something will eventually break. Either you or your business, or more likely both, will at some point cease to function properly. At best, your business most certainly will not achieve its full potential. Giving in to the need for this kind of "control" will guarantee that you will never have the good kind of control, the one that gives you a business that works for you, instead of you being a slave to it.

The emotional need for this kind of "control" is based primarily in the fear that everything will just fall apart if you take your eyes off the ball just for an instant. If you're the only juggler, then it's easy to see why you would feel this way —there are just so many balls you can keep in the air at one time. Yet if you had a team of expert jugglers, each with their own set of balls they were concerned about, you could accomplish so much more and your business could grow by simply adding more jugglers. Unless, of course, you distracted them by standing over their shoulders every second to make sure they were juggling properly!

> *Feeling the need to do (or supervise) everything yourself is actually a prison that guarantees to hold you back from realizing and enjoying the full potential success of your business.*

Feeling the need to do (or supervise) everything yourself is actually a prison that guarantees to hold you back from realizing and enjoying the full potential success of your business. Fortunately, however, you hold the key to leaving this prison forever, and it's just a matter of turning that key to be free.

One Small Step at a Time

The key to getting out of this prison is to take just one small step at a time. Dip your toe into the virtual waters just enough to test it out. Then, when you're comfortable with that, wade in up to your ankles and stay there until you're completely confident that this "virtual stuff" actually works as advertised. Pick a project or support task that's small enough so that if it doesn't work out, it's not the end of the world. The main thing is to start! Just keep it simple and measurable so you can objectively see if it's working out the way you expected. Eventually, you will be swimming with the best of them and enjoying the full benefits and competitive advantages Virtual Outsourcing has to offer.

On the other hand, if you like to fully plunge into things, avoid the temptation of virtually outsourcing everything right from the start. Using Virtual Consultants and Virtual Assistants is a skill set that you will become better at over time. Give it the time and experience to let it mature. Jumping in all at once and outsourcing everything right from the start is a recipe for disaster. It's much wiser to take a structured, incremental approach. That is, start by outsourcing one support function, and when that appears to be working and stable, outsource another one. This way you'll always feel in control and your business won't get out of hand because you went in too many virtual directions at once.

I am often asked what the best way to get started is. How do you pick the first thing that should be outsourced? Well, that depends upon what your biggest "pain" happens to be. You see, on a day-to-day basis, there are only three kinds of business "pain": 1) not enough income, 2) not enough free time, 3) doing things you don't like doing. For most business owners, it will be some combination of the three. It's important, however, to consider which of the three are causing you the most distress; this will help you determine what to outsource first. And if you're not clear about this, you could end up outsourcing tasks that will cause you even greater pain.

For example, during a workshop for a large group of real estate agents, I posed the question: "What is stopping you from having an absolutely fabulous real estate career?" One lady raised her hand and said, "I handle 70 – 90 property listings at any one time, get only two to three hours of sleep a night… and I hate my life!" I didn't know it at the time, but she was one of the top rated agents in her state —and completely miserable. While her sales and income were the envy of every other agent in the room, their admiration quickly turned to compassion when they saw how close to burnout she was. They all could relate because her level of business was where each of them wanted to be, yet none were willing to pay so dearly for it. Because I could see that "Janet" was truly hurting and quite frankly in a prison of her own making, I decided to work with her specifically as an example for the others in the room.

One of the exercises I had the participants complete was to pick three tasks or functions they would be willing to virtually outsource immediately. When I asked Janet which three she picked, she proudly declared that she would outsource activities that would generate even more business. Yep, just what she needed: more business leading to even more overwhelm, less sleep and more misery. Clearly, this gal did not need more business. What she did need was to get her life back, but she was so blind to her own pain, she simply didn't see it. Actually, it was a little more complicated than that. At that point in the conversation, on a whim I asked her which day of the week she found to be the most difficult. It was no surprise to me that without hesitation she picked Sunday. Why Sunday? Because it is the traditional day of rest, and for Janet that meant not being a top rated sales agent, which in her mind at some level meant she "ceased to exist." Janet was a perfect example of a business person who defines who they are by what they do. And when they are not "doing," they become essentially (or is that existentially?) "nothing" —a rather scary thought indeed.

At my insistence, Janet decided to switch from outsourcing the business-generating tasks to those that would immediately relieve some of her stress. She must have taken it to heart because the very next day she hired a VA four states away to start the process. A month later, I received a message from her saying that she had virtually outsourced over 75 percent of those tasks that were causing her overwhelm. As a result, she was getting a full eight to 10 hours of sleep a night and loving life!

So being clear about what your biggest day-to-day business pain happens to be is the first step on the path to successful Virtual Outsourcing. Now let's take a look at each of these three types of pain and explore some possible first "virtual" steps to relieving them:

- **Not Enough Income** – Most people who run small businesses are usually very good at delivering whatever value they have to offer in exchange for money. However, marketing is often not one of their strengths. Effective marketing can make a big impact on the number and quality of new leads that are generated for your business. And of course, once these leads are converted to sales (another issue we'll address shortly), they generate additional income. Here are some ways you can outsource your marketing:

  - *Create a Written Marketing Plan* – Hire a Virtual Consultant to develop a strategic marketing plan. This should include a SWOT (Strengths, Weaknesses, Opportunities and Threats) analysis. It should identify your key existing and potential new target markets and answer the question, "What's in it for me?" from the perspective of those target markets. It should also addresses how your products and/or services will differentiate themselves from those of your competitors. Once written, a marketing plan needs to be executed consistently in order to maximize the intended results.

- *Implement Your Marketing Plan* – This could involve many types of tasks depending upon your plan. For example, if advertising is involved, you could hire a VA copywriter and VA graphic designer to create the required ads for your plan on an ongoing basis. Any direct mail can be typically handled by a VA who specializes in direct response marketing. If your plan involves participating in trade shows and/or putting on special events, there are VAs and VCs you can find who specialize in just such activities. And, of course, there are countless virtual experts who can help you with any kind of Web-based marketing or e-commerce.

  If your marketing plan is extensive, you will want to hire a VA marketing specialist who will oversee the smooth execution of your plan and report back to you on a regular basis. This VA will also be responsible for hiring other virtual talent as necessary. With this approach, you essentially have your own virtual VP of Marketing, without any of the usual strings attached (i.e., high costs, long-term commitment to a key employee, etc.).

Assuming your plan was well conceived and implemented, you will see a stream of new leads. However, this is just the first step to generating income because these leads need to be converted to sales and the product or service fulfilled.

- *Telemarketing* – The phone is a powerful sales instrument in the hands of a properly trained salesperson. Fortunately, it's relatively easy to find good inbound and outbound telemarketers using the VA and VC resources mentioned in this book. And, with the help of the tools mentioned at the end of this chapter, you will be able to have an entire sales team work the phones without having to add a single line to your existing system.

- *Fulfillment* – Efficient delivery of the products/services sold is a crucial part of the marketing/sales process. If drop shipment is a possibility, this function can be easily managed by a VA. In fact, nearly every aspect of fulfillment that does not require someone to physically be onsite can be facilitated virtually.

These are just some ideas of how you can dramatically boost your company's income using the resources of Virtual Outsourcing. But what if "income" is not your biggest pain? Then chances are, it's that you're so busy, you don't have a life…

- **Not Enough Free Time** – This complaint (i.e., "pain") is the next step up the business version of Maslow's Hierarchy of Needs. Once the threat of insufficient income has been addressed, most business owners start feeling the pinch of not having a life because they're working all the time. This state of affairs is usually the result of trying to wear too many hats (or that "control" thing again!) To address this problem effectively, it usually requires that you step back from your business a few paces to have a look at the big picture. Then, you can see what's out of whack and fix it. This typically requires outside help, such as:

  - *Hire a Business Coach* – Business "coaching" for small business is now big business. There are many fine business coaches you can hire from a distance (i.e., virtually) to help you get back and stay on track. They typically will conduct an initial assessment of the way your business is currently operating, help you explicitly define where you want it to be in three, five and 10 years, make suggestions for corrective action and then usually hold you accountable for implementing them.

    If you don't want to get that deep into seeing the "forest for the trees" process, you may just want to revisit your organizational chart to see how resources can be shifted in a way to lift some of the burden off your shoulders.

  - *Refine Your Organizational Chart* – Sometimes when working with audiences of small to midsized business owners, I have them go through the exercise of creating their company's organizational chart. The most important part of this exercise is to objectively identify those functions or positions that either *a)* are being done by the business owner, or *b)* are currently not being done at all, but should be. Most people who complete this exercise are quite surprised at how many job functions for which they have taken personal responsibility. For some, it's exhausting just looking at their chart!

If you're not sure about how to create your organizational chart, there are many Virtual Consultants who can help you do this in a snap. Once set up, you will want to look at each job function and ask yourself (as honestly as possible), "Can this be done virtually?" If so, label it as such and keep doing this until you've gone through your entire organizational chart.

The next step is to prioritize which support functions (you labeled as capable of being done virtually) you will outsource first. Pick the one thing that will remove the most overwhelm from your shoulders while still feeling comfortable with outsourcing it. Then give yourself and the Virtual Assistant a chance to settle in to make sure it's consistently working the way you want. Once you have successfully outsourced your first choice, go to the next and so on. Using this very simple yet structured approach, your sense of overwhelm will be gone in no time.

Now, with all this extra free time on your hands, you may just start wondering whether you even enjoy what you're doing in your business. This of course, is the third and final "pain" to be addressed.

- **Not Enjoying What You Do** – Being good at something is not necessarily synonymous with enjoying it. As business owners, we inevitably start out by wearing many hats, and even become highly proficient at several things outside of our "core competency." Your core competency is something you are passionate about doing that brings high value to your company. If you find that you're spending most of your time doing things outside of your core competency, you'll eventually resent your business, no matter how much money you make or free time you have. That's because your core competency, by definition (assuming you really are passionate about it), is the pathway to feeling fulfilled. And achieving fulfillment within your business puts you at the highest level of the business version of Maslow's Hierarchy of Needs. Now, not everyone is in touch with what their core competency happens to be within their business. If this is the case for you, consider hiring a good virtual business coach as mentioned above and get really clear about this —and the sooner the better.

Figuring out what your biggest business "pain" is and then systematically using Virtual Outsourcing to eliminate it one step at a time is a great way to get started. By first relieving your pain, you'll receive powerful feedback as to the efficacy of Virtual Outsourcing, and it will give you the confidence to outsource even more of your business support functions.

Using Teams of VAs Within Your Business

Once you get started and become comfortable using Virtual Outsourcing (especially ongoing support through Virtual Assistants), you will soon see other ways to incorporate them into your business. Remember, the better VAs are specialists, so this means hiring a different VA for each type of support. Do not make the mistake of hiring one, being absolutely thrilled with how well they're working out and then dumping more and a broader scope of work on them as time goes on. This is an almost certain recipe for disaster. First of all, if your first VA agrees to do work outside their specialty, then they're not very professional or haven't been in the business very long. The true pros realize the importance of sticking to what they do best, rather than trying to be everything to everybody. And, if they are unwise enough to actually take on the extra work you give them (outside of *their* core competency), they will eventually get in over their head and start making mistakes. The quality of their work will likely diminish and you will start hearing excuses as to why deadlines are missed or important tasks fall through the cracks. I have seen this happen time and time again where a business owner is initially thrilled with the results of using a VA, and then everything melts down after giving them work outside their specialty.

It's very tempting (and very normal) to hire a great VA for one thing initially and then just want to give them more and more responsibilities. Yet, as mentioned earlier in this book, it's important to have a written business process for each support function that a VA does for you. This discipline will quickly disappear into a mist of good intentions as soon as you try to broad-scope any of your VAs.

As you hire additional VAs for different support functions, you will eventually have a team of them. Keeping in mind that they require very little management, having multiple VAs doing ongoing work for you should not be a problem. However, at some point (probably after you have hired your third VA), you'll want to have someone run and continue to grow your virtual team for you.

Your Virtual COO

An executive level VA is someone who is highly skilled and experienced in providing strategic support, including project management, "virtual" human resources (i.e., hiring and terminating other VAs and VCs as needed), writing business processes for each member of your virtual team, and making sure they stay on track as per their written objectives. They also strive to understand the "big picture" of your business and focus on making sure you achieve your goals and objectives using available resources. Think of them as your "Virtual COO."

Depending upon the size and complexity of your business, this key VA will typically not have to spend a great deal of time watching over your business. In most cases, you would only need to chat with them about once a week. They report to you on how well your other VAs are doing their job and discuss what other types of virtual support you may be needing in the near future. With this kind of support at your side, you now have a key VA who will hire and manage other VAs and VCs for you. Now that's virtual leverage!

At this point, you might be thinking, "Why don't I just hire an executive level VA and let them take care of the rest?" That certainly is an option. This is a key position in your company and any potential candidates must be evaluated very carefully. They must have extensive experience assisting businesses from the strategic, operational and human resources perspectives. If you are new to Virtual Outsourcing, then handing over this level of responsibility to someone you have never met may seem a bit, well... scary. If that's the case, then I suggest you start with "small steps" of hiring VAs for specific, measurable tasks as mentioned earlier. After you have two or more working with you and everything is going smoothly, then consider hiring an executive level VA to grow your virtual team beyond that point.

Another option is to hire an executive level VA just to document your various business processes. This way you get the benefit of their experience and organizational abilities without feeling you are handing over the "keys" to your company. Also, by using this kind of VA instead of a VC to create your processes, this VA will be intimately familiar with how your company functions when you're ready to hire them for more of an ongoing key management position.

How to Avoid Freaking Out Your Onsite Staff

If you currently have onsite staff that you want to keep (I never said get rid of them all), then you may want to consider a bit of "positioning" for their benefit before your first virtual hire. A couple of years ago, a business owner brought me in as a consultant to see how he might incorporate Virtual Outsourcing into his operations and better support his several hundred salespeople. Apparently word got out to his onsite administrative staff that I was coming and the rumors of mass firings went through his company like wildfire before I even arrived. In retrospect, I should have counseled him on how to position his current staff on the whole notion of using Virtual Outsourcing as a way to "augment" and complement their current efforts. Some of his staff were already in the overwhelm stage and they must have thought they were going to be replaced by some nameless, faceless VA from afar. Actually, that was the intent for some, but certainly not all of his staff. However, having rampant rumors and fear mongering running through his entire staff certainly did nothing to improve morale.

If you have in-house employees you value and expect to keep no matter how "virtual" you take your organization, it's very important that you keep them in the loop during the VA/VC hiring process. Help them see that by having VAs and VCs handle the more routine support functions, they'll be freed up to do higher level work. You want your onsite staff to welcome the extra help that comes with having VAs do some of the work. Ideally, you have your key people participate on the VA/VC hiring process. It's important for them to realize that the VAs and VCs are there to help them do a better job, not take it away.

Even with best intentions and Herculean efforts of managing your onsite staff's expectations (and fears), you may end up having one or two of your current staff resenting the "invasion" of virtual people (remember, they are employees after all —enough said). Keep a sharp eye out for any behavior that may point to this possibility. An onsite employee who is secretly fearful of the changes that come with Virtual Outsourcing can quickly sabotage your efforts at going virtual. This is especially true if your VAs or VCs must interact with your onsite staff.

If you see this happen, ask those individuals to identify which of their current tasks they dislike the most. Then explain the benefits of having a VA handle this part of their work. Help them see that it frees them up to focus on the more important and interesting, high-leverage aspects of their work. And, help them see that this makes them even more valuable to your company. If it appears that this little "heart-to-heart" still doesn't sink in, then it's time to re-evaluate whether this employee is still one of the "keepers" or not.

OK, let's assume you prepped your staff (the "keepers") and they enthusiastically support using Virtual Outsourcing to take your business to a whole new level. Now is a good time to explore some of the "tools" you and they can use to maximize your Virtual Outsourcing experience.

Virtual Outsourcing Tools and Procedures

All of the "tools" you and your business will utilize to facilitate working effectively with virtual support are information transfer tools to one extent or the other. They fall into one of three basic categories: Internet, phone and fax. And, their proportionate uses are typically in that same order. You will use the Internet as your primary means of communicating and collaborating with your virtual team, then the phone and occasionally the fax.

As we investigate some of the specific tools within each of these categories, certain technology vendors will be mentioned that, as of this writing, currently provide these tools and services. Since the majority of this book is based upon sharing the relatively timeless principles of incorporating Virtual Outsourcing into your business, mentioning specific vendors here, that can come and go at any time, makes me just a tad bit uncomfortable. In an effort to give you specific examples of interacting with your virtual team, I have mitigated my discomfort in the following ways. First, rest assured that I receive no compensation whatsoever from any the following vendors mentioned here. Second, you can see a more comprehensive list of products and services within these categories on my Virtual Outsourcing resource Web site at http://www. virtualoutsourcing.org. Now with that out of the way, let's explore how you can maximize the benefits of working with virtual support talent…

Using the Internet

There are many different ways to use the Internet to facilitate the productive interaction between you and your virtual team. However, there is one Net-based tool that stands out above all others as the true workhorse when it comes to using Virtual Outsourcing:

- **E-mail** – It is by far the most important tool you will use when working with your virtual support staff. It's fast, efficient, costs practically nothing and, unlike the phone, is non-interruptive (i.e., you use it only when you choose to). The beauty of communicating via e-mail is that it allows them (and you) to get work done without interruption. And, you will find that you're interacting with them far less than if they were in the office. This translates into much higher levels of productivity, less disruption and far less time expended on management. As great a tool as e-mail is, here is how you can make it even better:

a. Create a "folder" within your e-mail software for each member of your virtual team. Storing all of your inbound e-mail from them within their respective folder makes it much easier to find and organize their messages. Most professional-level e-mail programs like Microsoft Outlook give you the ability to create these folders.

b. If any of your virtual team interacts with your prospects, customers or suppliers, then have them use your e-mail signature and/or stationery (with their name, not yours) when they communicate online on your behalf. I also suggest that you issue them an e-mail address using your company's domain name, which they should use every time they send e-mail on your company's behalf. In addition, consider giving them a credible title (i.e., identifying their position within your company) that is also reflected on their e-mail signature/stationery. This is important for a number of reasons. First, it will extend and promote your company's "brand" every time they send a message. Second, it will clearly show them as part of your staff.

Just in case you were wondering, an e-mail signature is a block of text (for text-only e-mails) or Web code (for HTML e-mails) that includes information about who you are, the name and location of your company, and all other contact information, including phone, fax and links to your e-mail and Web site. Once set up, it gets added to the bottom of all your outbound e-mails automatically. E-mail stationery, on the other hand, is a graphical "wrapper" around your e-mail message. It can be designed to look like just about anything you want. Think of it as your company's electronic corporate stationery that is uniquely branded and identifies the message as coming from your organization.

If you currently don't have branded e-mail signatures and stationery for your company, get them —it is a nearly costless way to advertise your company. And of course, it's not hard to find a VA or VC who can create these for you in no time!

Another very useful function of e-mail is to send digital documents and files as attachments. As you probably already know, however, there can be problems sending attachments because many ISPs (Internet Service Providers) put a restriction on the size and/or number of e-mail attachments per message. This can be an annoying issue if you work with a VA or VC who is doing any kind of graphic design or multimedia work for you, as these files can be quite large. One way around this is to use a service like WhaleMail (http://www.whalemail. com), which allows you to send just about any size file (within reasonable limits) and avoids altogether the typical issues surrounding the sending of e-mail attachments.

Here is how it works. First, you need to set up your WhaleMail account (very affordable) which gives you space on the WhaleMail server for the files you want to send. Let's say you want to send an old PowerPoint presentation to your VA for updating, but it's over 15 MBs in size, which is too large to send as an e-mail attachment. You simply log into your WhaleMail account on their Web site, upload the file to the server, and use the system to send an e-mail to your VA with a link they can use to download the file. By clicking that link, they go to a special place on the WhaleMail server site. From there, they can immediately start the download process. The best part is that the recipient does not have to have a WhaleMail account to receive the file you sent them. Keep in mind, however, that most VAs will typically have something similar to WhaleMail that they use to send large files, especially if it's something they do all the time (they have to get the updated PowerPoint presentation back to you after all). *NOTE: There are a number of other services similar to WhaleMail, which are currently free. However, I hesitate to recommend free online services given that they have a nasty tendency to go out of business before my books hit the bookstore shelves.*

While e-mail will almost certainly be your primary means of communication, some VAs and the people they work for like to use a more immediate form of connecting.

- **Instant Messaging** – Often referred to as IM, it's a way of sending written messages, well... instantly, between you and your remote staff. This is great if you or your VA needs an answer to something right away. However, I personally try to have my businesses run so there is little if any urgency, which allows me to avoid interruptions as much as possible. Many VAs and business people swear by IM. I rarely use it so that I don't end up swearing at it whenever that #&$%!* message window pops up, interrupting whatever I happen to be focused on at that moment. There are many feature-rich IM tools available that even include voice and video messaging, many of which are free. Certainly one of the more ubiquitous is Microsoft's Instant Messenger which you can download from MSN.com (http://www.msn.com).

Using the Internet to communicate with your virtual team is just one way it can be used. There are also several other Internet-based collaboration tools you can use to enhance the benefits of working with your virtual team.

- **Intranet** – This is your business's private, password-protected "home base" where all your staff can access important documents and other information vital to the running of your business —no matter where they're located, using only a Web browser. This is a powerful, collaborative virtual work environment that is central to the successful operation of my own companies. There are essentially two ways to get an intranet for your company. The easiest and quickest way is to use an intranet service company that allows you to set it up in literally minutes using just a Web browser. You typically pay by the month, per "seat" (i.e., number of people in your organization that have individual access to it). There are several such companies that offer this service, with WebEx WebOffice (http://www.weboffice.com) being one of the better known ones.

Another alternative is to host your intranet on your own Web server. You can have it custom-built to your specifications (time-consuming and expensive —not recommended), or use a pre-packaged solution that can be installed on your server without too much time or hassle. If your Web server happens to be using the Microsoft Windows operating system, then Microsoft's Share-Point Services (http://www.microsoft.com/sharepoint) is a powerful and sophisticated intranet application to consider. However, it will require the services of a SharePoint expert (which you should be able to easily find on Elance.com, Guru.com or other VSPMs) to install and customize it for your company's particular needs.

Generally speaking, most intranets will contain the following standard features:

- *Group Calendar* – For scheduling purposes, usually with automatic e-mail reminders of upcoming items. This way, your entire team is working off of the same schedule.

- *Document Storage* – Allowing access to documents and files that are critical to the day-to-day running of your business. The more full-featured intranets will allow for the intranet's administrator to have set access privileges for each folder (group of documents) or individual documents as needed. Some will also have a document check-in/check-out feature that prevents two people from modifying a document at the same time. And, some have document "versioning," which keeps track of the modification history of any document so that if you ever need to access an earlier version, you can easily do so. By having this kind of centralized, secure and controlled document repository, you will never again have to ask, "Who has the latest version of our proposal template?"

- *Database* – A convenient way to store lists of information that's accessible to your team members, depending upon their permissions setting within the intranet. In most cases, these databases are very simple "flat files" (i.e., two-dimensional tables where each column is a field and each row a record, similar to a spreadsheet). However, some may offer more sophisticated, relational types of databases (i.e., consisting of multiple tables that are connected or related).

- *Announcements* – A simple and quick way to send a message to all the members of your intranet. They will typically receive it as an e-mail and see it on your intranet's home page.

- *Discussion Forum* – A way for you and your virtual team to post and reply to various topics and ideas important to your business. You can think of it as a form of asynchronous (i.e., not in real time) brainstorming. As members of your team post thoughts or questions, the others can take their time to reply. This is a great way to seamlessly distribute knowledge throughout your organization, no matter where your staff (virtual or otherwise) are located.

In addition to the above, some of the more sophisticated intranets can also offer the following:

- *Task Management* – Allows you to manage small projects online. This feature usually includes personnel allocation, deadline tracking and reminders, progress reporting, etc.

- *Contact List* – A convenient way to store and update information about all your prospects, clients and vendors. Some services will even allow you to synchronize your intranet contact list with your computer and/or handheld PDA.

- *Expense Reports* – An especially useful feature if your VAs bill you for their out-of-pocket expenses. This way you have a unified way to track and report staff business expenses.

While intranets are a powerful way to connect and collaborate with your virtual team (and your onsite staff, too, for that matter), they are by no means the only way...

- **Web-based Applications** – It used to be that the only kind of software you could use had to be physically installed on your computer. Not any more. Thanks to the advent of quite powerful and feature-rich Web-based applications offered by Application Service Providers (ASPs), everyone can be on the same digital page, no matter where they happen to be. A few notables in this space include Intuit.com with their QuickBooks Online product. As I mentioned earlier, it is QuickBooks Online that allows my virtual bookkeeper in Kansas (or occasionally from Florida when deep sea fishing) to keep my various companies' books up-to-date. It also allows me to access my financial data from any Web browser.

Another very big player in the Web-based application business is SalesForce.com, one of the most sophisticated Customer Relationship Management (CRM) packages available. SalesForce was founded by Mark Benoff, a former top sales executive at Oracle software. He is the most passionate evangelist for the power of Web-based applications, and is famous for his brash marketing, including his famous "No Software" symbol.

Sophisticated CRM solutions used to be accessible only to large enterprise corporations because of their expense and complexity. What SalesForce.com and its competitors have done is *a)* made the power of a full-featured CRM affordable to even the smallest of companies, and *b)* made it simple and intuitive enough so that it doesn't take an IT degree to run it. Think about this for a moment. No matter what size your company happens to be, you now have access to sales-enhancement solutions that only the "big boys" used to enjoy.

Just to give you an idea of how powerful this can be, there is a 100 percent virtual company in Columbus, OH (well, that's where the CEO lives anyway) that provides virtually outsourced telemarketing services. By going completely virtual and incorporating SalesForce and other powerful Web-based tools, owner Jack Sands is able to attract best-of-breed workers, dramatically reduce his turnover and overhead, and under-price his competitors. In so doing, he won the Ernst & Young Entrepreneurial Award two years in a row …

It's Your Call

In a way, we have re-invented the wheel —within a wheel —within a wheel. The key to keeping our virtual business oiled and rolling is hiring people from all across the country to work for us from their homes. Intrep, Inc. is unique in that it uses an elite population of savvy telemarketers/salespeople, hired on a national basis, to perform the same services of employees working in traditional, onsite call centers. In general, these facilities are often reconverted retail establishments, cheaply gutted and fitted with appropriate technology. The pay scale matches these lavish physical trappings, at a whopping, average hourly wage of $8. We pay $15 per hour. The yearly turnover rate in a congregate business environment is 100 percent. Ours is 15 percent.

For my concept to work, our employees needed access to a sophisticated, Web-based database application and automated phone system. I had to effectively merge diverse technologies in a brand new way. One of the most important tools for us, to find the right kinds of employees, has been our use of Elance.com. I found an "Elancer" in the Ukraine who developed a proprietary software system, suited and customized to our needs. Late one evening, I suddenly realized that I needed a PowerPoint presentation for a meeting the next day. Since Elance allows me to quickly access the best specialists in the world, I posted the project and a provider in India delivered it to my inbox by 9 a.m. the next morning. I was literally outsourcing the creation of the tools I would need to outsource labor for Intrep.

Many of these contractors are women. Some are on maternity leave from high-profiled executive jobs, but desire the challenge of work-at-home opportunities at hours they choose. Others are perhaps highly experienced executive wives, joining their spouses on location. On the whole, this population encompasses a diverse cross-section of people who are specifically looking for part-time employment that can be performed from the comfort and convenience of their own homes. Everybody loves to make money, but a good portion of our people simply want to be a part of a worthwhile business association. Competitive salaries paid to people working on their own time schedules, in their own surroundings, provides a more satisfying work/life balance.

Managing a remote work force is challenging, yet the solution to closing the gaps is sophisticated, state-of-the-art technology, which enables us to exercise control, tap into the system in use and measure employee performance. Everything we do is Web-based, courtesy of SalesForce.com. The employee, home training system allows them to log into a series of sessions, which they can use at their own pace. We tout the selling process offered in these sessions because we consistently glean high-caliber people who have usually been in sales and have the keen ability to listen, understand customer feedback, and use mature, real-life skills in phone interactions. A few hundred people may apply for a job with us and maybe one will be hired. We search for and hire the "best of the breed."

Another crucial requirement for the success of operations such as ours is the enlistment of a very strong recruiting agent, which is a necessary tool in the management of a remote work force. We receive hundreds of resumes, which are processed and entered into our Web site database. The system is set up to invite final candidates to call us, talk to us, and literally "sell" themselves in a phone call. If you can't put a sentence together on the fly, it's highly unlikely that you'll be chosen.

As the CEO of Intrep, Inc., I have the same capability of a call center, but I don't own its responsibilities, its overhead, its computers, its phone lines or its technology. Management costs can be cut as well, because you don't need 15 supervisors when you're working with pros.

Jack Sands, CEO
Intrep, Inc.

The trend of companies shifting toward the use of Web-based applications is not going away. What will eventually go away is the use of shrink-wrapped software. That includes software powerhouse Microsoft, which intends to offer many of its industry standard Office programs via a Web interface. All of this is great news for any company contemplating using Virtual Outsourcing. That's because powerful software, the very engine of information processing, is now ubiquitously accessible to anyone, anywhere who's connected to the Net.

- **Remote Access** – Just like being there! Web-based versions of this kind of service allow you (or anyone to whom you give permission) full access to your office computer as if you were sitting right in front of it. So how could this work with a trusted member of your VA team? Well, imagine you had a big presentation tomorrow that included a formal, printed proposal and customized PowerPoint presentation. You simply contact the VA who typically does this for you and give them the necessary details to complete the work. Then, before heading home for the night, you leave your computer and printer on (filled with the necessary paper for the report) and put a blank CD into your computer's burner. While you're at home with the family, eating dinner and relaxing, your VA is busy creating the necessary documents and slide presentation. Assuming your office computer has been set up to be remotely controlled through a service like GoToMyPc (http://www.gotomypc.com), LogMeIn (http://www.logmein.com) or some other Web-based computer access service, your VA will be able to print out your proposal and burn the PowerPoint presentation to the CD you left in the burner. The next morning, you come in, pick up the printed copies of your presentation, put the CD into your laptop and away you go.

Remote access extends the capabilities of your VAs in ways that just would not be possible without it. Another practical example is if you have a VA run your direct mail campaigns. In this scenario, they can do the mail-merge from your contact database on your computer (remotely), yet print the pieces on *their* printer, thereby handling all aspects of the direct mailing from their end. You never even have to touch the paper that gets sent to your customers and prospects.

Most Web-based remote access services can be very secure because they use a two password system to prevent unauthorized access to your computer (assuming you use sufficiently complex passwords). Obviously, you would only give this kind of access to someone you completely trusted. To be on the safe side, it's a good idea to set up your VA as a separate "user" for your computer where they have to log in as that user before accessing your computer's files and programs. This way you can assign specific restrictions to that user, thereby effectively creating a "sandbox." This approach lets them into the areas of your computer for which they need to do their job, while preventing them from seeing or doing anything else.

In addition to remote access, there is another kind of Web-based collaborative tool you can use with your virtual team that gives them restricted access to your computer screen, but for an entirely different purpose.

- **Web Meetings** – You will find that there will be times when it would be extremely helpful to have a "virtual" meeting where all the parties can see and share your computer screen in real time, regardless of their location. For example, you may need to train your staff on how a particular application works, or conversely, your VA may need to train you! Sometimes it's important to be on the same "digital page" (an application, business process, spreadsheet, report, etc.) when discussing it during a meeting. Or, being able to present an important proposal to a prospective new client without having to travel to their offices. Web meetings can also be used as a quick way to have technical support where a technician can access your computer (as a meeting member), diagnose and fix the problem while you watch it happen!

There are many Web meeting services available that offer a fairly rich set of capabilities in all different price ranges. One of my favorites is GoToMeeting (http://www.gotomeeting.com), which I have found to be extremely easy to use and quite affordable. It's fast, too. I can set up a Web meeting in about 10 seconds flat before sending out the e-mail invites to the other members. Most Web meeting services typically offer the following standard features:

- *Application and screen sharing* – the ability to show whatever is on the meeting presenter's computer screen;

- *Commenting* – the ability for the presenter to mark up or highlight whatever is on their screen for purposes of emphasis;

- *Assign keyboard and mouse control* – the ability of the presenter to give control of their keyboard and mouse to one or more of the other meeting members at any time;

- *Presenter switching* – the ability to switch on-the-fly who is presenting and thus sharing their screen with all other members of the meeting;

- *Meeting recording* – the ability to record both audio and video of everything that was said and shown on the presenter's screen. This is very useful for training purposes because you give the training live once, record it and allow your newer staff to view it as necessary.

Another important yet often overlooked benefit of presenting meetings this way is that, by definition, all the parties to the meeting are in different physical locations. This tends to make your meetings more highly focused on the issues at hand and less likely to stray into unnecessary tangents. Also, the human dynamic is very different in a Web meeting versus your traditional onsite meeting. As mentioned earlier in this book, there are many nonverbal cues flying around a physical meeting room which can be distracting and often exacerbate organizational politics. Web meetings, on the other hand, create a significant buffer between the attending personalities and what needs to be accomplished. That's just another way of saying Web meetings can be considerably more effective and efficient than traditional ones.

> *Web meetings can be considerably more effective and efficient than traditional ones.*

Without question, the Internet is by far the most important means of communicating and collaborating with your virtual team. And, you can expect even more innovative solutions in the future. As powerful as the Internet is, however, we will always need voice communications (whether traditional land line, digital cell or Voice Over IP) for some aspect of our businesses. Fortunately, there are some interesting and quite affordable solutions to the problem of integrating the phone with your virtual staff.

Using the Phone

Conventional use of the phone in a business environment meant having wired handsets with tons of buttons at each desk. And there had to be enough dedicated lines to adequately support the size of your onsite staff. Thanks to technology, this is no longer the case, no matter how large your virtual organization becomes.

- **Virtual PBX** – A traditional PBX is a fairly complex affair that allows you to customize and grow your phone capabilities along with your company. Plan on spending plenty of money and time buying, installing and being trained on the necessary equipment, wiring and software if you go this route. Alternatively, a "Virtual" PBX requires no added equipment, wiring or software and can be operational in just minutes for very little cost. Most importantly, however, is the fact that it can be used to connect all of your staff to your prospects, customers and suppliers no matter how geographically far flung they may be. There are several companies that offer this kind of service. The one I have been using for years, and certainly one of the larger players, is called FreedomVoice (http://www.freedomvoice.com). Another very full-featured service is quite appropriately named Virtual PBX (http://www.virtualpbx.com).

These services can usually be configured to your company's needs directly on the phone, using a touch-tone keypad or using a password-protected, Web-based control panel. Here is how they work:

    a. Upon sign up you are given a toll-free number, or if you have one already, that can be used as well. This number will be the one that the public uses to contact your company;

    b. You are given the number of "extensions" as needed for your staff (virtual or otherwise). These are typically password-protected with a separate password for each extension and a master password (that only you have) that gives access to all the extensions, their voicemail boxes and setup parameters;

    c. Each of these extensions can be set up individually with its own greeting, call forwarding, call following, voicemail box and message forwarding. This means that your VAs can have all calls forwarded to their own phone if answering live is critical to the kind of support they are providing you (i.e., customer or technical support for your products or services, etc.) If this is the case, it is important that they can distinguish calls coming in from your company versus others they are helping so they can give the appropriate greeting;

    d. You can also set up your own on-hold music and a touch-tone directory listing of all your staff that have separate extensions.

If you're like me and don't appreciate being interrupted by the phone or having to call in for messages, you can usually set these systems up to save a voice message as a compact MP3 file and have it sent as part of an e-mail announcing the received call. This means you can play back your messages from anywhere you can connect to the Net.

This also makes it easy to forward the message (via e-mail) to anyone else that needs to hear it, whether or not they have direct access to your Virtual PBX system.

While the initial setup for these systems is relatively straightforward, they can be intimidating. One solution, of course, is to hire a Virtual Consultant to do this for you. Make sure they document all the extensions, passwords, and procedures for staff use. With this kind of system, you can grow the virtual side of your company to literally any size without having to spend a dime on equipment or installation. Having a Virtual PBX is clearly a critical necessity for any company that plans on operating virtually.

The Birth of an Idea

Pregnancy is a natural condition for most women, yet it is that special time in a woman's life when everything she's known or taken for granted about her physical constitution is suddenly examined under a microscope. Every breath, every twinge, every unfamiliar physical sensation is questioned —all with the intention of bringing into the world the healthiest, happiest, perfect little baby. For mothers-to-be, the timing of these questions aren't confined to a physician's office hours.

I am an OB/GYN nurse and have teamed with my colleague, Anne Afshari, to provide a service dedicated to answering questions from pregnant women, discussing their concerns, and educating them about their specific issues of care. Since its inception in 2003, our business, Exclusively RNs, has eased the communication between patient and doctor by providing a 24/7, toll-free, call-in service, hosted by qualified OB/GYN nurses across the country. The use of a Virtual PBX phone system enables us to answer calls anytime, from anywhere, with seamless precision. It also allows us to grow our staff of OB/GYN nurses to any size without having to invest in additional phone lines, hardware or software.

The idea for such a business sparked during a brief exchange between doctor and nurse. Anne and I were both working in a hospital's labor and delivery unit. We were trying to talk to a particular doctor over the repeated interruptions of his pager going off. Anne asked him why he had to return all those calls, without knowing the nature of each and every one of them. His answer was simple. "Because I haven't found anybody to do it for me." Now, we jokingly refer to that moment as the jumping off point for our business. Several weeks later, we went into his office with our business proposal for "triaging" and answering his calls. He warmed to the idea immediately. Before long, we were taking calls for his entire practice, including the six additional doctors who worked with him.

Our business is not a public information center. We contract directly with the physician's office and every incoming call is documented, which provides an upscale benefit for doctors when they review patient progress and information. Doctors usually don't write things down when they talk to patients because they don't have time or they take the call at awkward times and places. Our staff of 25 virtual nurses records the patient's demographic information, what she called about and what information she was given. This kind of response service not only allows specially trained OB/GYN nurses to talk directly and immediately to patients, but to also triage and prioritize the nature and/or urgency of calls —something that doctors can't do each time their pager goes off. Nurses who have contracted with us from New Jersey, Florida, North Carolina and other states, program their own phone numbers into the Virtual PBX system so calls can be forwarded to them. Patients have the security of knowing that a real person is taking their calls, but don't know that our nurses are working remotely. We take our service one step further by offering specific options as to how offices want us to handle their calls. They can forward a certain branch of their calls, if not all of them, or have patients receive a customized, outgoing message, or utilize a traditional answering service that screens calls for us and prioritizes the needs of each caller.

We have taken our nursing skills to a different level in that we can use the same professional judgment we used on the hospital floor to minister to patients' concerns from our own homes. Twelve-hour hospital shifts are common today, taking nurses away from family activities. Working from home makes us more available for these quality times. One of the nicest aspects of our business is that Anne and I share our strengths and weaknesses in our own areas of expertise. We excel where we are most comfortable and rely on the other's individual skills to cover and overlap. Add our contracted nurses to the equation and we have a thriving business which utilizes the best niche skills of all. There is such a sense of relief in not having to manage everything! This is especially true for the six doctors we work with —who are sleeping very well at night!

Laura Hagler, Co-Founder
Exclusively RNs

- **Conferencing** – there are likely to be many times when you will need to have a conference call with one or more of your virtual staff and/or customers. "What's the big deal? I already do this," you may say. Well, none really, unless you want to save a ton of money. For example, I use the services of FreeConference.com (http://www.freeconference.com) to quickly and easily set up phone conferences with up to 100 people at a moment's notice (or pre-schedule one for later). The best part is that there is no cost whatsoever for the service other than the usual long-distance fee every participant pays to access the conference. This is a great way to have multiple-party phone meetings where everyone can hear each other just fine (unlike some small business phone systems that offer conferencing capability for at most three people).

Using the Fax

Remember when the fax machine represented the latest and greatest business communications tool? In today's highly digitized office environment, sending and receiving faxes is the low man on the electronic communications totem pole. That's primarily because faxing is restricted to transmitting scanned images of documents rather than a digital version that allows them to be easily manipulated after receipt. Despite its limited utility, faxing is still an important part of office communications and will continue to be so for at least another decade. And until recently, you needed dedicated fax lines to send and receive faxes via dedicated fax machines. If this were still true today, arranging to have each of your support VAs have their own fax number, that you controlled, would be an expensive affair.

Thanks to the Internet and services like eFax (http://www.efax.com) or MyFax (http://www.myfax.com) however, even the lowly fax has become much more nimble, affordable and VA-friendly. And, here's the best part: You don't even need to have a fax machine or dedicated fax line to send and receive faxes through these services. Here's how they work. When you establish an account online through their respective Web sites, you are immediately given your own dedicated fax number. That number can be toll-free, local to your business, or local to just about any other area you want. When anyone faxes a document to that number, the fax is automatically converted to a digital image (usually in industry standard Adobe Acrobat PDF) which is then sent to you as an e-mail attachment. Upon receipt, you can view, annotate, forward or even re-fax the document to others, all without ever having to print it out.

There are some other benefits as well. Since you receive your faxes via e-mail, this means you can pick them up no matter where you are in the world. No more ringing your hands in frustration because you happen to be where your fax machine isn't. Also, they can be stored digitally within your e-mail software folders, rather than having to print and file them manually.

So how does all this impact your VAs' ability to receive faxes on your behalf? Tremendously, as it turns out. Let's say you have a team of five VAs who are in a position of working with your prospects, customers or vendors. Simply acquire a separate fax number for each VA which they are allowed to use only on your behalf. It's quick, inexpensive and a highly effective way to control the fax number which will remain the same even if you have to replace the VA that it is currently assigned to. And, since most of these services allow you to view faxes sent and received to a particular number through their Web site, you can always check to make sure your fax number is not be used for anything other than your business.

It's Not the Tool, It's the Tool User

The above ways to enhance your communication and collaboration using the Internet, phone and fax with your virtual team are certainly very useful and will help you realize even greater benefits from Virtual Outsourcing. Yet, this covers only a small part of the available technology tools that you may use day-to-day in your business. For example, businesses that are very sales-oriented may heavily use a contact management system, or its big brother, Customer Relationship Management (CRM) systems. And there are some industries (securities, insurance, real estate, construction, etc.) that rely on very industry-specific solutions to get the job done.

> *let the "tool expert" (i.e., VA) choose the best tool for the job and handle the details of accomplishing your objectives.*

As I travel the world speaking to various business audiences, I am often asked what the best tool to do "X" is. My response is, "Not the one you use, rather the one that is used for you." Ideally, you let the "tool expert" (i.e., VA) choose the best tool for the job and handle the details of accomplishing your objectives. For example, instead of trying to figure out which contact management or CRM system is best for your business, hire a VA who specializes in those areas and let them get the job done using the tools they know well.

This approach allows you to get up and running much faster without having to agonize over which solution is the best. It also allows you to avoid most of the steep learning curve associated with trying to implement it yourself.

If They Can, You Can Too

So far in this chapter, it has been all about starting, growing and managing your business's foray into the world of Virtual Outsourcing. Now let's take a look at how a wide range of small businesses have already done so very successfully...

Extreme Virtual Outsourcing

Call me the virtual poster child. I like saying, "I don't know." It's a relief. I like saying that I don't know every answer to every question that is put to me, because I surround myself with advisors and outsource partners who are a hell of a lot better at what they do than I could be and they have the answers. I can't imagine doing business any other way, and I am always eager to point out the benefits, profits and scalability factor to entrepreneurs and investors in situations similar to mine. We are a small company that has basically outsourced our entire schedule of finance functions —CFO, controller, accounts payable and accounts receivable. We outsource sales, marketing and business development to a company in New York. We've outsourced finance to a primary source in Texas, Web hosting to a company in Colorado and technology to a company in Cambridge, Massachusetts. In fact, *The Wall Street Journal* did a story on us, referring to our business as being at the forefront of "extreme outsourcing," making it sound like an Olympic event in the small business category.

We provide corporate weight management programs to employees working for any number of big companies, which aids them in controlling their dietary and nutritional needs. It is built on financial incentives, tracking on the Web, and the incorporation of a large number of diet and exercise partners into the equation. We aim to customize the individual's experience and success by offering the right combination of techniques, particular to each person.

Five years ago, if I found myself toying with the idea of starting and running a business, I probably would have had a harder time trusting the concept of outsourcing and explaining it to other people. But, I come from the technology field. I was CEO of an Internet company that provided outsourced e-commerce solutions. So, I am more than familiar with and supportive of such a business model. Getting our business off the ground was simplified because we agreed from the start that we wanted to outsource everything that was not core to our operation. When we asked ourselves if paying bills and managing financial statements was something that we wanted to handle directly, and a chorus of "no" filled the air, we knew we were on to something better. We even outsourced the commercial branding of our product. I am known for coming up with notoriously bad marketing suggestions when it comes to names and catch phrases. Good! Here's something else I didn't have to address. I spend 10 percent of my time on administrative matters and 90 percent working with clients, current business and mapping out long-term strategic issues. Why would I want to spend the better part of a day arguing with the accounting department about some issue or agenda? Or some potential coup from HR? The differences in doing business the traditional way and a better, more convenient and sensible way by outsourcing, are like night and day.

If you are considering making the jump to outsourcing, be sure you really understand what it is that makes your business different from any other business and those of your competitors. Consider cost effectiveness, conservation of capital, and a low-cost model that can scale and save countless headaches, problems and dilution, in the future. Then, define and monitor the services you are looking for; assess and review your outsource partners as you would evaluate onsite employees. Learn to identify your strengths and limits and you will eventually attain admission into that blissful state of judgment, where you can defer to somebody who knows something better than you do.

Aaron Day, CEO
Tangerine Wellness

In the case story above, Tangerine Wellness chose to outsource their non-core functions to primarily U.S. based Virtual Support Organizations (VSOs), which works great for them. However, the beauty of Virtual Outsourcing is that you are not restricted by geography, which means the world truly is your oyster...as our next case story so cogently illustrates.

It's a Small World After All

Has the world gone virtual when a guy like me, from a town with a population of 500, can drive to McDonald's, pay $3, get Wi-Fi, open up my TeamLeader collaboration system and work with a virtual team in Russia and India (as well as Philly, Cleveland, Fairmont and Morgantown, West Virginia)?

Well! You know the answer is a resounding yes! The reality just continuously blows me away!

It feels pretty incredible to me that I've been outsourcing software development to Russia since 1999, yet Virtual Global Technologies has never had a single verbal conversation with a Russian team member! Our team is 100% virtual.

Here I am, in a small town, working out of my country home, presenting a big company image, while doing business with people around the world, especially in Russia and India! Amazing!

I'm a native son and a huge "fan" of Green Spring, West Virginia. But, after earning a college degree in computer science, I ended up taking a job working on a roof to earn money! Like many graduates of small town colleges, I had to relocate to find better jobs.

West Virginia is not exactly known as a hub for information technology. I admit I have a pet peeve related to the misperception, a topic about which I am very passionate.

I feel I have paid my dues, by initially having to move to find a good job — which is not very different than people in India relocating to bigger cities for better opportunities.

These people eagerly embraced their newfound opportunity to work remotely via the Internet, and plumped up their economy by $17 billion, yet West Virginia has not capitalized on the same opportunity. If working remotely in India is a successful, proven model, surely we can do a heck of a lot better here!

I love what I do. I don't enjoy anything more.

We're also doing some work for NASA, where they are looking into how virtual communication could be maintained if the government's transportation were ever shut down again, as it was following 9/11. The project was launched to reduce reliance on travel for security reasons. Interestingly, travel reduction has an even bigger meaning nowadays with the soaring gas prices.

There is so much more that we can do as a country. Even though virtual employment affects hundreds of thousands of jobs in the United States each year, the Department of Labor does not seem to have a government body in place to explore the specificity of such jobs.

Even though the business of virtual teams involves enormous security issues, the Department of Defense does not seem to have a dedicated organization to oversee this.

Virtual Global Technologies strives to see the biggest picture possible in our mission to help NASA, other government entities, and businesses of all sizes around the world become more virtual by developing collaboration programs such as TeamLeader along with other necessary software solutions.

A very persuasive argument can be made that Internet traffic is just as significant as physical transportation. If we can have a Department of Transportation, we can and should have a Department of Internet Traffic.

Entrepreneurial "laggards" in rural America coin the existence of virtual businesses as an "interesting concept," when it is, in fact, a $100 billion per year, worldwide reality.

In response to those who frown on American businesses who use virtual overseas teams, I can only suggest that they peruse the latest Fortune 500 company list and choose one such successful, multibillion-dollar candidate they don't want in their state.

We are on the precipice of an increasingly rich economic reality, one which enables us and virtual workers from all corners of the globe to choose where they will earn their money to improve their lifestyles and have the best of both worlds.

We are always afraid of the unfamiliar. My advice to anyone who has been flirting with taking the virtual business route is, just do it! Take the mystery out of it.

When people ask me, "How do you work with an Indian company?" I reiterate the simple truth. "I get their phone number and I call 'em!"

Cary Landis, President
Virtual Global Technologies

As you can see, opinions about Virtual Outsourcing can be quite strong. When on the road speaking about it, audience reactions range the full gamut from an exuberant, "Wow, this is incredible!" to a fierce "Those #%$&@'s are stealing our jobs!!" There seems to be very little in between and the color of the reaction is largely determined by the location of where I happen to be speaking. In areas that have recently experienced large corporate layoffs, this topic is a lightning rod for the audience's frustration. In the final chapter, "The Future of Virtual Outsourcing," I'm going to address this issue at greater length and show why Virtual Outsourcing is a win-win for everyone.

Ever get to the point where it seems that your business is running you? That happened in a big way with the business owner of our next case story. She found redemption in using not one, but seven different VAs to handle different aspects of her business...

A Big Fish in a Little Pond

For over a decade, my business, FrogPond, has been the leading free content provider for the real estate industry. Yet, even with this distinction, my small business was not growing as fast as I would have liked. Looking back, I now know that the business was running me! I realized that the only way to expand our profits was to develop additional products, but I was still overwhelmed with the cost of creating them and the time it would require to do so.

My only solution for improved efficiency and cost-effectiveness was to outsource my development needs to Web experts —in my case, in Pakistan—and hire Virtual Assistants to handle the daily, multiple tasks needed to keep up with current responsibilities and client needs.

We decided to implement this change. Our "risk" was instantly rewarded with the successful launch of our software, FrogPond Publisher, an online magazine and newsletter software program designed for small businesses that do not have an IT department, but understand the importance of increased branding and product awareness in the digital world. It's as simple as "point and click" but as sophisticated as CNN.com and other highly-trafficked Web sites. The software offered countless advantages and possibilities for its users, to the point where its success was outpacing my ability to oversee all of its applications and operations. When I became aware of the many benefits of using Virtual Assistants to absorb and rein in the overflow, I heaved a big sigh of relief.

The perks of using our site and software allows subscribers to capture the essence and core spirit of their companies in the following ways: To market and sell products and services, to feature easy networking between company and community activities, to create company news bulletins and reports and video training modules, to build political and charitable fundraising promotions, and to publicize events, conferences and online registrations. Whew! No wonder I was tired!

Ten years ago, I could not have accepted the prospect of outsourcing elements of my business in any way that did not fit the traditional brick and mortar business model. I liken it to the satisfaction of pumping gas for the first time or successfully using your microwave oven for the first time. You may resist something new, but seeing is believing; once you've done it, you can't imagine going back to the way you did things before.

I do not hire full-time employees. I contract with virtual specialists to perform very specific business tasks. This option for small businesses like mine is ideal. In my opinion, the use of Virtual Assistants is increasingly cost-effective and redefines the concept of excellence in business practices and productivity. I pay only for time and material spent on outsourced projects. I do not have to pay employment benefits or taxes. My professional, certified virtual partners and I operate in a climate of mutual respect, trust, confidentiality and impeccable business ethics.

I use seven different Virtual Assistants, each of whom specializes in their own area of expertise, including executive assistant (California), technical support (Texas), customer service, product development (based in Pakistan), product sales (based in Georgia, Texas and California), writing (California), editing, accounting (Texas) and monthly interviewing (Canada). Each VA uses their own office equipment and supplies. Not having repairmen traipse through your communal office daily, disrupting the flow of business, is another small blessing!

One of the largest hurdles to overcome is changing one's mindset about the concept of Virtual Outsourcing and allowing time for it to prove its value in your particular business situation. You can always start small, monitor revenues, the quality of projects headed by VAs and the time saved in assigning work this way. When I assessed these factors, I was bowled over by the amount of time saved in virtual assistance. We cover a lot of time zones with people working all hours to help us meet our goals. This allows us enormous flexibility to keep chugging along!

Susie Hale, CEO
Frog Pond, Inc.

Your ability to achieve these kinds of results for your own business depends solely on your commitment to having your company (whether it happens to consist of one person or many) incorporate the benefits of Virtual Outsourcing as quickly and effectively as possible. So let's take a quick review to lock these ideas in...

Key Ideas and Chapter Review

- Fear of losing "control" is the number one reason why businesses hesitate to outsource;

- You don't gain control by doing everything yourself, that's called "chaos" —real control is making sure it gets done by the people who know how to do it best;

- The first step to incorporating Virtual Outsourcing into your business is to take "that first step" —one that is relatively small, has easy to measure results, addresses your current "pain" and frees you up to spend more time on your "core competency";

- There are only three kinds of pain related to day-to-day business: *1)* not enough income, *2)* not enough free time, and *3)* not enjoying what you do, or some combination of the three;

- Your "core competencies" are those business functions you love to do that bring real value to your company's bottom line;

- A successful strategic approach to Virtual Outsourcing is to virtually outsource everything that is outside of your core competency and that can be executed offsite;

- Hire VAs for ongoing support based upon their specialty, not their versatility —avoid the temptation of giving your VAs work beyond their core competency;

- Once you have hired three or more VAs, consider hiring an executive level VA to manage and grow your entire virtual team for you;

- Be sure to manage the expectations of your current onsite staff prior to bringing on any VAs to do ongoing support work —otherwise your efforts to go virtual may be sabotaged by key staff who feel threatened by the Virtual Outsourcing process;

- Internet, phone and fax are the primary ways of communicating and collaborating with your virtual support staff;

- E-mail is the most important tool when communicating with your virtual team members because it is non-interruptive (which makes you and your staff more focused and effective) and automatically documents the trail of messages;

- Whenever you have a VA send e-mail on your behalf, they should be using your e-mail signature and stationery (with their contact information);

- An intranet is your virtual team's "home base" of operations that can be used for document storage, maintaining a calendar, databases and collaboration between team members;

- Using a "Virtual PBX" allows your company to scale to any size with respect to phone communications, with no installation of hardware of software, no matter where your staff are physically located;

- E-mail based fax services allow you to give each of your VAs their own fax number which you control;

- When considering special purpose software or Web-based tools/ services, focus more on finding the virtual expert "tool user" rather than the tool itself.

Building a virtual team that just does their job, the way it's supposed to be done, on time and without management or training hassles, is very straightforward and easy to do. And, the more you incorporate this incredible resource into your business, the easier it will be to use it throughout nearly every aspect of day-to-day and strategic support. The result is having a business and career where you do only what you love to do, make a great living doing it and have all the free time you want to enjoy that success. A business that truly is your faithful servant rather than your master.

The Future of Virtual Outsourcing

Trying to predict the future of anything in this age of rapidly accelerating innovation and change is always a risky affair. However, this task can be made a bit more manageable by understanding that predicting the future growth of any industry is essentially equivalent to predicting its supply and demand curves. Both supply and demand must grow in close synchronization with each other, otherwise the growth of the industry will be attenuated.

Future Supply

Of the two primary categories of virtually outsourced support, only the project-based Virtual Consultants are currently truly supply-side scalable. The Virtual Service Provider Marketplace (VSPM) online transaction based model (as used by Elance, Guru, etc.) is readily equipped to absorb (and also provide) essentially an unlimited number of virtual service providers. This is because *a)* domestic talent, not currently in the pool of service providers, will continue to become more and more aware that becoming a VC and bidding on projects is a viable option for them, and *b)* the VSPMs haven't even scratched the surface of available offshore virtual support talent. China, India, Africa, South America and the Balkan States represent literally tens of millions of potential virtual service providers that have yet to make their talent accessible through these systems.

Also, the number of projects completed through these VSPMs can easily scale from the current tens of thousands per year to millions. This is because the online-based nature of these systems are inherently scalable and businesses essentially "self-serve" when using them. This is an important point because this means that VSPMs like Elance or Guru do not have to grow their own staffs in proportion to the number of virtual projects completed. The result is that just a few VSPMs can serve the demands of the entire worldwide market place for virtually outsourced project-based work, no matter how large or fast it grows.

Since the VSPMs are already successful and scalable, it's not likely that the fundamentals of their model will change significantly over the next five to 10 years. Instead, how business owners interact with these systems and manage the project completion process is likely to evolve via incremental improvements.

The scalability of VSPMs is good news, because the other category of virtual outsourced support (Virtual Assistants) is currently anything but scalable. As mentioned earlier, fractionalization, small numbers, and lack of standards relegates ongoing support via Virtual Assistants to a cottage industry. Certain things will need to happen before this part of the Virtual Outsourcing equation can support large-scale demand from small to midsized businesses:

- **Scalable Training** – Most of the training available for people wanting to become Virtual Assistants is through non-accredited and often ad hoc sources. Some of the VA communities attempt to provide some semblance of training for people interested in joining. There are few if any real standards, and though the word "certification" is bantered about within the context of these training programs, it is essentially meaningless. None of these groups are equipped to act as a genuine skills certification authority such as BrainBench.com or handle large numbers of students.

  Also, there are currently only a handful of accredited community colleges around the country that are offering Virtual Assistant training classes. It's only a small fraction of the 1,100 or so community colleges in the U.S.[40] Clearly it will take some time for this kind of training to become standardized curriculum throughout the community college system.

  One potential solution to the VA training standards and bottleneck issues is if accredited online schools such as University of Phoenix or Kaplan University offered the necessary courses. In addition to having a proven track record of delivering quality education online, they also have the bandwidth to facilitate large numbers of students. Hopefully, these kinds of progressive adult learning institutions will avail themselves to the potential of satisfying the explosive demand for Virtual Assistant training and certification.

The sooner, the better, too. As demand for this training grows, so will the numbers of "work at home" scams. These mostly online fly-by-night operations will prey on people who see becoming a VA as a dream come true, which it certainly can be. Unfortunately, these predators will more often than not turn these dreams into nightmares. They will typically offer one or more of three basic promises: *1)* we will train you, *2)* we will help you find clients, and as a result *3)* you will get rich while working at home. While the integrity of the training offered is often questionable, the cost will not be —it's almost always expensive from these sources. Placement with potential clients will likely consist of a one or two page list where the newly minted VA can advertise their services. And, while successful individual VAs can make a good living, they will not get rich by delivering support services from their home.

If the accredited online education institutions jump into the VA training business with both feet, it still does not adequately address the issue of specialization. These online universities will likely start out offering general administrative Virtual Assistant training and certification programs. That's because it's the type of support service most sought after by businesses and requires the least capital-intensive training to set up and deliver. These organizations will take a hard look at their ROI before offering a wide range of highly specialized and/or vertical market types of VA specialist training programs.

And even if they did, it still does not address how "experience" within a highly specialized virtual support role is acquired. Business owners do not want to be the training ground for a VA who is supposed to already know their stuff. As mentioned in a previous chapter, a "guild" system within Vertical Market-Specific VA Communities is a potential solution to this problem.

- **Scalable Delivery Systems** – There are some VA communities and organizations that give business owners the ability to post RFPs (Request For Proposals) when looking for VA support.

However, none approach the level of sophistication found in the typical VSPM online systems. Also, since all of these VA organizations are quite small, they would be quickly overwhelmed if large numbers of businesses posted their support requests all at once.

As mentioned previously, one potential solution to the scalable delivery of virtual support services is the Virtual Staffing Agency model. While there a number of VA staffing agencies that each offer a very specific type of VA support (i.e., for call centers, transcription, medical billing, etc.), I'm currently aware of only one VA staffing agency that offers a wide range of types of VA support (Team Double-Click^{sm}).

A significant advantage of the Virtual Staffing Agency model is that it provides a convenient source of clients for the vast majority of VAs who just want to get paid for providing their services, and not spend time marketing to build their client base. Unlike the VSPM model however, businesses don't "self-serve" when requesting support through them. They must first speak with a live customer service representative to discuss needs, budget, etc. prior to hiring any VAs. This obviously takes manpower, virtual or otherwise, to support this kind of service. One company alone, no matter how successful they become, cannot handle the virtual ongoing support needs of a significant percentage of U.S. based small to midsized businesses. It will require many such agencies. And if this model proves viable, there eventually will be many virtual staffing agencies making it easy for business owners to hire a wide range of Virtual Assistant support.

If it were not for the already highly scalable VSPMs like Elance and Guru, the supply side of virtual support would look rather bleak. Fortunately, these resources allow any number of businesses to tap into the power of Virtual Outsourcing *now*, at least on a project-by-project basis.

The availability of ongoing support through the use of qualified Virtual Assistants will continue to grow over time. How fast that growth occurs depends on many factors. The most important of which is the entrepreneurial vision and capabilities of those companies and learning institutions that are needed to support that growth.

Future Demand

The *potential* demand for Virtual Outsourcing is incredibly huge. In the U.S. alone, there are over 25 million small to midsized businesses that could easily take advantage of the many benefits it has to offer. For the most part, though, this demand still goes largely unrealized, for two primary reasons:

- **Lack of Awareness** – The vast majority of businesses are simply not aware of the option to hire remotely located independent contractor talent. As mentioned earlier, a study conducted for Elance, the largest of the VSPMs, found that over 99.5 percent of all U.S. small to midsized businesses don't even know they exist;

- **Status Quo** – The use of Virtual Outsourcing in one's business represents a major paradigm shift from the traditional model of using only onsite employee staffing. Unlike disruptive technologies that can effect almost immediate change, new paradigms tend to take their time in the beginning stages of establishing themselves. People don't like change, never have and never will. This fact alone is a key reason for the initial slow adoption rate of any new idea.

Lack of awareness by the general business community is the result of *a)* VSPMs relying (so far) mostly on word of mouth to grow their business —both their base of service providers and the businesses that use them, *b)* the Virtual Assistance movement is still very much a cottage industry whose voice is not yet large enough to be heard, and *c)* no one, until now, has attempted to bring the concept of Virtual Outsourcing to the forefront of the consciousness of mainstream business in a big way. In fact, this last point is the main purpose for this book. If it (and the others like it that will undoubtedly follow) succeed in gaining traction and the attention of contemporary business "thought leaders," then the lack of awareness issue goes away.

> *First movers will immediately see virtually outsourcing their non-core functions as an enormous opportunity.*

In today's world of instant news, flash crowds, Web 2.0 dilettantes and hair trigger tipping points, the time period to go from "Virtual what?" to "Of course!" can be as short as a few months, weeks or even days. But as stated above, awareness is not enough; businesses must incorporate Virtual Outsourcing into their day-to-day operations in a much bigger way if it is to come into its own.

There is no better lubricant to cut through the rust of status quo than the combination of opportunity and threat. First movers will immediately see virtually outsourcing their non-core functions as an enormous opportunity. One that will help them save both hard and "soft" staffing costs and provide access to a range of highly affordable talent that's simply not available to their competitors. These people are largely already, or will soon be, in the game using Virtual Outsourcing to one degree or another.

Since first movers typically reside on the feather-edge of the business owner distribution curve, their numbers alone are not enough to get the ones on the "bulge" to move. However, if you add ubiquitous awareness to the proven success of the first movers, then you have those in the bulge perceiving a growing threat they cannot ignore. If I were to guess (which is always a hazard when prognosticating), it will take three to five years (i.e., by 2010 to 2012) before most U.S. small businesses are at least aware of Virtual Outsourcing and perceive that it's something they seriously need to consider. Not long after that (say around 2015 – 2017), virtually outsourcing at least some non-core functions will be a requirement to stay in business.

Also, as the supply of virtual service providers and virtual service organizations grows to meet the demand, they themselves will virtually outsource more as well. Whether a company of one or 100, they still have all the needs that come with being in business. And who better to use Virtual Outsourcing for support of non-core tasks than the same ones that provide Virtual Outsourcing services to others. This fact will greatly accelerate the growth of Virtual Outsourcing after a critical threshold of mainstream adoption has been crossed.

There is another factor to the demand side of the equation that, ironically, will likely be the last to manifest itself (domestically), but undoubtedly will still happen. Enterprise outsourcing has been a long accepted way of doing business by large corporations. However, the use of virtually outsourced resources at the departmental level is still relatively rare. The reason for this is that within a typical "command and control" large corporate structure, departmental heads are not usually given free reign to find and use "nontraditional" support resources. They are also the least likely to even be aware of them since most large company departments support needs are provided from higher levels up within the organization. Therefore, they seldom even consider other possibilities. Nevertheless, at some point, large companies are going to wake up to the advantages of using Virtual Outsourcing at the departmental level and give their department heads the freedom to use it.

And lastly, small to midsized businesses in the European Union and the U.K. have been slow to utilize virtually outsourced talent. This is particularly interesting given their overall high cost of plant and labor, especially for those located in the EU. This is bound to change as these firms start realizing that the only way they can remain competitive in the world market is to virtually outsource as many of their non-core functions as possible. This of course will release yet another wave of demand for virtual support.

Future Services and Tools

As greater numbers of businesses begin to use Virtual Outsourcing, new categories of support specialization and tools used to interface between businesses and their virtual service providers will emerge. Here are some thoughts as to what these might look like:

- **Services** – Clearly, one of the first to emerge will be specialists who shepherd the entire Virtual Outsourcing process from needs analysis to finding the best virtual resource to get the job done. Most business owners intuitively know what their needs are, but either have trouble articulating them or feel uncertain about their own ability to navigate the Virtual Outsourcing process. "Virtual Outsourcing Contractors" (who themselves are virtual, of course) will interface between businesses that desire to use Virtual Outsourcing and the talent that is available.

  This position can be best described as similar to a construction contractor for virtual services. They will need to understand, at the "big picture" level, a very broad range of business support requirements. This includes being quite adept at finding the appropriate virtual resources (whether project-based through the VSPMs or ongoing support using VAs) for the job. A current analog to this is the use of executive level VAs to hire and manage other VAs for ongoing virtual support, as mentioned in an earlier chapter.

  The involvement of these Virtual Outsourcing Contractors could range from simply finding the virtual talent, to taking over entire virtual projects and seeing them all the way to completion. How they will be paid is likely to be similar to the traditional construction field as well. In most cases, it will be either "time and (virtual) materials" or they themselves will be responsible for the entire project in which their bid includes built-in profit, adding in costs to cover all their "virtual subcontractors." Interestingly, this kind of "virtual project management" service is already happening, but on a very small scale and is not widely advertised. Due to potential strong demand, this service category could easily become the basis for a viable, rapid growth industry. One that acts as the "go between" for small to midsized businesses and the virtually outsourced support services from which they could benefit.

This kind of service will open up the benefits of Virtual Outsourcing to many more businesses that otherwise might be too intimidated to use it. Also, it creates the possibility of "Ephemeral Virtual Project Teams" proffered by Elance CEO Fabio Rosati, when asked about the future of Virtual Outsourcing. These are teams of virtual service providers that come together for the purpose of completing specific complex projects, most likely for larger companies. When a project is completed, the virtual team "evaporates." A new virtual team is formed based upon each particular project's needs. These teams will need a "Virtual Team Leader" which requires essentially the same skill sets as the Virtual Outsourcing Contractor described above. Ironically however, at the enterprise level, this position is likely to be held in-house even though it could just as easily be outsourced.

As for other types of services in the future, well, only time will tell. Without a doubt, in the next five years there will be services offered that have not been dreamt of yet. One thing is for sure though, anything that can be virtually outsourced, will be;

• **Tools** – Expect virtual collaboration tools to become only more sophisticated and easier to use. The ability to create real-time virtual meetings where attendees appear to be in the same room is not far from becoming a reality. As this becomes widely available, it will be interesting to see if these meetings will become a breeding ground for organizational "virtual politics" and other forms of CYA that inevitably result from traditional onsite meetings. I still hold that an exchange of powerful nonverbal communicative nuances will occur when team members regularly see each other (virtually or otherwise) and is therefore a distraction from effective management by objective.

The relentless march toward improved Internet bandwidth and reliability will allow future virtual service providers to affect the people that hired them in very real physical ways. For example, a surgeon in Boston can operate in real time on a West Coast patient through the use of robotic surgery tools. These devices allow a degree of precision for certain types of surgery that is simply not possible by even the best surgeons in the world working directly on the patient. Now imagine this same surgery being performed by a highly trained but much less expensive New Delhi surgeon. A recent study has shown that 500,000 Americans traveled to India and Mexico for major surgery that was on average less than one-tenth of what it would cost in the U.S. [41] These patients would not have to travel to India, yet would receive nearly the same benefits in cost and quality as if they had. This could be an ideal way for the hundreds of surgery centers around the country to expand the range of their services and fill a vital need. "Virtual Heart Surgery" —what a concept! (Better check those past user ratings pretty carefully though...)

Sometimes small to midsized businesses need to prototype new ideas and products, which can be an expensive affair. Thankfully, not for long since rapid virtual prototyping of mechanical or electronic products is a very real future possibility. Already there are 3D "prototype printers" that will build three-dimensional plastic prototypes of real objects based upon a CAD (Computer Aided Design) file practically while you wait. Likewise, there are "integrated circuit printers" on the horizon (similar to high resolution ink jet printers) that can do the same with prototyping chips and circuit boards. Marry these capabilities (and their likely future improvements) to virtual prototype designers located anywhere in the world and you have substantially reduced your prototyping development time and costs.

Once again, as there will be virtual services we cannot even imagine provided in the next five years, the same holds true for the tools that will support virtual collaboration.

The future for Virtual Outsourcing is very bright indeed. As you have seen, it provides nearly unlimited possibilities to the businesses that incorporate it as part of their day-to-day and strategic operations. The direct benefits of Virtual Outsourcing from a business owner's perspective are big and undeniable. Now let's take a look at something even bigger —how it will affect everyone else.

Future Impact (on Society)

As this is being written, I'm trying my best to stay cool. This is a losing battle despite my overhead fan whirling furiously away. That's because of the heat pouring out from under my desk where my desktop computer resides. The problem is that this waste heat has no place to go since it's about 87° F outside. While this temperature is hardly unprecedented for the central coast of California, this is considerably warmer than what is typical for the second week of November.

OK, so I'm a little damp under the arms, big deal —right? In just a few years time, it could end up being a very big deal. There is little doubt that global warming is real, accelerating and if not checked soon, will have an incalculable impact on the way human beings live and work on this planet. Being uncomfortably warm will be the very least of our problems. And, there is very little remaining doubt that it is due in large part to our addiction to fossil fuels. In some ways, however, this is a good thing because at least we can do something about that.

Ironically, tomorrow happens to be mid-term elections, two years before the big presidential election in 2008. In California, the world's sixth largest economy, this means mega-billion-dollar propositions on the ballet for massive expansion of our state's infrastructure. The political ads talk about the importance of investing in our state's future through expansion of freeways, so even more billions of gallons of gas can be wasted each year in ever larger gridlocks (obviously this last part was not included in any political ad). Instead of widening ribbons of concrete that will literally end up being the road to a hell on earth, why not add ribbons of glass fiber? We could spend far less to build out our information infrastructure so we don't need to have so many people on the road commuting to and from work. And while we are at it, start rewarding companies, big and small, that proactively reduce the number of employee vehicles on the road. Whether it's aggressively encouraging the use of remote employees or virtually outsourcing to independent contractors, it's feasible today and can be done.

We're not talking about a Herculean Manhattan Project effort here. Intelligent implementation of a global warming, gas credit trading system may be all that is required. In fact, the U.S. Environmental Protection Agency Telework and Emissions Trading Study (known as the eCommute Program) is exploring the feasibility of just such a system.[42] Businesses that became adept at using non-commuting workers could sell their credits to those that have yet to do so. This would be a powerful incentive for small to midsized businesses to shift their support staff to telecommuting or Virtual Outsourcing. In addition to all the other benefits realized by going virtual, they would be helping to fight global warming, reducing pollution, congestion and wasted time during commutes, all while getting paid to do it. A "win-win" just doesn't get much better than that.

For many business contexts, especially service-based industries, the notion that all staff must *a)* be employees, and *b)* work under the same roof is frankly quite antiquated. As more companies shed this throw-back to the old command and control ways of running a business, the use and hence value of urban office space will likely be affected.

High-rise office towers are typically one of the most expensive ways for organizations to provide employee workspace. While undoubtedly there will always be a need for the imposing urban corporate edifice, the impact of Virtual Outsourcing will likely reduce the amount of total space required by each company. Virtual outsourcing also allows service providers to do their work from well... virtually anywhere, which gives them full flexibility to live where they want. Given this option and the continued trend toward cocooning, I suspect relatively few people will resign themselves to a dystopian lifestyle within the concrete jungles of modern cities. This means the value of a good portion of urban office space could take a hit. This will not happen overnight, but certainly may over the next 10 – 20 years.

Another major societal impact of Virtual Outsourcing is the perfection of the worldwide talent marketplace. "Perfection" in any marketplace is an idealized condition where buyers and sellers have equal access to all the relevant players and the same knowledge when transacting with each other. The more a market place approaches perfection, the more efficiently it works and in aggregate, buyers and sellers each receive the highest value for their respective parts in any transaction. This condition can only be approached, but never fully attained. Stock exchanges are a good example of markets that are always striving for "perfection," at least in principle.

Highly scalable VSPMs, such as Elance or Guru, represent the possibility for some semblance of perfection of a worldwide marketplace that consists of buying (i.e., using) and selling (i.e., providing) talent. As it stands today, that ideal is a long, long way off, primarily because only a tiny fraction of the world's population is able to participate. But that's changing. On October 13, 2006, Muhammad Yunus, an Indian economist and the Grameen Bank which he founded, were awarded the Nobel Peace Prize for establishing the foundation of the worldwide "microcredit" initiative.[43]

Who would ever have imagined that lending miniscule amounts of money, often less than US $30 to dirt-poor women in Bangladesh would make a difference? These unsecured loans made solely on trust were for the purpose of helping these women create "businesses" to help lift themselves out of poverty and become financially self-sustaining. It takes a true visionary to see things that others don't and a hero to see that vision through to fruition. This program was not some idealistic Ivory Tower fantasy. Since 1983, Yunu's Grameen Bank has lent over US$5.72 billion to over 6.7 million Bangladeshis in over 70,000 villages. It is an awe-inspiring strategic victory over poverty and one of the first steps to giving these people access to the global marketplace.

The "One Laptop Per Child" (http://www.olpc.org) is another initiative aimed at eliminating poverty in developing countries. This is the brainchild of Nicholas Negroponte, founder of the prestigious MIT Media Lab. His vision is to provide all the world's impoverished children with an affordable, dependable computing device that will give them access to educational resources they otherwise could never have. Powered by a built-in, hand-pull generator and accessible to the Internet via Wi-Fi technology, these computers will not need a wired infrastructure to operate. Once again, like most visionaries, his ideas were dismissed early on as impractical and unattainable. Yet before this book goes to print, 5000 test units are slated to roll off a production line in Taiwan.[44]

> " if the majority cannot come out of poverty, peace cannot prevail. "

Now imagine combining the microcredit and One Laptop Per Child initiatives (and others like them) with the efficiencies of VSPMs. By doing so, you have the foundation for a way the other impoverished two-thirds of the world can bootstrap themselves into a decent standard of living. While this may take a full generation or two, ultimately the forgotten, strife-torn parts of the world population become our stable trading partners, even down to the individual level. And in so doing, we all win. In awarding the Peace Prize to Muhammad Yunus and his Grameen Bank, the Nobel committee said that if the majority cannot come out of poverty, peace cannot prevail. There are very few fundamental truths in this world; I happen to believe this is one of them.

Future Impact (the Individual)

So how is Virtual Outsourcing going to impact you personally? Possibly in more ways than you can now imagine. Sure, as a business owner you are going to be able to compete more effectively through lower costs and greater access to talent. You will be able to grow your business, like so many of the case stories presented here, in ways that otherwise just wouldn't be feasible. You will be able to spend more of your time doing what you do best, while virtually outsourcing the rest to people you will not have to train, manage or provide logistic support for. You will likely make more net income, work less and enjoy the process more than you ever thought possible. And, without having to become a gifted manager, you can finally have a business that is your faithful servant, rather than a merciless tyrant that drives you relentlessly nearly 24/7.

It will also free you up to consider, perhaps for the first time, what you are here "to give, before you go." Once again, Maslow's Hierarchy of Needs kicks in. After the issues of money (survival) and having a life (time) are sufficiently addressed, most human beings start thinking more about what truly fulfills them. Call it purpose in life, self-actualization or just a sense of deep inner peace and contentment; it is something that all human beings strive for when their basic needs are no longer an issue.

They say that no one on their deathbed ever wishes they had just one more day at the office —unfortunately, I think I've met a few that would. When consistently applied, Virtual Outsourcing becomes perhaps the very first practical tool that allows everyday ordinary human beings to achieve what is important to them. The key is to be clear about what that is.

Writing this book has been part of a journey for me that started nearly 13 years ago. It was borne out of frustration that there had to be more to business and life than just making money doing things I didn't particularly enjoy while taking short-lived solace during vacations. It was further fueled by the constant annoyance that the necessary talent to help build my dreams was, in the traditional sense, expensive, hard to find and difficult to manage.

By fully embracing Virtual Outsourcing since the mid-1990s, I have been empowered to live my dreams, while avoiding most of the nightmares associated with having one's own business. By sharing these practical ideas and insights about Virtual Outsourcing, my journey completes one milestone and begins another. Now it is your turn. Don't let the possibility of Virtual Outsourcing be just another "great idea" that you put on the shelf of "someday I'll get to it" —because that someday almost never comes. Make a commitment to implement even just one small step, so you can experience firsthand the revolutionary possibilities for yourself. Once that first step is taken, it will undoubtedly lead to many more. And in so doing, you will find yourself embarked on your own journey that leads to a total transformation in the way your business serves you.

Resources

The resources mentioned in this book are but a fraction of what is available to help you incorporate Virtual Outsourcing into your business. As in any industry, this list is rather dynamic in that it will be constantly changing. New ones being added all the time and existing ones occasionally going away.

Trying to list all these resources here would effectively make this part of the book obsolete before it even went to print. Instead, I elected to create a Web portal dedicated entirely to the support and growth of Virtual Outsourcing and its use by businesses.

You can find this resource portal at **www.virtualoutsourcing.org**. Within this site you will discover comprehensive lists of VSPMs, Virtual Assistant organizations, Virtual Staffing Agencies, Virtual Outsourcing related online tools and organizations offering accredited Virtual Assistant training. Think of this as your virtual "home base" for anything related to Virtual Outsourcing. Enjoy!

Index

Endnotes

Chapter 1

1   Document Title: Job Fulfillment Tops Total Compensation on Executive Wish List
Publisher: TheLadders.com
Publish Date: November 22, 2004
Link: http://www.theladders.com/press/abouttheladderspressdetail_112204

Document Title: Work vs. Fulfillment is a Top Concern
Publisher: Star Bulleting (StarBulletin.com)
Publish Date: September 11, 2006
Link: http://starbulletin.com/2006/09/11/business/bizbriefs.html

Document Title: The Gallup Poll – Fulfillment Frequently Cited as a Top Job "Like"
Publisher: The Gallup Poll
Publish Date: August 7, 2006
Author: Jeffrey M Jones
Link: http://news.aol.com/gallup/story/_a/fulfillment-frequently-cited-as-a-top/20060809121209990001

Document Title: SHRM 2006 Job Satisfaction Survey
Publisher: Society of Human Resources Management (SHRM)
Publish Date: June, 2006
Author: N/A

2   Document Title: Worldwatch France
Publisher: SHRM Global HR Library
Publish Date: Revised 08/2005
Link: http://www.shrm.org/global/library_published/country/GlobalWorldWatch%20-%20Europe/FranceTOC.asp#TopOfPage

Document Title: Worldwatch Germany
Publisher: SHRM Global HR Library
Publish Date: Revised 08/2005
Link: http://www.shrm.org/global/library_published/country/GlobalWorldWatch - Europe/GermanyTOC.asp

Document Title: "Learning from Our Overseas Counterparts"
Publisher: HR Magazine
Publish Date: February, 2004 (Vol 49, No. 2)
Author: Paul Falcone
Link: http://www.shrm.org/hrmagazine/articles/0204/0204falcone.asp

Document Title: A Shorter Workweek Indicates Lower Employee Productivity
Publisher: Career Journal.com
Publish Date: November 23, 2004
Link: www.careerjournal.com/myc/workabroad/20041123-sterling.html

3   Document Title: Employer Costs for Employee Compensation- June, 2006
Publisher: Bureau of Labor Statistics
Publish Date: September 22, 2006
Link: http://www.bls.gov/news.release/ecec.nr0.htm

4   Document Title: Staffing Research - Recruiting Benchmark
Publisher: Society of Human Resource Management
Author: John Dooney, Manager, Strategic Research
Date Published: Summer, 2006
Link: http://www.shrm.org/research/staffresearch_published/Recruiting%20Benchmarks%
20-%20Defending%20and%20Improving%20Recruiting%20Performance.pdf

5   Document Title: ASTD 2005 State of the Industry Report
Publisher: American Society for Training & Development
Publish Date: 9/26/2006
Link: http://www.astd.org/NR/rdonlyres/BBDACF82-C50F-44AA-A179-
9FD5825EE766/0/ASTD_StateoftheIndustry_2005_ExecutiveSummary.pdf

6   Document Title: TeleWork Fact
Publisher: Telework Commission
Link: http://www.telcoa.org/id33.htm

7   Document Title: Employer Costs for Employee Compensation- June, 2006
Publisher: Bureau of Labor Statistics
Publish Date: September 22, 2006
Link: http://www.bls.gov/news.release/ecec.nr0.htm

8   Document Title: Employer Costs for Employee Compensation- June, 2006
Publisher: Bureau of Labor Statistics
Publish Date: September 22, 2006
Link: http://www.bls.gov/news.release/ecec.nr0.htm

9   Document Title: Hidden Costs in In-House TCO for Payroll - Are you accounting for all of
your expenses or only the most obvious?
Publisher: ADP National Account Services
Link: http://www.nas.adp.com/.aspx/0/2.1457b2/Hidden-Costs-TCO

10 Document Title: Calculating the High Cost of Employee Turnover
Publisher: Taleo Research

Author: Yves Lermusiaux
Link: http://www.taleo.com/research/articles/strategic/calculating-the-high-cost-employee-turnover-15.html

Document Title: How Much Does Your Employee Turnover Cost?
Publisher: Center for Community Economic Development
Author: William H. Pinkovitz, Joseph Moskal and Gary Green
Link: http://www.uwex.edu/CES/cced/publicat/turn.html

11 Document Title: SHRM – Management Practices
Publisher: Society of Human Resources Management
Link: http://www.shrm.org/hrresources/faq_published/Management%20Practices.asp#P18_4011

12 Document Title: Organizational Entry: Onboarding, Orientation And Socialization
Publisher: Society of Human Resources Management
Author: Belin Tai and Nancy R. Lockwood, SPHR, GPHR
Publish Date: October 2006
Link: http://www.shrm.org/research/briefly_published/1Organizational%20Entry_%20Onboarding,%20Orientation%20And%20Socialization.asp

13 Document Title: The Law of Accelerating Returns
Publisher: KurzweilAI.net
Author: Ray Kurzweil
Publish Date: March 7, 2001
Link: http://www.kurzweilai.net/articles/art0134.html?printable=1

Chapter 2

14 Document Title: 15 Top Reasons Why a Business Fails
Publisher: AMANet.org
Article Publish Date: Unspecified but link indicates February, 2005
Author: Barry Thomsen (publisher/editor of Small Business Idea-Letter and Small Business Advisor)
Link: http://membersonly.amamember.org/smallbiz/2005/feb_01.cfm

Document Title: "75% of Senior Managers Lack "Soft Skills"
Publisher: AMAnet.org
Article Publish Date: Not specified but link indicates 11/2002
Author: Not specified
Link: http://membersonly.amamember.org/management/2002/nov_01.cfm

15 Document: MEETING MANAGEMENT FOR BUSINESS RESULTS
Publisher: Society of Human Resources Management
Date: September, 2005
Author: Rebecca R. Hastings, SPHR
Link: http://www.shrm.org/hrresources/whitepapers_published/CMS_014058.asp

Article: Microsoft: Workers Waste 2 Days Out Of 5
Publisher: Information Week

Date: March 15, 2005
Link: http://www.informationweek.com/story/
showArticle.jhtml?articleID=159900390

16 Document Title: Group Dynamic: Theory Research & Practice - Meetings and More
Meetings: The Relationship Between Meeting Loan and the Daily Well-Being of
Employees. – Study byAlexandra Luong and Stephen Rogelberg
Publisher: Educational Publishing Foundation
Publish Date: 2005
Link: http://interruptions.net/literature/Luong-GDTRP05.pdf (Page 3)

Chapter 3

17 Document Title: "Top 50 services vendors fail to match market growth rate"
Publisher: Computer Business Review-Analysis Center: Outsourcing & ASP
Publish Date: April 24, 2006
Author: Staff Writer
Statistic: Top four IT service vendors: IBM, EDS, Fujitsu, and Accenture
Link: http://www.computerbusinessreview.com/article_news.asp?guid=3A5ED25D-5886-
4CBD-A1C1-F1E8773C3C11&z=rc_OutsourcingandASP)

18 Document Title: Now in Offshoring's Sights: High-Level Professionals
Publisher: Careerjournal.com
Publish Date: March 23, 2004
Author: Kris Mahler
Link: http://www.careerjournal.com/myc/survive/20040324-maher.html

19 Document Title: Briefly Stated – Telecommuting
Publisher: SHRM (Society of Human Resources Management)
Publish Date: 2003

Document Title: TELECOMMUTING: THE WORKPLACE OF THE 90'S
Publisher: The National Institute of Mental Health, Bethesda, MD
Publish Date: 1998
Author: Thalene T. Mallus
Link: http://lbc.nimh.nih.gov/people/mallus/ttmSUGI24.pdf#search=%22TELECOMMU
TING%http://www2.sas.com/proceedings/sugi24/Posters/p214-24.pdf

20 Document Title: Traffic Reports From Your Cell Phone - Civil Engineers Track Roaming
Cell Phones to Monitor Traffic
Publisher: Discoveries & Breakthroughs Inside Science
Publish Date: March 1, 2006
Link: http://www.aip.org/dbis/stories/2006/15139.html

Document Title: The Role of Road Pricing in Reducing Traffic Congestion -Testimony
before the Joint Economic Committee
Publisher: PPIOnline.com
Publish Date: May 6, 2003
Author: Robert Atkinson
Link: http://www.ppionline.org/ppi_ci.cfm?knlgAreaID=141&subsecID=299&contentID
=251568

Document: The Quiet Success - Telecommuting's Impact on Transportation and Beyond
Publisher: The Reason Foundation
Publish Date: November, 2005
Author: Ted Balaker
Link: http://www.reason.org/ps338.pdf

21 Document Title: Well-Designed Telework Policies Help You Reap Benefits
Publisher: SHRM
Publish Date: March 2001 / Reviewed Jan. 2004
Author: Linda Thornburg
Link: http://www.shrm.org/hrtx/library_published/nonIC/CMS_006493.asp

22 Document Title: Transportation and Global Climate Change: A Review and Analysis of the
Literature 5 Strategies to Reduce Greenhouse Gas - Emissions from Transportation Sources
Publisher: Federal Highway Administration
Publish Date: December 1, 2005
Link: http://www.fhwa.dot.gov/environment/glob_c5.pdf

23 Document Title: Selecting The Home-Based Business Option
Publisher: SmallBiz.ca (Canada)
Publish Date: 2006
Author: Douglas Gray
Link: http://www.smallbiz.ca/2006/07/03/selecting-the-home-based-business-option/

Document Title: Are You Ready to Become One of the New Entrepreneurs
Publisher: TheNewEntrepreneurs.com
Publish Date: N/A
Author: Rene Reid Yarnell
Link: http://www.thenewentrepreneurs.com/tnepresentation.shtml

24 Source: Revolutionary Wealth – How it will be created and how it will change our lives
Author: Alvin and Heidi Toffler
Publish Date: 2006

25 Document Title: SHRM Workplace Forecast
Publisher: Society of Human Resources Management
Publish Date: June, 2006
Author: Jennifer Schramm
Link: http://www.shrm.org/trends/061606WorkplaceForecast.pdf

26 Document Title: "Nearly 1.5 Million Back-Office U.S. Jobs Seen Moving Abroad"
Publisher: "Information Week"
Publish Date: October 27, 2006
Author: Eric Chabrow
Link: http://www.informationweek.com/news/showArticle.jhtml;jsessionid=3TQQO10DR
OAW0QSNDLPSKH0CJUNN2JVN?articleID=193402615

27 Document Title: "Women in the Labor Force in 2005"
Publisher: US Department of Labor Women's Bureau
Publish Date: August 23, 2006

Author: NA
Link: http://www.dol.gov/wb/factsheets/Qf-laborforce-05.htm

Document Title: "Women in the Labor Force: A Databook"
Publisher: US Department of Labor, Bureau of Labor Statistics
Publish Date: May, 2005
Link: http://www.bls.gov/cps/wlf-databook2005.htm
Statistical Table: http://www.bls.gov/cps/wlf-table1-2005.pdf

Document Title: After the Time Out - How to navigate the return to the workforce
Publisher: Newsday.com
Publish Date: September 10, 2006
Author: Patricia Kitchen
Link: http://pqasb.pqarchiver.com/newsday/results.html?st=basic&QryTxt=After+the+
Time+Out+-+How+to+navigate+the+return+to+the+workforce&x=39&y=7

28 Document Title: Degrees conferred by degree-granting institutions, by level of degree and
    sex of student (Table)
    Source/Publisher: U.S. Department of Education, National Center for Education Statistics
    (NCES)
    Publish Date: July, 2005
    Link: http://nces.ed.gov/programs/digest/d05/tables/dt05_246.asp

    Document Title: School Enrollment--Social and Economic Characteristics of Students:
    October 2004
    Publisher: Census.gov
    Publish Date: Released October 2005
    Link: http://www.census.gov/population/www/socdemo/school/cps2004.html

    Cited Table: Table 10, All Races
    Statistic: Of 4,715,000 total entering first year of college, 2,319,000 are women represent-
    ing 55.87%

29 Document Title: Gauging the labor force effects of retiring baby-boomers
    Publisher: Monthly Labor Review Online, Divison of the Bureau of Labor Statistics
    Publish Date: July, 2000 Vol 23, No. 7
    Author: Arlene Dohm
    Link: http://www.bls.gov/opub/mlr/2000/07/art2abs.htm

30 Document Title: Baby Boomers Envision Retirement II: Survey of Baby Boomers' Expec-
    tations for Retirement – Research Report
    Publisher: AARP
    Publish Date: May 2004
    Author: Sarah Zapolsky, AARP Knowledge Management
    Link: http://www.aarp.org/research/work/retirement/aresearch-import-865.html

31 Document Title: How Many Home-Based Businesses Are There?
    Publisher: National Association for the Self-Employed (NASE)
    Publish Date: Not dated (Listed under Media Resources)
    Link: http://news.nase.org/news/homebased.asp

Document Title: Want to Start a Business? Join the Crowd
Publisher: Entrepreneurial Connection
Publish Date: January, 2005
Link: http://www.entrepreneurialconnection.com/Trends/issue26.asp

Document: HOME-BASED AND MICRO BUSINESS TRENDS
Publisher: University of Kentucky – College of Agriculture
Compiled by Patty Rai Smith, Extension Specialist for Home Based Business
Publish Date: September 2003
Link: http://www.ca.uky.edu/fcs/trends/business.pdf

Chapter 4

32 Document Title: How Much Money Does it Take to Start a Small Business?
Publisher: Wells Fargo/Gallup Small Business Index Study
Publish Date: August 15, 2006
Link: https://www.wellsfargo.com/press/20060815_Money?year=2006

33 Document Title: SBA Frequently Asked Questions
Publisher: Small Business Administration
Link: http://app1.sba.gov/faqs/faqindex.cfm?areaID=24

34 Method and apparatus for an electronic marketplace for services having a collaborative
workspace
United States Patent 7069242 issued on June 27, 2006
Link: http://www.patentstorm.us/patents/7069242.html

Chapter 5

35 Document Title: Virtual Assistance Chamber of Commerce – 2006 Virtual Assistant Survey
Publisher: Virtual Assistance Chamber of Commerce
Publish Date: August, 2006
Link: http://www.virtualassistantnetworking.com/survey.htm

36 Document Title: Wasted Time At Work Costing Companies Billions
Publisher: Salary.com
Publish Date: N/A (date of referenced survey way May – June 2005)
Author: Dan Malachowski
Link: http://www.salary.com/sitesearch/layoutscripts/sisl_display.asp?filename=&path=/
destinationsearch/personal/par542_body.html

37 Document Title: ASTD 2005 State of the Industry Report
Publisher: American Society for Training & Development
Date: 9/26/2006
Link: http://www.astd.org/NR/rdonlyres/BBDACF82-C50F-44AA-A179-
9FD5825EE766/0/ASTD_StateoftheIndustry_2005_ExecutiveSummary.pdf

Cited: "For BMS organizations in 2004, average expenditure as a percentage of payroll
did not change from the previous year, remaining at 2.34 percent, but increased from 2.05
in 2003 to 2.20 in 2004 in BMF organizations. The average expenditure as a percentage of

payroll in 2005 BEST Award winners was higher than BMS and BMF organizations at 3.2 percent."

38   Document Title: Movin' On Up – Relocation specialists are broadening their offerings as employers consolidate vendor base.
Publisher: HRO (Human Resources Outsourcing) Today
Date: November 2005
Author: Andy Teng
Link: http://www.hrotoday.com/Magazine.asp?artID=1100

39   Document Title: Workplace interruptions cost US economy $588 bn a year
Publisher: BaseX
Publish Date: 1/9/2006
Link: http://www.basex.com/press.nsf/0/E53F4C6142D119A6852570F9001AB0EC?OpenDocument

Document Title: 'Interruption Science': Costly Distractions at Work
Publisher: NPR.com
Publish Date: October 14, 2005
Link: http://www.npr.org/templates/story/story.php?storyId=4958831

Document Title: Meet the Life Hackers
(References Clive Thompson's article of the same title from the New York Times)
Publisher: LifeHack.org
Publish Date: October 18, 2005
Link: http://www.lifehack.org/articles/lifehack/meet-the-life-hackers.html

Document Title: Social Interruption and the Loss of Productivity
Publisher: CubeSmart, Inc.
Publish Date: 2002
Link: http://www.cubedoor.com/docs/cs_productivity_wp1.pdf

Document Title: You Only Have 11 Minutes to Work in the Office
(References Brian Donnelly's article called "Why Modern Offices Only Let You Work for 11 Minutes from the Scotland Herald)
Publisher: LifeHack.org
Publish Date: October 31, 2005
Link: http://www.lifehack.org/tag/interruption

Chapter 7

40   Document Title: National Profile of Community Colleges: Trends & Statistics 3rd Edition
Publisher: American Association of Community Colleges
Link: http://www.aacc.nche.edu/Content/NavigationMenu/AboutCommunityColleges/Trends_and_Statistics/InsightintoCommunityColleges/Insight_into_Community_Colleges.htm

41   Document Title: Businesses May Move Health Care Overseas
Publisher: Associated Press
Author: MALCOLM FOSTER and MARGIE MASON

Publish Date: November 2, 2006
Link: http://news.yahoo.com/s/ap/20061102/ap_on_he_me/outsourcing_health

42 Link: http://www.ecommute.net

43 Document Title: Bangladesh honors Nobel peace laureate Muhammad Yunus
Publisher: International Herald Tribune
Publish Date: November 5, 2006
Link: http://www.iht.com/articles/ap/2006/11/05/asia/AS_GEN_Bangladesh_Nobel_Lau-
reate.php

44 Document Title: This PC wants to save the world
Publisher: CNNMoney.com
Publish Date: October 24, 2006
Author: David Kirkpatrick
Link: http://money.cnn.com/magazines/fortune/fortune_archive/2006/10/30/8391805/
index.htm